TEARDROPS OF TIME

TEARDROPS OF TIME

BUDDHIST AESTHETICS IN THE POETRY OF ANGKARN KALLAYANAPONG

ARNIKA FUHRMANN

Cover design by Wonderwhale

Original drawing:
Angkarn Kalyanapong
Melting Men
1976
Charcoal on paper, 110 × 89 cm
Collection of National Gallery Singapore
Image courtesy of National Heritage Board

Published by State University of New York Press, Albany

© 2020 State University of New York

All rights reserved

No part of this book may be used or reproduced in any manner whatsoever without written permission. No part of this book may be stored in a retrieval system or transmitted in any form or by any means including electronic, electrostatic, magnetic tape, mechanical, photocopying, recording, or otherwise without the prior permission in writing of the publisher.

For information, contact State University of New York Press, Albany, NY
www.sunypress.edu

Library of Congress Cataloging-in-Publication Data

Name: Fuhrmann, Arnika, author.
Title: Teardops of time : Buddhist aesthetics in the poetry of Angkarn Kallayanapong / Arnika Fuhrmann.
Description: Albany : State University of New York Press, [2020] | Includes bibliographical references and index.
Identifiers: ISBN 9781438480732 (hardcover : alk. paper) | ISBN 9781438480749 (pbk. : alk. paper) | ISBN 9781438480756 (ebook)
Further information is available at the Library of Congress.

10 9 8 7 6 5 4 3 2 1

Contents

ACKNOWLEDGMENTS		vii
1	INTRODUCTION Buddhist Aesthetic Modernity	1
2	ONTOLOGY Time as Conflict: Angkarn Kallayanapong's Buddhist Temporal Modernity	35
3	HISTORY The Dream of a Contemporary Ayuthaya: Angkarn Kallayanapong's Poetics of Dissent, Aesthetic Nationalism, and Thai Literary Modernity	55
4	SUBJECTIVITY Modern Manifesto: Poetry as Redemptive-Therapeutic Action in the World	87
5	LANGUAGE Transnational Poetic Modernity: Linguistic Innovation and Religious Borrowings in the Work of Paul Celan and Angkarn Kallayanapong	121
6	POLITICS One Night in Bangkok: Angkarn Kallayanapong and Allen Ginsberg	143

7	CONCLUSION	165
	Performing a Redemptive Present	

APPENDIX 171
Translations of Angkarn Kallayanapong's Work on Time

NOTES 223

BIBLIOGRAPHY 245

INDEX 255

Acknowledgments

Countless individuals facilitated the completion of this multidecade project. It is a pleasure to express my gratitude to Suchitra Chongstitvatana, who first introduced me in depth to the poetry of Angkarn Kallayanapong and inspired me to continue to study his work. At the University of Hamburg, Klaus Rosenberg, Klaus Wenk, Bahrend Jan Terwiel, Patcharee Kaspar-Sickermann, Lambert Schmithausen, Albrecht Wetzler, and Michael Zimmermann spent countless hours teaching me how to read Thai poetry, Sanskrit, and Pali. Among my dedicated teachers at the Faculty of Arts at Chulalongkorn University in Bangkok, Ing-orn Supanvanit, Bunlom Manothai, and Trisilpa Boonkhachorn have my special appreciation.

Much later, at the University of Chicago, Sheldon Pollock prompted me to ask questions about the sociopolitical import of Angkarn Kallayanapong's poetry. Pali and Buddhist studies with Steven Collins taught me how to think about Buddhist philosophy in literature. Guy Leavitt and Andy Rotman tirelessly critiqued and supported my work.

While preparing this book for publication, I had the great pleasure to get to know the poet's daughter, Khun Qwan (Ormkaew Kallayanapong). I thank Adele Tan at the National Gallery Singapore for the introduction. I thank Ormkaew for generously granting translation rights for the poems printed here. I thank Sulak Sivaraksa for taking the time to have a long, insightful conversation about Angkarn with me and Anuk Pitukthanin for facilitating this meeting.

I am grateful to Peter Hale at the Ginsberg Foundation for taking an interest in my work and providing me with information about Allen Ginsberg's travels in Southeast Asia. Without the help of Tim Noakes, head of Public Services, Special Collections, at Stanford University Library, who invested time searching the Ginsberg papers for me, my comparative analysis would not have been possible. I thank the Wylie Agency in New

York for subsequently granting permissions for the first-time publication of passages from Ginsberg's journal about his experience in Southeast Asia: excerpts from the Allen Ginsberg Papers at Stanford by Allen Ginsberg. Copyright © 1963 by Allen Ginsberg, used by permission of the Wylie Agency LLC.

Karl Gerth, Wasana Wongsurawat, and Tony Day furnished valuable feedback on a paper titled "One Night in Bangkok: Ideological Convergence in Angkarn Kallayanapong and Allen Ginsberg's Cold War Poetics," delivered in the panel "Cold War Cosmopolitanisms: Arts and Cultures that Transcend Ideological Boundaries," at the Association for Asian Studies Annual Convention in Washington, DC, in March 2018.

A faculty fellowship in 2015–2016 at Cornell University's Society for the Humanities allowed me to finish large sections of this manuscript. Tim Murray and my colleagues in the Department of Asian Studies generously supported my work. I also wish to acknowledge an Association for Asian Studies, South East Asia Council Translation Subvention Grant (2013).

Any shortcomings in translation or analysis are my sole responsibility, but I thank Kong Rithdee for casting his sharp eye on my translations and Daniel McNaughton for carefully reviewing my manuscript and creating the book's index. I thank Raven Schwam-Curtis and Manasicha Akepiyapornchai for their contributions to the proofing process.

Finally, I was fortunate to have in Christopher Ahn and James Peltz editors who shepherded this project with great enthusiasm, as did Diane Ganeles as project editor. I am grateful to the press also for enlisting the expertise of the sharp and engaged anonymous readers whose review improved my manuscript immeasurably. Chusak Pattarakulvanit is one of the press's reviewers who has allowed me to thank him by name. I would like to express my gratitude to Ajarn Chusak for his generous, insightful engagement with my work. I would like to extend the same heartfelt thanks to the second, anonymous reader, whose succinct review likewise allowed me to improve the book tremendously.

I am very grateful to Renée Staal and Adele Tan of the National Gallery Singapore and to Ormkaew Kallayanapong for providing permission to use an image from Angkarn's *Melting Men* (1976) as the cover image of this book.

A version of chapter 3 first appeared as "The Dream of a Contemporary Ayuthaya: Angkhan Kalayanaphong's Poetics of Dissent, Aesthetic Nationalism, and Thai Literary Modernity," *Oriens Extremus* 48 (2009),

271–90. B. J. Terwiel, Thak Chaloemtiarana, and Martin Hanke provided insightful feedback on this chapter.

I thank Ek, Sutham Thamrongvit, for directing me to the work of Wonderwhale. I am very grateful to the designer Wonderwhale for his conceptualization of the book's cover.

It was my father, Gunther, who, in his inimitable way, prompted me to complete and submit the manuscript for this book. I thank him and my mother, Malve, for their humorous and unstinting support.

⇜

A note on romanization: In agreement with his daughter, Ormkaew Kallayanapong, I use the official transliteration into English of the poet's name, Angkarn Kallayanapong. Other scholars' transliterations vary throughout the text.

1

Introduction

Buddhist Aesthetic Modernity

In his 1969 poem "Wela Khue Chiwa" ("Time Is Life"), modern Thai poet Angkarn Kallayanapong (1926–2012) presciently combines the cultural critique of a globalizing, commercializing, and art-averse era with a remedial vision. As a piece of modern Thai poetry, "Time Is Life" stands out in that it incorporates all at once a critique of the contemporary world, an expansive ontology that includes the cosmos, and a Buddhist-informed reparative vision:

> Heaven has given us Time,
> Like a lord of heavenly status.
> Every single minute is life,
> Destroying time is destroying oneself.
>
> Does this existence have ideals,
> Or is the heart evil, dissolute, without aim?
> Worse yet, scores of lowly creatures,
> Are carelessly enmeshed in the refuse of worldly entanglement.
>
> One day, feel deeply about something,
> Cut a newer gem of wisdom.
> All over the earth there is no taste of divine efflorescence
> As food for the soul.
>
> The Wheel of Time will approach slowly,
> Abducting life and executing it.

Should one merely eat, sleep, reproduce to one's heart's content
Before the end of this life, before death?

Greedy, infatuated, insatiable, crazy for wealth,
The spirit, sorrowful, disintegrates.
The glow of life adverse diminishes,
Lacking dignity, the glow of the heart is lost.

Awake, arise and seek value,
Traces of the way of the great Bodhisattva.
Render the value of your life to the world,
Offer it for everlasting miraculous happiness.

Revolutionize the view of philosophy,
So that the world be pure like heaven.
Have loving kindness and pity, don't kill one another,
Turn the flow of blood into the planting of flowers.

Salvage the heart to the height of the incomparable stars,
Like glimpses of great dignity,
Immortal, far above the turning of the Wheel of Transmigration,
Sacred new power, brave knowledge of discursive thinking.

Clearly perceive the entire value of earth, water, sky,
Long until the day of the *kalpa*'s end,
For contentedness throughout time eternal,
For the universe's calm, to erase suffering and peril.

In *Teardrops of Time*, I investigate how Angkarn Kallayanapong's poetry makes Buddhist concepts available to the creation of a modern Thai aesthetic and ethical imaginary. The poem "Time Is Life" represents an example of the ways in which Angkarn adapts Buddhist temporal frameworks to create scale for cultural critique, to inform modern ethical paradigms, and to invent a lexicon and poetology that adequately reflect the dilemmas of a transforming country and region.

In a primary oeuvre that spans the late 1940s–late 1980s, Angkarn inhabits scales of temporal enormity as his poetry simultaneously moves through a contemporary global world, through the universe, and through Buddhist eons—the *kalpa* that "Time" references. This immensity of time serves to underline both the vehemence of the poet's critique of the present and the magnitude of the alternative worlds that he envisions. Angkarn works through questions of time in Buddhist philosophy, negotiates a literary historical legacy, and wrangles with subjectivity in the contemporary world. What is more, his work presents a diagnostic of an era in which US Cold War policy leaves an indelible mark on Thailand.

The use of imperatives in "Time Is Life" points to the fact that Angkarn's poetry aims to build modern, postcolonial ethical paradigms, taking seriously the question of cultural continuity and inquiring into what proper action for a postcolonial individual might look like. One of the important conceptual moves that the poet makes is that he resacralizes temporality and reenchants the modern world. The contemporary world that has become claustrophobic in his view is thus expanded to encompass the dimensions of an enchanted universe. In this universe, which the poet claims as distinctly Thai, it is possible to inhabit the same time as "the great Bodhisattva." What is more, this universe even offers the possibility of an existence that is "immortal, far above the turning of the Wheel of Transmigration"—a prospect that confers dignity upon and opens up opportunity within a dispiriting modern existence.

For those reading in Thai, "Time" exemplifies the ways in which Angkarn creates a novel poetic language that captures the problematics of globalization from the location of Southeast Asia: a poetry that wields the lexicon of a Buddhist universe with such facility that it manages to label the shortcomings of contemporary culture with precision, while outlining a redemptive scenario of artistic and ethical endeavor.

My analysis in *Teardrops of Time* further provides insight into the transformation of the cultural and political imaginary throughout the history of Thai authoritarian governance since the late 1950s and the exigencies of an increasingly globalized economy in the 1980s. During this entire period, Angkarn's work centrally debates Buddhist notions of time, refunctioning Buddhist ontologies and engaging pedagogies related to the Buddhist truth of impermanence.[1]

In five analytical chapters, I examine how Angkarn's poetry engages fundamental problems in Buddhist thought about temporality to propose desirable *ontologies* for the present; draws on the *historical* temporality of the Ayuthaya period (1350–1767) to furnish modern ethical and aesthetic standards; debates the status of the modern *subject* in time; introduces a novel poetic *language* to address the vicissitudes of Thai modernity; and how the poet's cultural critique and formal innovation produce a lyrical postcolonial *politics* that engages global concerns. With the aid of these building blocks, Angkarn shapes a comprehensive poetic and philosophical framework for the Thai present.

As the formally most innovative Thai poet, Angkarn at the same time centrally mobilizes the literary, artistic, and intellectual pasts of Thailand. Thus, his poetic lexicon stems from Thai Buddhist cosmology and classical literary heritage and makes these available as aesthetic and ethical features for the present. Christian Bauer describes the seemingly incongruous features of the poet's work succinctly:

> Formally it is consciously marked by the use of older meters, familiar from the canon of classical Siamese poetry.
>
> . . .
>
> His great innovation lies in his simultaneous systematic break with the conventions of traditional poetics: on the one hand, he explodes metrics through varying the number of syllables—but retains the 'correct,' that is, the expected, rhyme schemes—, on the other hand, he combines opposing expressions with each other, and includes even the use of obscenities. Readers were at first perplexed by this breaking of taboos: the literary dictate of 'euphony' (Thai *bayrauḥ*), or the expectation of the reader, is challenged by the content in this oeuvre.[2]

What I append to this widely held understanding of the character of Angkarn's work is the argument that, while his poetry is marked by strident critique of the hybridization of Thai culture that has taken place as a result of globalization, it advances a language that is itself exemplary of such hybridity. His work thereby combines an intentional content that conjures the image of an early modern Thai cosmopolitanism with a poetics highly reflective of present-day globalization. What results is an experiment in a Thai Buddhist cosmopolitan aesthetic modernity. As one of the globally most significant poets of the twentieth century, Angkarn thus not only pioneered much of Thai modern prosodic development, but his work also provides unique insight into a non-Western literary modernity and modern Buddhist aesthetics.

In its linguistic innovation, Angkarn's work aligns itself with contemporaneous trends in poetry across the globe. In chapter 5, I therefore draw Angkarn's work in relation to Paul Celan's. The Thai poet even drew the attention of American Beat poet Allen Ginsberg, who proceeded to translate three of Angkarn's poems into English, a textual and personal encounter that chapter 6 explores.

In this book, I label Angkarn's concern a postcolonial one. Official versions of Thai history continually foreground the country's noncolonization, but critical historical work has persuasively detailed its semicolonial status.³ I describe Angkarn's poetry as postcolonial not only in accordance with official or nonofficial designations of Thailand's colonial status, however, but due to this poetry's overriding focus on cultural survival and its very preoccupation with time. My analysis includes first-time translations of poetry and poetic prose from the poet's entire oeuvre.

Temporality

In Angkarn's large-scale project of cultural recovery, Buddhist frameworks of temporality assume an especially important role in the critique as well as the remedial ontologies that he develops for Thai modernity. In 1969, the poet writes "Su Krasae Chara," a poem in the volume *Lamnam Phu Kradueng*, the title of which translates as "Against the Stream of Aging" or "Fighting the Process of Aging." The following three stanzas of the poem detail the immensity of time's power and the poet-narrator's efforts to transcend its destructive power.

> The universe combats time's endlessness,
> Brave for the timeless ages to come.
> The human race may presently become extinct,
> But Time will always be paired with the earth.
>
> Why should the heart tremble in fear,
> Leading the defiled world to utter sadness?
> I, floating higher than the clouds fly,
> Am used to grazing the spectrum of the stars.
>
> Taking the mountains, streams, forests, and oceans,
> As divine medicine, a tribute to heaven,
> The manifold diverse precepts of all of eternal nature,
> Come like magnets with the power of a miraculous, sacred heart.

"Against the Stream of Aging" moreover further elaborates the world that Angkarn's poet-narrators inhabit. Rather than traverse merely the world of the social or of feeling, the poet inserts the speaker into a world in which the universe as a whole plays a role and natural phenomena appear as philosophical agents ("The manifold diverse precepts of all of eternal nature"). To build such a world for his readers, the poet draws on Thai Theravada Buddhist as well as Mahayana Buddhist—and Hindu—imaginations of cosmology. These Buddhist and Hindu paradigms are marked by the vast dimensions of space and time that they delineate. Thus, the *kalpa*, or Buddhist eon, that the poet references in "Wela Khue Chiwa" ("Time Is Life," 1969) above, designates the age of a world and spans billions of years—4,320,000,000 years, to be exact.

The majority of Angkarn's publications stem from between 1964 and 1987. His first collection of poetry, *Kawiniphon Khong Angkarn Kallayanapong* (The Poetry of Angkarn Kallayanapong), was published in 1964. However, this collection also contains poems that were originally published in the 1950s—and the earliest even dates to 1947. Throughout his writing from the 1950s until the 1980s, the theme of time emerges as an overriding concern. This becomes evident throughout Angkarn's first volume of poetry, *Kawiniphon*, as well as throughout the subsequent volumes, *Lamnam Phu Kradueng* (Kradueng Mountain Song, 1969), *Bangkok Kaeo Kamsuan Rue Nirat Nakhon Si Thammarat* (Lament for Beloved Bangkok or Nirat Nakhon Si Thammarat, 1978), *Panithan Kawi* (The Poet's Testament, 1986), and *Yad Nam Khang Khue Namta Khong Wela* (Dew Drops Are the Tears of Time, 1987).

In these works, time becomes the trope that unifies the poet's aesthetic, historical, and ethical concerns. The poet works through quandaries regarding time in the ontological sense of "What is time?" and in the sense of "How much time do I have in the face of time's passing?" Angkarn begins his poem "Kala Khue Arai" ("What Is Time?," *Lamnam Phu Kradueng*) as follows:

> Time, a rapid powerful current, what is it?
> Why is it great, all over the skies?

That the title and beginning of the poem take the form of questions is apt, as the poet addresses issues of temporality in the format of a problematic, rather than as something already known. In particular, Angkarn's work takes up the problem in Buddhist philosophy of whether time is to be regarded as substantial or not. Thus, in the 1987 prose poem "Nimit Nai Sai Rung" ("*Nimitta* in the Rainbow") the poet writes about the nature of time: "It is possible to say that it has a self and possible to say that it has not."[4] I direct detailed attention to this question regarding time's substantiality in chapter 2.

In addition to debating the substantiality of time, the poet experiments with temporal scale, setting vast cosmological temporalities and Buddhist temporalities of impermanence against the minuteness of human life. These inquiries into the nature of time then prompt the poet's concern with the role and destiny of humanity in the present. In "Laeng Wanakhadi" ("Devoid of Literature," *Kawiniphon*) the poet asserts:

> Devoid of literature this life is
> As though the auspicious spirit is no longer to be found.
> Without the precious jeweled rainbow—
> Light of the soul in the world.
>
> Buying status and riches,
> Flooding and feeding the charnel ground.

As early as in this 1964 poem, the notion of art's essentiality to human life looms large. In a further step, the poet's signature laments over cultural loss motivate reflection on the status of the art-producing individual and the endurance of the arts within time. It is in this context that his poetry also acutely grapples with ethical questions. One ethical path that could be pursued within a Buddhist system is that of striving toward the timeless state of nirvana. This individual soteriological solution does not entirely satisfy Angkarn, however, and he calibrates the possibilities of a Buddhist practice that is oriented toward a collective soteriology instead. It is here that the poet confronts one of the most difficult problems in the ontology that he attempts to design for the present. The notion of impermanence (Thai. *anijjang*; Pali, *anicca*) that is at the heart of Buddhist philosophy presents an obstacle to the meaningful life centered on the production of art and the striving for knowledge that the poet proclaims as humanity's highest goal, a dilemma that has garnered much attention in Thai literary criticism. During the poet's working through this ethics of artistic practice, both art and the artist acquire cosmological and soteriological significance. Angkarn's poetry thus constantly oscillates between the injunction to adhere to Buddhist principles and heed the law of impermanence—and his desire to transcend impermanence for the sake of producing lasting, ethical work. The problem is never entirely resolved, and this produces the tension that gives his poetry its contemporaneous and ethical-philosophical charge.

A poem in the 1986 volume *Panithan Kawi* presents some of the paradoxes of the ontology the poet seeks to build and illustrates the challenges for an individual who seeks to retain a culturally specific and Buddhist worldview in the present.

"Phutharom" ("Buddhist Spirit")[5]

I would like to wrap myself in the wind, the sky, and the great ocean,
In a second, a hundred years of human lifetime become empty, nothing.
The coffin helps to let go, o soul,
When the world is in turmoil, heaven leaves us the cemetery of the universe.

Taking sky and earth as a home,
The brilliant stars and the rays of the moon as torches,
Misty clouds drop down as a blanket,
Enveloping wisdom, singing to sleep the sky.

Crazy possessions all over the sky and universe,
Throw them away, bestow good fortune on the burial ground.
The soul abandons the remains of grief, that hidden cemetery,
Forgetting to wake up in the next existence, weary of transmigration.

Ever since the sun illuminated the sky,
The golden clock was not time watching the world.
Slavelike humanity, don't be vile, be still.
Attain the core of brave heroic truth, sharp discursive thinking.

Assume a brave and miraculous attitude,
The heart sparkling with the strength of merit,
Buddhist *dhamma* illuminating the spirit.
Place the universe under the sole of voidness.

> In a Buddhist spirit, for the instance that an elephant shakes
> his ears,
> A snake sticks out its tongue, contemplating this immense value,
> Making merit to expel preposterous, shameful arrogance,
> Contempt toward others that rots the soul.

In "Buddhist Spirit" the poet at first enjoins us to submit to the law of impermanence or the inexorable, all-annihilating progression of time. Here the poem seems to speak in accordance with Buddhist orthodoxy and its doctrine of *anattā*, or nonself. Already the second stanza, however, positions the speaker as an important cosmological actor, "taking sky and earth as a home." In this stanza, the poem invokes a notion of individual possibility and even grandeur that seems to be at odds with the prior Buddhist exhortation. In the stanzas that follow, the reader is encouraged to discard possessions and instead to turn to the production of art as a proper ethical pursuit. At first this again seems to be a truly Buddhist injunction:

> Buddhist *dhamma* illuminating the spirit.
> Place the universe under the sole of voidness.

The poem further speaks of a weariness of existence and the desire to escape the cycle of transmigration—all proper Buddhist sentiments on the path of individual soteriology. However, all lines of the poem that speak of the individual's actions also assume yet another dimension. Thus stanzas 4–5 exhort us to

> Attain the core of brave heroic truth, sharp discursive thinking.
>
> Assume a brave and miraculous attitude.
> The heart sparkling with the strength of merit.

Although presented in the context of meritorious action, these lines may be read to stand in contrast to the Buddhist injunction to let go. The mandates that "Buddhist Spirit" sets forth also assume the symbolics of individualism, hinting at such characteristics of an individual as superior talent and training as well as diligence.

While others have designated Angkarn's apotheosis of the artist a version of Bodhisattvahood, this poetic vision always also possesses qualities that exceed Buddhist formulations.⁶ As much as it may be oriented toward Buddhist action, this vision, as instantiated by "Buddhist Spirit," underlines the individualist bent of Angkarn's philosophy, a fact that Marc Weeks and Frederic Maurel presciently note and draw into comparison with writing on individual will by Friedrich Nietzsche.⁷

As such, Angkarn's poetry lends itself precisely to an inquiry into contradictory notions of the self under conditions of Thailand's growing engagement with global capitalism in the period under consideration. I investigate the poet's interrogation of modern Thai subjectivities through the lens of time in chapter 4. On a further level of analysis, we can understand the poet's vision as also furnishing evidence for the confluence of Buddhist and individualist-capitalist delineations. Thus, Angkarn's poetry is uniquely suited to an investigation of the paradoxes of life in a globalized, neoliberal world.

Rather than assume that Angkarn's poetry presents only a coherent, purely Buddhist ethics for the present, consideration of the contradictory elements in his work allows us to ask what the particular challenges to the individual are in the Thailand of the 1950s–1980s. Thus, the strength of Angkarn's poetry is not that it furnishes logical closure, but rather that it keeps open the question of how to live in a present in which cultural survival is constantly under threat.

My analysis of the coexistence of divergent temporalities in Angkarn's work is informed by systematic critiques of the linear, rationalized time of clock and calendar undertaken by scholars such as Bliss Cua Lim, Dipesh Chakrabarty, Harry Harootunian, and Pheng Cheah. Thus, Chakrabarty's critique of temporality aims to "situate the question of subaltern history within a postcolonial critique of modernity and history itself."⁸

Lim argues that "modern homogeneous time has come to seem increasingly natural and incontrovertible, assuming the guise of a ready-made temporality." This temporality "synchroniz[es] people, information, and markets in a simultaneous global present." The problem that such a streamlining of time creates is the following:

> Modern time consciousness is a means of exercising social, political, and economic control over periods of work and leisure; it obscures the ceaselessly changing plurality of our existence in time; and it underwrites a linear, developmental notion of progress that gives rise to ethical problems with regard to cultural and racial difference.⁹

By contrast to such forcible rationalizations of time, Lim calls attention to the ways in which heterotemporality persists in the present. Her remedial strategy is to highlight the critical, historically reparative perspective that the recognition of divergent temporal strata may engender.

In Angkarn's poetry, Buddhist temporal strata are called upon to perform the work of expanding the time of the present. I will argue that the function of Buddhist temporality in this work is not merely to represent an *other* dimension to a dispiriting present, however. Rather, Buddhist temporality is as much of the present and erupts from within it as it links to other temporal strata (such as the past).

I argue that the centrality of time in his oeuvre alone makes Angkarn's a postcolonial project. In this argument, I rely on the work of Pheng Cheah, who locates temporality at the center of a postcolonial reconceptualization of world and worlding. On the most basic level, the focus on time, rather than space, enables an intervention into colonial and neocolonial capitalist mappings of the world, according to this author. Cheah's framework understands "time [as] the original opening, the first and ongoing relation to exteriority" and "the world as an ongoing work."[10] It complicates both teleological models of the world as well as the facile championing of heterotemporality. Within this model of world and worlding that focuses on temporality, postcolonial literature holds a special place.[11] Two avenues for decolonization have been pursued in this literature and in postcolonial political projects more broadly—revolutionary decolonization and the championing of heterotemporality. Cultural survival occupies a central place within these endeavors: "One of the aims of revolutionary decolonization is the struggle against cultural genocide. It ushers a new temporality that reworlds and opens another world for a people in the face of colonial violence."[12]

The greatest intervention that Cheah makes into postcolonial models of worlding and deployments of time is to position heterotemporality—the existence of multiple temporalities that are distinct from the "homogeneous empty time" of modernity and colonial, capitalist expansion—not as extraneous but as situated within the temporalities of globalization, nation, and capital:

> Multitemporality is not the interruption of the homogeneous empty time of capital by another, nonsecular temporality. It is instead the intensification of an already existing heterogeneity by the forces of hybridization generated by global capital flows.[13]

Seeking to show that this is precisely the move that Angkarn's oeuvre undertakes, I argue that he is at once the modern Thai poet who engages most directly with the global and thinks most stringently about how to make the temporalities of cosmology and Buddhist soteriology available for critique in the present.

Angkarn's poetry further engages historical temporalities by inquiring into the significance that one particular period in Thai history might have for the present. In particular, he consistently contrasts the Ayuthaya period (1350–1767), which he deems to have been the high point of Thai cultural achievement, with the present Bangkok period. I discuss the question of what kind of worldview emerges from this orientation toward Ayuthaya in chapter 3.

In other poems on time, Angkarn highlights poetological questions, focusing with great intensity on what modern Thai art should look like and what the role of the art-producing individual should be. In this debate, the poet inquires into the individual's status within the temporalities of modernity, setting these into relief against vast cosmological frameworks of time. What is noteworthy is not only the degree to which Buddhist thought enters into these debates, but also the extent to which the poet develops further Buddhist thought on time, the self, and the arts.

Although Angkarn's poetry and poetology are distinctly Thai and frequently bear cultural-nationalist overtones, this work is at the same time intricately connected with poetological concerns across the globe. Thus, like several of his contemporaries internationally, Angkarn is singularly absorbed in questions of cultural continuity, or rather, in an updating of Thai cultural resources for the present. Although he frequently declares his aversion to foreign cultures, Angkarn is also the first Thai poet presciently to address issues of globalization in a concentrated manner.[14]

In his poetic critique of the present, especially where "Bangkok" is concerned, the poet's work at times appears xenophobic. He has further been said to eschew reading in foreign languages. His daughter, Ormkaew Kallayanapong, by contrast, describes Angkarn as a vivacious, cosmopolitan intellectual who enjoyed the exchange with foreign poets and read voraciously, attempting to do so even in languages of which he did not have extensive knowledge.[15] At an event in the 2000s, Angkarn himself affirmed, "I read everything like an ocean takes everything in; but mostly literature."[16] This biographical information will become important for understanding the cosmopolitan character and references of the poet's work.

Subjectivity

At great length, Angkarn's work deliberates on impermanence as the base condition of subjectivity. The creator of art, especially, oscillates between sacrificing life and gaining ascendancy over impermanence. The poet moreover situates modern Thai subjectivity in a world of capitalist pressures, but also highlights aspects of personhood that supersede these. Rather than understanding the temporalities of the contemporary, Cold War world as diametrically opposed to those of Buddhism, I argue that they converge in Angkarn's poetry and the social fields that it addresses.

As a prescient poet of globalization, Angkarn grapples with the question of what a desirable modern Thai subjectivity might look like. Angkarn's preoccupation with a self that on the one hand possesses immense powers of agency, while it is on the other hand constantly subject to dissolution, is part of his philosophy of vocation, but must also be examined in relation to political change from the 1950s until the late 1980s. In the 1970s the poet's contemporaries were singularly concerned with creating poetics that they understood as aimed toward democratization, while Angkarn seemed oblivious to the political agendas of his leftist colleagues. At the same time, he set his sights on a broad philosophical horizon of cultural renewal early on, a postcolonial cultural politics. The poet's deliberations on subjectivity represent an important component of this agenda. What does a desirable modern Thai subjectivity look like? How is this subject positioned within time? What temporalities might be accessible to him?[17] What is a culturally postcolonial subject to do?

I argue that the new, multifaceted demands that persons in Thailand face in the constantly changing political, economic, and social environments of the 1950s–1980s vitally motivate Angkarn's focus on the ideal contours of ethical selfhood. The poet conceptualizes subjectivity along two main axes that I investigate in two chapters. Chapter 2 approaches Angkarn's concept of subjectivity by examining how he positions the self in relation to Buddhist doctrinal thinking about impermanence. Chapter 4 returns to this question with a focus on the role of the artist and an investigation into the social and economic factors that make increasingly contradictory demands on the individual in the 1950s–1980s.

While subjectivity is not merely a matter of historical cultural forces, but also of psychic economies and pleasure—all of which one could read from Angkarn's work—I restrict myself primarily to investigating the poet's concept of subjectivity in relation to new stipulations for personhood in the decades under review and to analyzing the notions of subjectivity put forth in the manifestos drafted by Angkarn and other poets.

Manifestos

Closely connected to questions of temporality, subjectivity, and Angkarn's deployment of Buddhism is the discussion of modern poets' artistic credos. My discussion of manifestos in chapter 4 is inspired by Suchitra Chongstitvatana's work on the modern manifesto and its literary predecessors.

In the 1980s and 1990s, Thai literary scholars pursued the question of an indigenous literary theory. Suchitra notes that there are few extant treatises on literary theory per se; therefore, scholars turn to the investigation of the literary theory inherent in treatises on versification and in thought about the role of literature expressed in the literary works themselves. In 1984 Suchitra pioneered this trend with an inquiry into the "formation of Thai poetical convention and Thai concepts of poets and poetry."[18] In chapter 3, I pursue a similar historically grounded analysis with regard to the poetics and politics of the *nirat* genre.

With respect to the modern period, scholars note the tendency of Thai poets to put forth manifestos declaring the aims of their work—as well as exhorting others to heed particular literary standards and ideological ideals. Investigating the predecessors of modern poets' manifestos, Suchitra asserts that statements of poetic purpose are not an entirely modern invention, but in some respects follow upon a tradition: "Thai poets in the Ayuthaya period demonstrated a 'convention' of expressing a high esteem for their own work and wishing it to remain forever."[19] She provides three examples: "This 'convention' can be seen from the early poetical works like *Lilit Yuan Phai*, *Thawathotsamat*, and *Lilit Phra Lo*."[20] Suchitra observes that modern poets follow in the traces of these classical dedications, but modify them to a great extent: "This 'convention' still survives in the works of modern poets like Angkhan and Naowarat. . . . Although these two modern poets seem to follow the 'convention' they extend it further to a deeper dimension of their own."[21]

Trisilpa Boonkhachorn relates modern poets' manifestos to the declining role of poets in society and considers the new relation to the social that modern poetry evinces:

In the "advanced" technological society, the status of poetry seems to lessen. However, an interesting phenomenon is that in contemporary Thai poetry some poets, e.g. Angkhaan Kalayaanaphong and Naowarat Phongphaibun express the philosophical themes of poetry by emphasizing the meaning, the status, and the function of poetry. For the first time in the history of Thai literature poets struggle with a declining role in society. Poets now declare their "Poetic Testaments" to restrengthen the power of poetry in creating a better society and world.[22]

What my analysis adds to this important conversation on modern poetics is the sociopolitical contextualization of modern literary manifestos and the investigation of changing notions of subjectivity in a neoliberalizing world.

A Cultural History of the 1950s–1980s

Teardrops combines a methodology of close readings of Angkarn's poems and poetic prose pieces with discourse analysis and thereby embeds its thematic analyses in the cultural history of the period in which the poet works. Most of Angkarn's writing is published at the height of the Cold War, during a time of predominant US influence and, later, of Japanese economic engagement in Thailand. More specifically, the poet begins to write, with regularity, in the 1950s. The late 1950s marks the beginning of a period of authoritarian, developmentalist rule under Field Marshall Sarit Thanarat (1958–1963). This period proved foundational for structures of governance in subsequent decades. I thus examine how Angkarn's poetry positions itself in relation to standards that emerged as the Thai state increasingly consolidated itself as a military polity and expanded government control over the provinces.[23] I further investigate how we might understand Angkarn's poetic innovation and philosophical outlook in comparison with the left-wing Art for Life poets whose works dominate the tumultuous 1970s, the decade in which prodemocratic citizens rise up to challenge the military state and are ultimately brutally suppressed. Finally, I argue that we must view Angkarn's work also in relation to the post-Cold War period of the 1980s when the Thai economy expands even further.

The historian Chris Baker and the economist Pasuk Pongphaichit provide a helpful account of the large-scale transitions that Thailand undergoes during the period that Angkarn's poetry addresses. What makes their presentation of the period from the 1950s until the 1980s especially valuable is that they investigate Thailand's history during these decades as always already transnational. Dating Thailand's "American era" to the 1940s–1960s as they do, these authors note that especially the 1950s and 1960s are marked by concerted US investment into establishing influence in Thailand—in the effort to make Thailand the primary ally of and a bulwark for the United States against the spread of communism in Southeast Asia and East Asia. Subsequent to Sarit Thanarat's military coup in 1958, the United States began its vigorous, long-term backing of anticommunist military regimes in the country.[24] Baker and Pasuk detail the far-reaching changes that US financial aid to Thailand effected in the country's bureaucracy and military.

Baker and Pasuk's history indicates the centrality that Thailand assumed for the US war in Vietnam in the years that followed: the first US airstrikes on Vietnam were flown from Thailand in 1964.[25] Subsequently, "three quarters of the bomb tonnage dropped on Northern Vietnam and Laos during 1965–1968 was flown out of seven bases in eastern Thailand."[26]

In close conjunction with consolidating Thailand's support of US geopolitical interests, these decades saw the introduction of the notion of *development*, which became the dominant paradigm of Thai economic, political, and cultural policy henceforth. In economic terms,

> The US set out to develop a free-market economy to cement Thailand into the US camp of the Cold War.
>
> President Truman introduced the word "development" in his inaugural speech in 1947. Sarit understood its role as a key concept of the US global mission, and as a new and powerful justification for the power of the nation-state—"progress" translated for the American era. His regime converted the new Thai coining, *phatthana*, into its watchword: "Our important task in this revolutionary era is development, which includes economic development, educational development, administrative development, and everything else."[27]

It is not difficult to see that the developmentalism of this era, with its tendencies toward standardization across educational, economic, administrative, and cultural fields, would provide a challenge to an artist concerned with cultural survival and Buddhist ethics and who possesses a keen sense for linguistic innovation.

The developmentalist period also set into motion a particular form of globalization of the Thai economy: "Sarit welcomed a World Bank mission to Thailand after his first coup. Its report was transformed into Thailand's first five-year development plan, launched in 1961." Importantly, this marked the transformation from state control of economic development to an emphasis on the private sector.[28] The shift to private enterprise brought with it whole new vocabularies of management and self-management, technology, and biopolitics as well as the development of coteries of professionals to support the new economic ventures that were to drive development forward.

Under US influence, Thailand undertook a far-reaching extension of the nation-state into the provinces. Although the "geo-body" of the Thai nation had been established earlier, the comprehensive administrative expansion of this geo-body only took hold in the mid-twentieth century.[29] At this time, Buddhism also became more centrally associated with the expansion of state control.[30] The Sarit era further saw the establishment of the monarchy as central to the new model of governance, especially to policies of development.[31] These policies inaugurated a blueprint for governance that became foundational for the national political structure.

I argue that the Sarit era is strongly reflected in Angkarn's writing. Even though his poetry may not feature this era by name, the extent to which the poet invests energy in inventing a countervision that eclipses the cultural, political, and economic paradigms of the Sarit regime stands out.

After the US defeat in Vietnam, the 1970s saw the US's gradual withdrawal from the region and from Thailand; this included the withdrawal of financial resources: "The U.S. remained Thailand's military patron, but at a much greater distance."[32] It is in this decade that Baker and Pasuk locate the initial foothold of "globalization and mass society" in Thailand.[33] The 1970s saw the shift to Japanese investment in and domination of the Thai economy. This was also the era of widespread farmers' and students' protests against military governance as well as the decade of communist insurgency and harsh state suppression of oppositional politics.[34]

A further focus of this book is the contextualization of Angkarn's work within a wider literary culture. Most relevant for comparison is the work of the left-leaning Art for Life poets of the 1970s, especially Naowarat Pongpaiboon's. The Art for Life poets' styles, thematic emphases, and stated ideologies differ fundamentally from Angkarn's and become instructive for considering the singularity of his political and poetological stances.

I also contextualize Angkarn's work within a longer literary history and consider how the poet improvises on form and develops poetic lexica, metrics, and genre. Thus, in chapter 3, I pay close attention to how Angkarn improvises on the historical *nirat* genre, a genre of travel poetry that the poet adapts to his discussion of themes of cultural departure in the present.

Finally, I believe that we must consider Angkarn's poetry also in the context of Thailand's increased entry into global networks of trade, finance, and cultural production in the 1980s. Angkarn continues to write into this decade, a period in which Cold War divisions begin to morph into new regional and transnational financial interests and neoliberal politics. With regard to the imbrication of Angkarn's focus on time with the economic change occurring during this time, Weeks and Maurel write: "Angkarn has lived and created through a period of unprecedented political and economic movement in Thailand, culminating in the breathtaking 'bubble' of investment and growth which began in the mid-1980s and ruptured in 1997."[35]

In this period, both politics and cultural production take a significant turn that provides an important background for Angkarn's deepening engagement with Buddhism. It is in the mid- to late 1980s that the poet writes his last well-known volume of poetry, *Panithan Kawi*, for which he is awarded the 1986 S.E.A. Write Award. In terms of economic activity, the 1970s had been the decade in which Japanese dominance began, but they also marked the initial reestablishment of trade ties with the People's Republic of China and the expansion of the global connections of Thai trade and finance.

In the early to mid-1980s, "Thailand lurched into the 'Asian model' of export manufacturing."[36] This shift was accompanied by extensive social change that included "rapid demographic transition," economic restructuring, economic growth, and urbanization that transformed Thailand from a still predominantly agricultural society into an industrialized and mediatized "mass society."[37] As Baker and Pasuk write, "The liberalization of first trade and then finance accelerated the pace of industrialization and urbanization, and incorporated Thailand more firmly within a global economy."[38] The authors summarize the abiding, fundamental transformations of Thai society that begin in the 1970s as follows:

> Over one generation during the last quarter of the 20th century, Thailand's society changed with unprecedented speed. Building on the foundations of urban capitalism laid in the American era, big-business families grew not only in wealth but also in social prominence. A new white-collar middle class embraced western-influenced consumer tastes and concepts of individualism. Capitalism drew into the city a much larger working class.[39]

What is more, during the last quarter of the twentieth century, the increased mobility that resulted from large-scale extension of the infrastructure and the expansion of print and electronic media had a significant social impact:

> National mass media created a social mirror in which the society could begin to see itself. The reflection revealed the variety of the society's ethnic make-up, the complexity of its history, the diversity of religious practice, and the scale of social divisions.
> The boom conferred by globalization and the emergence of a national society provided the background for challenges to the paternalist traditions of the nation's politics.[40]

Angkarn Kallayanapong's poetry keenly notes these massive transformations in governance and society. More than a critique of politics per se, Angkarn's poetry concentrates on cultural critique. What scandalizes the poet is not only the greed and despotism of military dictators; rather, he is concerned also with the emerging taste cultures, changing patterns of consumption, and cultural practices of modern Thais. A remarkable feature of this poetry, however, is that it does not only address these perceived social and political ills directly. While I will argue that Angkarn's work vitally revolves around the sociopolitical transformations of the 1950s–1980s, its focus lies on designing alternative artistic, philosophical, and political frameworks with distinctly Thai characteristics. In contrast to the Art for Life poets, who build socialist and social democratic poetic lexica, draw on popular poetic forms, and aim to integrate the rhythms of agricultural and working-class life into their poetry, Angkarn sets his vision on a wider poetic and philosophical horizon. The scope of his vision includes nothing less than the entire universe, and his interest lies in the redemption of all of humanity.

New Perspectives on Buddhism

Teardrops of Time seeks to contribute to understandings of a Southeast Asian, postcolonial literary modernity and provide insight into how this literature develops a Buddhist-informed aesthetics. The idea that Buddhism might perform functions other than those of religious pedagogy or philosophy is still a novel one. While the scholarship has drawn Buddhism into relation with Southeast Asian notions of power, logics of statecraft, and constructions of modernity, much work remains to be done on the ways in which Buddhist concepts, stories, and images provide frameworks for fantasy and desire, furnish rhetorical tools, represent means of psychological support, and diversify notions of self and agency in the everyday.[41]

I align my analysis with other new efforts, in Asian studies and beyond, to shed light on the work that Buddhism performs outside of the sphere of religious instruction proper—that is, the role that Buddhist concepts and forms occupy in media, cultural psychology, political rhetoric, affective repertoires, and literary and cultural imaginaries. What unites much of this new work in Buddhist studies is a focus on counterdoctrinal qualities of Buddhist cultural objects and practices. A long history of examining Buddhist practices as not conforming to doctrinal maxims precedes these works. In the Anglophone context, authors such as Richard Gombrich and Donald Swearer inaugurated a shift from the study of Buddhism as a South Asian textual tradition, in the languages of Pali and Sanskrit, to the study of Buddhism in historical context, as an element of the political order and as lived praxis in Southeast Asia.[42] Subsequent scholarship paid increased attention to practices and ritual in Buddhism, rather than only to its textual instantiations.

Recent investigations into the relation of praxis to text take the examination of counterdoctrinality even further, opening to Buddhist studies inquiry new domains such as media, psychology, and the built environment. Such new work undertakes the explicit theorization of Buddhist counterdoctrinality and expands the domain of Buddhism to include many vernacular practices and even the supernatural. Pioneering work in this vein includes Justin McDaniel's study *The Lovelorn Ghost and the Magical Monk*.[43] This monograph furnishes important insight into the counterdoctrinality of Thai Buddhist practices, as McDaniel makes clear that many practices, or indeed life goals, of Thai Buddhists are aimed toward attachment rather than detachment—a prime counterdoctrinal fact at the very heart of a living Buddhism.

The scholarship is approaching a point at which it is no longer the *fact* but rather the *how* of counterdoctrinality that is in focus, as authors pursue the question of what each counterdoctrinal deployment of a Buddhist concept effects and what it enables for their respective fields of inquiry. Recent publications that approach Buddhist studies from such new angles have included Julia Cassaniti's *Living Buddhism: Mind, Self, and Emotion in a Thai Community* and *Remembering the Present: Mindfulness in Buddhist Asia*; Andy Rotman's *Thus I Have Seen: Faith in Early Indian Buddhism*; Erik Davis's *Deathpower: Buddhism's Ritual Imagination in Cambodia*; my book, *Ghostly Desires: Queer Sexuality and Vernacular Buddhism in Contemporary Thai Cinema*; Justin McDaniel's *Architects of Buddhist Leisure: Socially Disengaged Buddhism in Asia's Museums, Monuments, and Amusement Parks*; and Francisca Cho's *Seeing Like the Buddha: Enlightenment through Film*. These works in cultural psychology, Buddhist studies, and cinema and cultural studies investigate the ways in which Buddhist texts and contexts provide aesthetic frameworks; idioms for how to talk about desire; and modern cosmologies or frameworks for how to talk about the world. In addition, many of these works link the study of Buddhist contexts to that of affect.

In *Teardrops*, I take up the question of how modern literature avails itself of Buddhist imaginaries. I am interested in how Angkarn adapts Buddhist concepts to ends that are not primarily directed toward religious edification. I investigate how this modern Thai poetry uses Buddhist frameworks to create scale for cultural critique, inform ethical paradigms, and invent a language that conveys the struggles of a region undergoing radical transformation.

Not surprisingly, it is Thai literary scholars who have carried out the most in-depth studies of Buddhism in Thai literature to date. In chapter 4, I highlight a debate in the 1980s and 1990s that concerns the status of the arts in Angkarn's work and the question of its compatibility with Buddhist doctrine. In this debate, Thai literary scholars pioneer the examination of Buddhism as a framework of thought that reaches beyond religious instruction or statecraft. The debate about the status of the arts in Angkarn's work may be the prime instance in which they showcase this important innovation in the scholarship.

That most of the relevant research on Angkarn's work and on modern Thai poetry and poetics would be carried out by Thai scholars and in the Thai language may also seem self-evident. Suchitra Chongstitvatana's English-language PhD dissertation, "The Nature of Modern Thai Poetry

Considered with Reference to the Works of Angkhan Kalayanaphong, Naowarat Phongphaibun and Suchit Wongthet," offers a rich compendium of analyses of the thematic and formal aspects of modern poetry. Most of this work is concerned with the poetry of Angkarn Kallayanapong, but Suchitra also devotes attention to the analysis of the poetry of his contemporary, Naowarat Pongpaiboon. She is moreover the first to analyze Angkarn's development of the *nirat* genre and conventions; consider the poet's privileging of nature as teacher; and investigate the genre of the modern poetic manifesto. Some of the sharpest formulations of these insights are contained in her 1987 article that examines the status of the arts in Angkarn's work in a Buddhist context, "Kawiniphon Khong Angkarn Kallayanapong: Sasana Haeng Sunthari" (The Poetry of Angkarn Kallayanapong: The Religion of Aesthetics), a piece of scholarship that I discuss in detail in chapter 4. Suchitra's 2001 book, *Phuthatham Nai Kawiniphon Samai Mai* (Buddha Dharma in Modern Thai Poetry), provides further invaluable examinations of Buddhism in Thai literature and analyses of Angkarn's poetry. Other Thai literary scholars who have focused on the poetry of Angkarn include Chetana Nagavajara and Trisilpa Boonkhachorn. Chetana is an important participant in the debate on the substantiality of the arts in Angkarn's work. Trisilpa's PhD dissertation also devotes attention to the Buddhist content of modern Thai poetry and discusses the form of the modern manifesto-poem.[44] Angkarn's poetry has drawn the attention of scholars outside of Thailand, and Christian Bauer, John Mattioli, Marc Weeks and Frederic Maurel, and Klaus Wenk all provide insightful analyses of his work.

Teardrops is the first monograph, however, that analyzes Angkarn Kallayanapong's work in English. There is a dearth of books on Thai literature in English more generally, but a fortunate recent set of publications includes Susan Kepner's *A Civilized Woman: M. L. Boonlua Debhayasuwan and the Thai Twentieth Century* (as well as her earlier *The Lioness in Bloom: Modern Thai Fiction about Women*); Martin B. Platt's *Isan Writers, Thai Literature: Writing and Regionalism in Modern Thailand*; Rachel Harrison's edited volume, *Disturbing Conventions: Decentering Thai Literary Cultures*; and Thak Chaloemtiarana's *Read Till It Shatters: Nationalism and Identity in Modern Thai Literature*.[45]

Although Angkarn was a National Artist and Southeast Asian Write Awardee, his work remains underrepresented in translation—and even in criticism in Thai. Only a few individual poems of Angkarn have been translated into German or English, while most of his oeuvre remains inaccessible to scholars and other readers of world literature. This book provides not only the first sustained analysis of this work in English but also first-time access to a substantial section of the poet's work in translation. In this comprehensive selection of Angkarn's poetry and poetic prose on the topic of time, my translation seeks to reflect the tone and style of the original. My analysis and translation are as much designed to make Angkarn's work accessible to an English-language readership as to contribute to research and teaching in world and global literatures, comparative poetics, literary modernity, and Asian literature.

Translation, Transnationality, and Political Orientation

Style and Composition of Translations

The appendix assembles in translation a comprehensive selection of Angkarn's poetry and poetic prose on the topic of time. In order to reflect the style of the original texts, my translation aims to transmit elements of the syntax, temporal indeterminacy, unique poetic lexicon, and customary absence of a distinct subject that mark the poet's work. Thus, my translation approximates a syntax that is frequently without a clearly delineated verb or agent. This is a grammatical feature of Thai, yet the poet maximizes the effect of this language's syntactic openness. Angkarn's poetry also does not codify tense as precisely as poetry in Thai could. One way in which I translate this openness of temporality and agency into English is by rendering some stanzas of Angkarn's poems without a clear subject and as using continuous forms of the verb. In other instances, I translate poems rather literally in order to preserve the tone and distinct lexicon of the poet's literary style.

The selection of translations that I have undertaken includes poems from Angkarn's earliest work in the late 1940s until his work in the late 1980s. During this period of over thirty years, Angkarn's poetry develops both in content and style. The late work sees a simultaneous increase of dedication to the world and forsaking of personal salvation as well as a more explicitly Buddhist orientation of philosophical content and poetic lexicon. At the same time, the late work is more heteroglot in its poetic vocabulary, combining the Greek and Latinate neologisms of an increasingly scientific and technocratic present with the most fundamental Buddhist terms of cosmology, ethics, and soteriology. In particular, my translations include two examples of Angkarn's *panithan*, or poetic manifestos: the 1959 "Pledge of the Poet" and the 1986 "The Poet's Testament" showcase some of the linguistic and conceptual changes that have occurred in this poet's work over the almost three decades that separate them.

A few of the poems featured in my analysis have been translated previously. Due to their prominence in the oeuvre and their relevance to the topic of time, I nevertheless include these poems in my selection. My translation is moreover radically different, aiming for more precise approximations of the original texts' tone and style. The previous translations in question include translations into English of three individual poems and two parts of poems:

1. Translation of "Sia Jao" ("I Lost You")—by Allen Ginsberg, 1980

2. Translation of "Jaruek Adid" ("Inscription from the Past")—by Chetana Nagavajara, 1986

3. Translation of "Panithan Khong Kawi" ("The Poet's Testament")—by Sulak Sivaraksa and Hiram Woodward, 1986

4. Partial translation of "Panithan Khong Kawi" ("The Poet's Testament")—by Allen Ginsberg, 1978.[46]

5. Partial translation of "Ayuthaya"—by Michael Wright, 1986

Thematically, I investigate aspects of translation in the last two chapters of the book. Thus, chapter 5 undertakes a comparison of Angkarn's work with that of the German-language poet Paul Celan (1920–1970). One intention in drawing Angkarn into relation to one of the most important—or the most important—European poet of the twentieth century is to treat Angkarn as a poet of similar stature and his poetry as of comparable global relevance. I argue that the two poets' works are united by their concerns with poetology, linguistic innovation, and the thematics of loss. I moreover set the global features of Angkarn's poetry into relation with scholarly work that considers translation in the context of Chinese prose poetry.

POLITICAL ORIENTATIONS

Among the handful of extant translations, the most astounding are the three by the American Beat poet Allen Ginsberg (1926–1997). Until I consulted cultural critic Sulak Sivaraksa, the circumstances of Ginsberg's translation of Angkarn's 1953 poem "Wak Thale" ("Scoop Up the Sea"), his partial rendition of Angkarn's 1959 "Panithan Khong Kawi" ("The Pledge of the Poet"), and his translation of "Sia Jao" ("I Lost You") from 1964 remained mysterious: Sulak confirmed that he himself translated (at least the first two) of the poems and Ginsberg then transposed them into his own poetic language.

The American poet had traveled to Thailand in May 1963, and the country subsequently continued to be on his radar due to its central role in US politics in Southeast Asia. Details of Ginsberg's encounter with Angkarn, and especially with his poem, "Sia Jao," remain unclear, but the appeal that the Thai poet's radical linguistic innovation might have had for the American poet, who was himself responsible for radical interventions into traditional poetics in the US context, is not surprising. Ginsberg's strong engagement with Buddhism furnishes a further compelling reason for his attraction to Angkarn's work, replete as it is with Buddhist iconography and cosmology.

Ginsberg and Angkarn were contemporaries—both were born in 1926, yet they inhabited radically different worlds and poetic traditions. Nevertheless, Ginsberg's experimentation with drugs and his rendering of those experiences in a novel, psychedelic poetic lexicon finds a parallel in the cosmogenic and at times hallucinatory poetry of Angkarn. What further unites the two poets is that both were affected by and reacted intensely to the US's Cold War politics in Southeast Asia—a factor that turned Angkarn's world around and ushered in a period of increased global interconnection and dependence for Thailand. For Ginsberg, too, it is US policy in Southeast Asia that draws his critique, albeit from the position of an American radical leftist.

Angkarn's encounter with Ginsberg points to a measure of reciprocity, in content and style, between Thai and American literary creation. Other broad transnational linkages can be discerned between Angkarn's poetry and that of Indian poets of the latter half of the twentieth century. Thus, the Thai poet's work finds parallels also in the poetry of India's "Bombay poets."[47]

My consideration of the encounter between Angkarn and Ginsberg rounds off the analysis of the transnational import of Angkarn's work in the final two chapters of the book. While comparison with Celan draws the focus to the global relevance of considerations of loss, temporality, and linguistic innovation in the second half of the twentieth century, the connection between Angkarn and Ginsberg sheds light on the thematics of Americanization and US empire and allows for the investigation of Buddhism as a globally relevant, alternative ideology. In this last chapter, I also use the comparison with Ginsberg to assess Angkarn's political outlook with more precision.

Because he does not produce a certain type of politicized poetry during the 1970s and 1980s, Angkarn has been suspected of harboring right-wing views or of being apolitical. Assessments of the poet's political stance frequently set his work in opposition to that of Art for Life poets such as Naowarat Pongpaiboon. Bauer summarizes this view as follows:

> Angkarn's poetology stands diametrically opposed to the Art for Life ('sinlapa phuea chiwit') of, for instance, Chit Phumisak—in interviews, he mocks politically engaged poetry; the critic Chetana Nagavajara even speaks of a "littérature désengagée" that remains too caught up in an idealized past.[48]

Elsewhere, Bauer remarks: "In contrast to that of Angkarn Kalyanapong's, Naowarat's late oeuvre is eminently political, although he, too, creates a field of tension to contemporary and modern content through his holding on to a traditional conventional poetics."[49]

While I, too, draw Angkarn's work into relation to that of the Art for Life poets, I do not designate one kind of poetry apolitical and the other political. By contrast, my analysis studies Angkarn as a poet who pursues a different critique than his contemporaries, but not a less politicized or perceptive one.[50] The poet's daughter, Ormkaew Kallayanapong, also sheds a different light on the poet's political orientation. She declares her father to have been a strong critic of the military regimes of the 1970s and 1990s, a claim that is corroborated both in details of biography and in several of Angkarn's poems and paintings (see chapter 6).[51]

In the Thai and international reception, some have taken Angkarn's poetry as functioning primarily (and merely) on a metaphysical, philosophical level while considering the work trivial in its political engagement. By contrast, my analysis takes seriously the seeming banality of the poet's political interventions. It is important that we also consider in earnest political ideologies that seem deplorable, misguided, or populist. To this end, I take into consideration Stuart Hall's thoughts on the "popular," but—with regard to the case of Angkarn—I take Hall's "popular" as analogous with the trivial. As the producer of difficult poetry—an elite cultural product—Angkarn cannot stand in for the popular as such.

However, his frequently quickly dismissed, seemingly right-wing political stance can be aligned with dominant, popular mainstream opinions that some discount as trivial.

In a well-known essay on "deconstructing the popular," Stuart Hall invalidates notions of the popular's constitution from above as well as understandings of the popular as representative of "the People's" will or as inherently authentic, progressive, or resistant. Instead Hall situates the value of the popular in its role as a domain of cultural-political contestation. It is here that he writes, "Popular culture is one of the sites where this struggle for and against culture is engaged: it is also the stake to be won or lost in that struggle."[52] Thus, rather than discount it as merely deplorable, misguided, or otherwise lacking in progressive elements, I take Angkarn's political expression seriously in order to understand the ways in which Thai poets in the latter half of the twentieth century sought to mobilize the domain of culture.

Gender

Finally, a note on the gender politics of Angkarn's poetry: throughout my analysis, I use the pronoun "he" to designate the figure of the poet or the artist that appears in his poems. I do so consciously and critically, with the intention of reflecting what I believe is the poet's perspective. The way in which Angkarn alternately refers to the poet, in the abstract sense, and to himself frequently does not distinguish between Angkarn's qualities and those of the ideal, cosmically significant producer of art that he describes. This amalgamation alone points toward an unexamined masculinist perspective.

While Angkarn's work is egalitarian in terms of class background, formal education, and ontology, it is generally not egalitarian in terms of gender. While, as Suchitra notes, the poet positions women in astoundingly egalitarian frames in some poems, other sections of his work are marked by a misogynistic attitude (see chapter 3). Overall, Angkarn's remains a masculinist vision. At points in the work, heteronormative presuppositions also shine through (e.g., in "Losing You," "Dew Drops Are the Tears of Time"). In the works represented here, this is rare, however, as they move almost entirely in the realms of Buddhist philosophy and are concerned with the creation of a modern Thai Buddhist temporal framework. This is not to assume that a philosophical endeavor cannot be haunted by misogyny and heteronormativity, but to note that Angkarn largely eschews the direct engagement with gender and sexuality in this body of works.

Chapters

This book explores issues of temporality in five analytical chapters, examining Angkarn's concerns with ontology, history, subjectivity, language, and politics and the transnational. In addition, it provides an appendix of translations of those poems and pieces of poetic prose in which the poet addresses issues of temporality.

Chapter 2, "Ontology: Time as Conflict: Angkarn Kallayanapong's Buddhist Temporal Modernity," investigates how Angkarn's mobilization of Buddhist temporal ontologies contributes to the creation of a Buddhist-inflected Thai literary and artistic modernity. His poetry centrally invokes Buddhist cosmologies and quandaries in Buddhist conceptions of time and makes these available as intellectual tools for the Thai present. I examine his poetry's convergence with and deviation from Buddhist doctrine, but I also investigate how the poet redeploys Buddhist thought to conceive of an ideal subjectivity and ethics appropriate to Thai cultural modernity. I argue that in the process, he folds seemingly incommensurable soteriological strands of Buddhist philosophy into everyday, lay practice—thereby transforming Buddhist doctrine and making it available to modern ethical praxis.

Chapter 3, "History: The Dream of a Contemporary Ayuthaya: Angkarn Kallayanapong's Poetics of Dissent, Aesthetic Nationalism, and Thai Literary Modernity," investigates the thematic and formal preeminence of the Ayuthaya period (1350–1767) in Angkarn's work. This chapter argues that by combining an intentional content that centers on Ayuthaya's early modern cosmopolitanism with a poetics that is reflective of present-day globalization, Angkarn achieves a forceful critique of the cultural present. While several scholars have analyzed the poet's use of the past, the relation of Angkarn's poetry to its own historical and political context remains underexamined. This chapter therefore also sets Angkarn's cultural criticism in relation to the reactionary modernism of the Sarit Thanarat regime (1958–1963) during which the poet began to write. It further draws into relation the poetics of the Art for Life poets who are Angkarn's contemporaries. I pay close attention to the significance of the poet's prosodic choices in struggles to define Thai cultural and political modernity. Focusing on the poet's adaptations of the classical literary genre of *nirat*, I investigate Angkarn's conservative political dissent as well as his poetic innovation.

In chapter 4, "Subjectivity: Modern Manifesto: Poetry as Redemptive-Therapeutic Action in the World," I examine the poet's manifestos, or statements of artistic intent, from the late 1950s until 1986. Building on a central discussion in Thai literary studies, I link Angkarn's extraordinary emphasis on the extra*samsaric*, supratemporal status of the arts and the redemptive role of the poet to an investigation of changing notions of subjectivity in the three decades spanned by his manifestos. Referencing especially the work of Thai literary theorist Suchitra Chongstitvatana, I investigate how Angkarn's poems concerning humanity in time, the status of the arts, and the self-understanding of the artist are interwoven with such shifts in notions of subjectivity and the poet's continually evolving, novel agenda for Thai cultural modernity. What happened in the three decades of his writing that motivated the intensification of Angkarn's poetic dedication to the point of forsaking nirvana, or personal salvation, toward the end of the Cold War? What social and political circumstances informed this change?

Chapter 5, "Language: Transnational Poetic Modernity: Linguistic Innovation and Religious Borrowings in the Work of Paul Celan and Angkarn Kallayanapong," investigates linguistic innovation and the relation of Angkarn's poetry to the transnational. Especially the heteroglossia of Angkarn's poetry increases throughout the three decades in which most of his writing is published. I link Angkarn's poetic innovation to transnational poetic trends of the second half of the twentieth century. While the historical positions of Angkarn and Paul Celan diverge radically, we can draw the two writers' poetologies and linguistic innovation into productive relation. Like Celan, Angkarn also grapples with language after loss—although this loss is of a different nature than the devastation of language and world after the Shoah. The Thai poet focuses on the revivification of language after what he perceives as momentous cultural loss. For the purpose of generating historically adequate language after great loss, both poets repeatedly turn to the vocabularies of religion—though they frequently invoke these for entirely nonreligious, or at least nondoctrinal, purposes.

Finally, chapter 6, "Politics: One Night in Bangkok: Allen Ginsberg and Angkarn Kallayanapong," takes as its subject the personal encounter of the two poets in the 1960s and its literary results, Ginsberg's translations of Angkarn's poetry. While the poets' explicit political orientations diverge, their poetry converges around shared concerns with the integration of Buddhism into radically egalitarian ontologies. I argue that both the American and the Thai poet write in a period that is overdetermined by US policy in Southeast Asia in the 1960s and after and examine their reactions to these Cold War politics.

The appendix features selected poems predominantly taken from the following works:

1964 *Kawiniphon Khong Angkarn Kallayanapong* (The Poetry of Angkarn Kallayanapong) (Bangkok: Khled Thai, 5th ed. 1986 [1964])

1969 *Lamnam Phu Kradueng* (Kradueng Mountain Song) (Bangkok: Sayam, 1991 [1969])

1972 *Bang Bot Jak Suan Kaeo* (Passages from the Crystal Garden) (Bangkok: Sueksit Sayam, 1972)

1978 *Bangkok Kaeo Kamsuan Rue Nirat Nakhon Si Thammarat* (Lament for Beloved Bangkok or Nirat Nakhon Si Thammarat) (Bangkok: Sayam, 1991 [1978])

1986 *Panithan Kawi* (The Poet's Testament) (Bangkok: Karat, 1986)

1987 *Yad Nam Khang Khue Namta Khong Wela* (Dew Drops Are the Tears of Time) (Bangkok: Thienwan, 1987)

History of Publishing and Circulation

The works listed above represent the main body of Angkarn's oeuvre—especially as regards the poet's concern with temporality. Bauer affirms my representation of the above titles as constituting Angkarn's main work. In his encyclopedia entry on Angkarn, Bauer appends only one later volume and omits the 1987 volume of prose poetry.[53] The 2011 volume *80 Pi Angkarn Kallayanapong* (80 Years of Angkarn Kallayanapong) features the same list, appending *Kawi Sri Ayuthaya* and two new editions of older works.[54]

Several factors contribute to the fact that Angkarn's work up until the 1986 conferral of the S.E.A. Write Award is more widely known.

Ormkaew Kallayanapong asserts that Angkarn never stopped writing and that this work was also published. However, changes in the publishing industry make Angkarn's poetic output appear less continuous than in previous decades. As Anuk Pitukthanin of the publishing house Khled Thai explains, "Since 1997, but definitely since 2002–2003, the market in poetry in Thailand evinced a downturn. However, this may not directly have been due to the economic crisis; rather, the market in books from other countries grew. Khled Thai did not publish any other books [than *Panithan Kawi*] of Angkarn's anymore." At the same time, Anuk confirms, *Panithan Kawi* is still in print and continues to be in demand by educational institutions.[55]

To an extent Bauer's, the volume *80 Pi Angkarn Kallayanapong*'s, and my argument above with regard to what constitutes the poet's main body of works are thus determined by features of the culture and publishing industries in Thailand since the late 1980s. Khled Thai, especially, had consistently published and reprinted Angkarn's work from the 1950s until 1986. After this time, publication of the poet's work became more diffuse and reliant on self-publishing.[56]

Additional collections of Angkarn's poetry were still published after 1987. However, as Ormkaew explains, with the diminished output of Khled Thai, the publishing process became more haphazard, and different editors compiled collections without coordinating with other publishers. Much of Angkarn's work after 1987 was published privately, with less distribution than previously.[57]

Angkarn's major publications after 1987 include the following: In 1992, after the brutal suppression of public protests against the government in May of the same year ("Black May"), the poet published a fervent defense of democracy titled *Rachasadudi Ming Khwan Prachathipatai* (Panegyric for Treasured Democracy). In 1994, he published an eighty-three-stanza poem, called *Sumalai Poralok* (Flowers of a Future World), for his teacher, Fuea Haripitak. In 1999, on Angkarn's seventy-second birthday, the publishing house Khled Thai launched *Kawi Sri Ayuthaya* (Poet of Ayuthaya), a volume that begins with republished older poems from as early as 1952 and further includes a loose collection of individual poems published in subsequent decades through 1998. *Kawi Sri Ayuthaya* represents the most significant collection of Angkarn's work after *Yad Nam Khang Khue Namta Khong Wela* (1987). The volume includes a foreword by Sulak Sivaraksa, lauding Angkarn as a quintessentially Ayuthayan poet and deploring the fact of his living in poverty in old age.[58] The new work in the volume includes a curious array of poems that on the one hand continue the work of mourning the loss of the cultural past, delineate the true, artistic vocation of humanity, and lament the present; on the other hand, the collection also includes poems that express virulent anticommunism ("Kamakon Khom Khuen Sak Sop Sau Tang Prathet"—"Workers Rape the Corpse of a Foreign Woman," 1992), concern about the evils of cholesterol ("Amnat Rai Khong Cholesterol"—"Evil Power of Cholesterol," 1995), and fervent prodemocratic sentiment (such as "Sith Isara Seri Khong Puang Pracharat"—"The Peoples' Right to Freedom," 1998). In contrast to Angkarn's previous volumes, *Kawi Sri Ayuthaya* is not as concerned with speculating on the ontological properties of time.

A collection of poems titled *Alangkan Jak Angkarn Kallayanapong* (Magnificence by Angkarn Kallayanapong), entirely in calligraphic script, was published in 2008 on the occasion of an exhibition of Angkarn's artwork. In 2008 Angkarn published a collection of poems supporting the rather undemocratic People's Alliance for Democracy (PAD), called *Makhawan Rangsan* (Makhawan Creation). Ormkaew designates her father's support of the PAD late in life as an aberration of his political beliefs, rather than as characteristic of his convictions. She attributes this to the influence of other poets who drew Angkarn into these circles. Ormkaew affirms her father's nationalism but considers his support of the PAD a misunderstanding.[59]

Finally, *Klap Ban Koed* (Returning Home), a kind of Festschrift-funeral volume that includes poems by Angkarn as well as the tributes and contributions of others, was published in 2013, a year after the poet's death, when his ashes were returned to his hometown of Nakhorn Sri Thammarat.

Short Biography of Angkarn Kallayanapong (1926–2012)

1926 Born in the province of Nakhorn Sri Thammarat in Southern Thailand

1941 Enters Vocational Artists School of Silpakorn University, Bangkok

1943 Enters Faculty of Painting and Sculpture, Silpakorn University, Bangkok

1972 Sathirakoses Foundation Prize

1989   National Artist Award

1986   S.E.A. Write Award

2012   Died 25 August

2

Ontology

Time as Conflict:
Angkarn Kallayanapong's Buddhist Temporal Modernity

In *Dew Drops Are the Tears of Time*, Angkarn Kallayanapong ends his poetic prose piece "*Nimitta* in the Rainbow" on the cautionary note that "Time always looks as though sleeping, but in that sleep it could turn out to be real awakening." The conclusion of "*Nimitta*" ("Portent") introduces us to the poet's intense concern with the ontological status of time in a Buddhist framework, to his preoccupation with the urgency of artistic creation against the flux of time, and to a cultural critique of the present that depends on the backdrop of vast historical and cosmological dimensions.[1] While the literary scholars Suchitra Chongstitvatana and Chetana Nagavajara have investigated the unusually high status that the poet accords to the arts and the ways in which this claim might contravene Theravadin Buddhist doctrine—a concern that I address in chapter 4—this chapter focuses on the ways in which Angkarn modifies Buddhist temporalities to lay the foundations for an ontological framework for Thai cultural modernity.[2]

Published in 1987, the volume of poetic prose *Dew Drops Are the Tears of Time* culminates the poet's preoccupation with time over at least three decades. From the 1950s until 1987, Angkarn pursues questions related to temporality in his volumes *Kawiniphon* (Poetry), *Lamnam Phu Kradueng* (Kradueng Mountain Song), *Bangkok Kaeo Kamsuan* (Lament for Beloved Bangkok), *Panithan Kawi* (The Poet's Testament), and finally in *Yad Nam Khang Khue Namta Khong Wela* (Dew Drops Are the Tears of Time). Throughout this oeuvre, the poet repeatedly returns to a concern with time, in the ontological sense of "What is time?" and in the sense of "How much time do I have in the face of time's passing?"

I argue that through his speculation on and manipulations of temporality, Angkarn develops a nondoctrinal Buddhist ontology of time and thereby contributes to the creation of a Buddhist-inflected Thai literary and artistic modernity. The fact that his poetry is suffused with a lexicon that stems from Thai-Buddhist cosmology, as well as continually invokes quandaries in Buddhist conceptions of temporality, testifies to the poet's commitment to making these intellectual tools available as aesthetic and ethical resources for the Thai present. This chapter thus pays attention to his poetry's convergence with or deviation from Buddhist doctrine, but more centrally investigates how Angkarn redeploys Buddhist thought to conceive of an expanded ontology, an ideal subjectivity, and an ethics appropriate to Thai cultural modernity.

The Ontological Status of Time in Buddhism

In the texts that address time directly, Angkarn identifies an essential conflict of defining time in Buddhism, a system of thought that espouses as its highest ontological truth the theory of nonsubstantiality. All Buddhist inquiry has to contend with the paradox of defining time that arises from the question of whether time has to be construed as an entity, and therefore as substantial, or whether it is to be interpreted as merely a mode and thereby as nonsubstantial. In early Buddhist inquiry, the schools of the Sarvāstivādins and the Sautrāntikas are representative, respectively, of positions that are weighted toward substantiality and nonsubstantiality.[3] The attempts at explanation of the diverse Buddhist schools range from these two positions to various gradations between these notions, but all find their basis in the necessity of having to reconcile their concepts of time with the basic Buddhist axiom of nonsubstantiality.

Angkarn's explicit speculations on time recapture this core paradox for the reader. In addition, they register a notion of time as conflict for the Thai cultural present. The poet's own conceptualization ranges from a theory of time as an entity to the understanding of time as nonsubstantial, and his poetry further calibrates all ontological gradations between these two positions. This is best exemplified by his text "Nimit Nai Sai Rung" ("*Nimitta* in the Rainbow").

In this piece, the time of night is portrayed as sleeping. It is classified in its spatial position in the universe as somewhere above the earth.

The early morning rays of sunlight meet with the mist and give rise to a luminous rainbow. A sign that appears in this rainbow is interpreted by means of a dream. In the dream, a conversation between a snail and the drops of dew first establishes a connection between time and the dew. The constant activity of the dew's painting during the night personifies the movement of time and its productive power. In the course of the piece, various stages of time of day, such as the dawn, or the moment before dawn, are subsequently personified.

The statement that time is probably only a dream lacking reality is immediately contradicted. The piece proceeds to discuss the obscure and unfathomable nature of time and finally arrives at what we can understand to be the core section of the discussion:

> Time is so great that we cannot conceive of it, cannot limit it, cannot perceive it. It is something profound and great. Even though time is a void thing. In itself it does not consist of anything. But in this not consisting of anything, which is *śūnya*, all things in the cosmos and the solar systems of other worlds are constituent parts of time in their entirety. It seems a huge dimension, beyond estimation, encompassing profound meaning, extending to all things as the highest unity.
>
> Above the multi-layered dimension of voidness that is *śūnya*, it is a powerful entity. It is possible to say that it has a self and possible to say that it has not. It is the highest purpose, entirely free in its non-attachment or in its attachment that seems to be non-attachment.

The piece queries time's contradictory nature, but does not make a final decision regarding its substantiality. Instead the text aims to transcend these positions and at once postulates time as *śūnya*—voidness—and as a dimension above the "multi-layered dimension of voidness." The passage's culmination in the statement that time is "entirely free in its non-attachment or in its attachment that seems to be non-attachment" accurately describes the breadth of the perspective on the ontology of time that becomes evident throughout Angkarn's oeuvre.

In this piece, Angkarn's presentation of the nature of time reflects the nonempirical and translogical position of the *śūnyavāda* school (the school that espouses the doctrine of emptiness), which sought to transcend both Brahmanical *ātmavāda* (the doctrine of a persistent self), and Buddhist *anātmavāda* (the doctrine of the nonexistence of a persistent self). The poet thereby draws on the most capacious position available within Buddhist philosophy to make room for two seemingly contradictory concerns. On the one hand, Angkarn is concerned with retaining vast, Buddhist-informed dimensions of temporality and configurations of cosmology for the Thai cultural present. The Buddhist account of impermanence (Thai, *anijjang*; Pali, *anicca*) represents a constituent part of the dimensions of this temporality, but is in this work not always deployed to teach detachment. On the other hand, Angkarn is intent on discussing the compression of temporality in the present and relating this to contemporary cultural loss.

In "*Nimitta*" as in others texts, we can read from the poet's work a notion of time-as-conflict in which time's essence is difficult to pinpoint and oscillates between that of mode and that of substance. At the same time, this engagement with time-as-conflict seeks to calibrate an era of attenuated cultural possibilities as well as to advance a remedial agenda. The poet will be shown to use seemingly incommensurable perspectives on time to resolve the quandary of how to inhabit the time of modernity and produce redemptive aesthetics in the particular location of Thailand.

Time as Dimension and Destroyer

In the pieces that feature time as protagonist, Angkarn delineates vast dimensions of time that remain evident throughout his work. Thus "Khwam Fan Khong Thueak Pha Luang" ("Dream of the Rocks") in *Kawiniphon* specifies "The Wheel of Time passes by with long periods of golden light years, their number a 1 with 42 zeros after it" and thereby draws on Buddhist conventions of outlining dimensions.

In the temporal architecture that the poet proposes, the vast dimensions of the timescapes that he delineates stand out. In addition to illustrating the magnitude of time, these poems serve to create the setting for the entirety of Angkarn's philosophical framework. The primordial, Buddhist-informed dimensions of time underwrite both the charge of the poet's acerbic cultural criticism and intellectual-artistic ethics.

Against the seemingly boundless dimensions of time, Angkarn's poetry contrasts the pressure of time on the individual. The action of "Kalajak" ("The Wheel of Time") takes place in a cosmic setting and what appears to be a prehistoric period. In the piece, time passes from a state of sleep to one of being permanently awake. Throughout the poet's oeuvre, such awakening signifies a historical rupture in temporality. In "Kalajak," this notion is supported by the story's assertion that time has a nightmare. Unfavorable events have taken place in the universe and push time into action, forcing it to give up its sleep and leisurely pace:

> Time woke up startled, not satisfied with its nightmare. From then on, Time never slept again, even if the cosmos was sleeping deeply. For a long time that can only be counted in eons, the Wheel of Time remained awake, like a watchman guarding the night and the day in the midst of eternity, which has no limit throughout all of time.

In the poetic prose pieces "Waeo Ta Khong Wela" ("The Eye of Time," 1960) and "Phlapphlueng" ("Lily," 1947), overwhelming temporal pressure likewise comes to replace a state of placidity: "The first *kalpa* was still sleeping; one day later the sun went out and fell down. Saturn crashed into the moon. A great meteor storm came blowing along to destroy the world" ("Lily"). Both pieces invoke associations with a prehistorical setting to further underwrite this transformation. These texts perform the shift from a period in history in which time passed at a purportedly more leisurely pace to modernity, with its self-understanding as an era marked by the accelerated pace of time and as distinct in quality from all that preceded it. It is this rupture that Angkarn deplores and for which he will propose reparative paradigms. As we will see, it is the poet's intent to distinguish the quality of this rupture in the Thai context from that of European modernity and to formulate a temporal ontology for the present that once again pays heed to the cosmological dimensions of time.

Angkarn's texts on the changing qualities and pacing of time moreover lay the ontological foundations for those pieces in which he will speak of the insurmountable pressure of time on the individual and especially for the artist. This pressure is further detailed in several of the pieces that feature time as protagonist in which it appears in the role of outright destroyer. Although Suchitra Chongstitvatana states that Angkarn also recognizes the productive power of time, much of his work foregrounds images of time's destructive potential.[4] Thus, "Su Krasae Chara" ("Against the Stream of Aging," *Lamnam Phu Kradueng*) urges the reader to combat and subdue time, the destroyer:

> Age thus comes in to take control,
> Is master over all of life, the mind and heart.
>
> Or one knows how to combat the current of aging,
> Awed by the great power divine,
> Erasing, letting the holy power of the inner core crumble,
> Hurrying to amend, becoming attentive to the divine.

Even more ominously, several pieces in which time appears as protagonist, such as "Wela Khue Chiwa" ("Time Is Life," *Lamnam Phu Kradueng*), presage:

> The Wheel of Time will approach slowly,
> Abducting life and executing it.

Poems such as this invoke the Buddhist notion of impermanence in one of its most uncompromising forms.

The Individual in Time

How then is the individual positioned in these ontologies of time? To begin with, Angkarn's texts on the individual in time feature several instances of a highly modest vision of self. Thus, the perspective on the self in "Raluek Thueng Phra Saphanyu" ("Remembering Phra Saphanyu," *Panithan Kawi*) appears exceedingly humble:

> My low self sticking to the grass,
> Offer my life to under your feet, praying,
> Asking that the world pass beyond suffering, danger, falsehood,
> Is blissful and peaceful for once.

In "Om" (*Kawiniphon*) the poem's speaker requests another fate in the next life: he asks to be the lowest possible being on earth. At the same time, he wants all his senses to be shut out and be relieved of perception as well as forego any knowledge of the beauty of the heavens. While the narrator's humility in the stanza from "Raluek" above also bears redemptive potential, the demand in "Om" seems geared primarily toward extinguishing the pain of individual existence:

Om, making a wish for the next life,
My small self asks to love, destitute,
Dumb, deaf, and blind,
To be a tree stump, a rain worm, a millipede.

I want to know nothing of the beauty of the world
And the heavens.
Unknowing, stupid, crazier than anyone,
My heart coarse like the surface of the earth.

Let my remains fall into the sand,
Scattering and disappearing,
For vultures, dogs, and crows to feed on.
Hear my words, o Gods.

While "Raluek" and "Om" showcase a sacrificial disposition as well as exemplify the Buddhist truths of impermanence and suffering, "Phi Phung Tai" ("Shooting Star," *Kawiniphon*) delineates a more ambivalent attitude toward the notion of a self:

In the burial ground of the gods,
Among the stars in heaven,
A soul is mumbling to itself,
Dreaming of the world uneasily.

I take the sky as a blanket,
Take wind for food, dejectedly,
Roaming about hazardously, without aim,
Reaching the next world of divine mood.

Forgetting my body on earth,
Long until every strand of hair is decomposed,
The light of the eyes blends into mud;
Covered by mud, I go under, become hard soil.

At this time, my heart
Has turned into a rock in a stream.
One day that rock will crack,
The stream of water eating away until it falls apart.

Who would there be in this world,
To mourn a stone?
They are used only to trampling on stones.
A pang of longing stirs the soul.

Glittering light going out,
A shooting star, trembling,
Disappearing into endless time,
Ending hopelessly, solitarily.

"Shooting Star" reflects the integration of the human individual and embodied subject into nature and the cosmos. On the one hand, the narrative evinces strong concern with the speaker's desolation but, on the other hand, it clearly envisions his existence across vast time periods and distances in the cosmos: the subject of the poem even appears as a soul residing in the heavens.

These texts show a human self that inhabits multiple worlds and is capable of mobility between heaven and earth, the cosmos and nature. Literature and the arts are shown to travel as well. As the narrator becomes a messenger of the beautiful and divine between heaven and earth, literature, analogously, becomes an emissary between these two spheres.

In many of Angkarn's pieces, the narrator's fate is tied up with that of the cosmos and the earth. Where next lives are concerned, his poetry also covers immense stretches of time. This is true of the individual's relation to others as well. In the 1964 love poem "Sia Jao" ("Losing You," *Kawiniphon*), the dimensions of the cosmos are put to a different use. In this poem, temporal dimensions are deployed in the aid of elaborating on the strength of emotion:

Losing you is like a brilliant gem cracking.
Whatever I had hoped for in this world,
My hopelessness now reaches the sky,
Lying face down on the ground eating sand.

I will hurt, remembering to the next world,
The cruel traces of sorrow will never fade,
Not minding how many skies I am born, how many times I
    sorrowfully die,
I cannot expect to receive your love.

If you are born in heaven,
I ask to burn, down at the end of the world.
If you are fire, I am wood,
Letting you destroy my soul completely.

Even the particles of dust are not compassionate,
Forgetting until the world crumbles.
If in any life I meet you,
I will be so tortured that I will tear out my eyes.

Dying I want to be under the soles of your feet,
So that you can trample on me for fun, like on blades of
    grass.
I will remember the myriad poisons of pain,
Until the end of the world.

As "Losing You" recounts the loss of love, the vast spatial dimensions that the poem's narrator inhabits and the presentation of the duration of individual consciousness across lives serve to detail the immensity of emotion.

In summary, the dimensionality of time and the cosmos that humans inhabit in Angkarn's poetry at once signifies human minuteness as well as creating scope for the description of emotion, expanding the agency of humans to avail themselves of cosmic dimensions, and fostering the ability to create meritorious works of art and lead ethical lives.

Buddhist Notions of Time, Consciousness, and Personhood

The Buddhist theory of *anātman* (Sanskrit; Pali, Thai, *anattā*) precludes the reality of a soul or self at the core of the individual. The theory of impermanence is closely linked to that of no-self. Thus, from *sarvam anityam*, all is impermanent, follows also *sarvam anātman*, all that is, is without substance or self.[5] Allowing for no category of an abiding substance in general, Theravada Buddhist thought also does not allow for any abiding mental substance.

The idea of a permanent and persisting self is incompatible with the all-pervasive doctrine of momentariness. Thus, Theravada Buddhist doctrine does not allow for a concept of subjectivity strictly speaking.

It admits only a flow of consciousness that is constituted by the serial relationship of individual psychic moments, or a succession of instants. Therefore, that which is perceived as the individual is interpreted as a temporary collocation of five groups of constituent factors, the five *khanda* (Pali; Sanskrit *skandha*). Steven Collins defines the *khanda* as "'constituents of personality,' in which the apparently unitary person is divided into five impersonal groups of elements."[6] Although these are in constant flux, they produce the impression of continuity. According to Collins, desire is the factor that ties these moments together. As its ultimate spiritual goal, Theravada doctrine stresses the transcension of the delusion of self. The relinquishing of desire, or attachment, represents the first step toward that goal.

As far as consciousness is concerned, time as a subjective phenomenon is understood as dependent on the *saṅkhāra*, or *saṃkhāra*, the fourth of the five "constituents of personality" (*khanda*). Collins explains the *saṃkhāra* as "'formations' or 'constructions' (Pali *saṃkhāra*) which in the process of *karma* and rebirth, create that composite which is the human being and which is wrongly imagined to be a 'self.'"[7] He further elaborates on the *saṃkhāra*'s relation to temporality: "Both the activity which constructs temporal reality, and the temporal reality thus constructed, are *saṃkhāra*."[8]

The *saṃkhāra*, or mental formations, are moreover part of the *paṭiccasamuppāda* (Pali; Sanskrit *pratītyasamutpāda*), the theory of dependent origination, which explains the "continuity of experience"—despite the lack of existence of a self—from another perspective.[9] Collins elaborates: "The fundamental function of the Dependent Origination list [. . .] is to express the Buddhist idea of the 'Wheel of Life' turning continuously without any self as a causal agent or persisting subject of karma."[10] In terms of temporality, the *paṭiccasamuppāda* reaches back infinitely (it is *anādi*, not having an end). In the direction of the future, however, it is precisely not infinite. Rather, the overcoming of ignorance, through knowledge or the attainment of nirvana (Sanskrit; Pali *nibbāna*), makes possible the cessation of consciousness and time.

In his investigation of Theravada Buddhist ideas of time, consciousness, and personhood, Collins further describes how the notion of self is thought in relation to larger social and ontological frameworks: "The conceptual framework of Buddhist thinking is addressed to the particular concern of elaborating an account of selfhood, persons, and their continuity, in light of the overall *saṃsāra-nirvāṇa* dichotomy, itself predicated on the social dichotomy of layman-monk; and how this account has embodied the hypotheses of the creation of temporality by the 'constructive' activity of *karma*, the need for a coherent picture of the cessation of such creative activity if the religious goal of release is to appear intelligible, and the supposition that such a cessation takes place in the consciousness of the religious virtuoso."[11] Angkarn's poems work through this "*saṃsāra-nirvāṇa* dichotomy" on several levels.

On the one hand, Angkarn's framework of thought puts forth a strong sense of temporality as the transience of the subjective being. Across poems and volumes, his works are marked by the notion that this temporality is the source of suffering for the individual. This idea of the intrinsically distressing temporality of subjective being is in agreement with Buddhist doctrinal conceptions. As Collins states, "Rebirth in *saṃsāra* is considered . . . as a form of suffering (*duḥkha*, Pali *dukkha*) in itself."[12]

The conformity to or departure from orthodoxy of the poet's panacea for temporally based suffering is more difficult to evaluate, however. Angkarn's work is suffused with the ambivalence between the desire to attain the self-transcending goal of timeless, eternal quiescence (or nirvana) and the urge to delay that goal. The poet's stance on subjectivity moreover oscillates between one that is exceedingly humble and stresses the transience of personhood and one that ascribes extreme prepotency (Thai, *ahangkan*) to subjectivity.[13]

"Dew Drops Are the Tears of Time"

The long prose piece "Yat Nam Khang Khue Namta Khong Wela" ("Dew Drops Are the Tears of Time") further clarifies the poet's philosophical concern with the manifold facets of time. In this text, the narrator is a father who conveys philosophical insights by way of didactic conversation with his children, whom he takes on an outing. He explains ethical, philosophical, and religious ideas to his young daughter and son through the contemplation of time and nature. As Suchitra writes, dew represents a prominent trope in the poet's work: "It is worth noticing that the poet repeatedly compares life to a tiny dewdrop or a drop of water, and thus establishes an underlying lexical pattern in the work."[14] At the end of the prose piece, the dew will be revealed to figure human lives. However, as the piece builds its argument, we can first understand the dew to concretize the more abstract concept of impermanence and to spark off discussions about central aspects of time.

"Dew Drops Are the Tears of Time" tells of time taking leave, disappearing in the "waves of the path of the universe" and never returning.

Where human time is concerned, time's taking leave and passing on to another world attenuates the duration of human life in the process. In the prose piece's movement between different aspects of temporality, it becomes clear that the poet does not view time as uniform and that his conceptualization of time retains a conflictual element throughout the discussion. In particular, the development of an unorthodox notion of impermanence (*anijjang*) becomes central to the text's philosophical enterprise:

> Every day in the early morning I, Father, take both of my children to greet the dew. Sometimes I talk about the special quality of these things and explain for both my daughter and my son to hear. For a new kind of inspiration, until both children are delighted, motivated, and interested in the different qualities of nature.
>
> I will usually point out the changing, uncertain states of the diamonds of dew drops which are touched by rays of sunlight from the moment before dawn until the rising of the sun in the early morning. I want my children to know that this being touched of the dew by the brilliant rays of the sun is a divine treasure that the sun has given to the world, as complete with beauty and different ethical teachings as anyone could imagine. To what degree can one develop consciousness? One will have no point at which one can stop searching, because one will think on and on. Until one becomes similar to the ripples of waves in the ocean, made up of miraculous elements. At that point, one will compile inspiring qualities, think of, dream of, and create miraculous elements for one's intellect, reaching divinity, able to discern auspicious desire. Knowing clarion reason from beginning to end, one will be able to create work of high auspiciousness from this inspiration. One will be able to think of and produce miraculously beautiful things, giving eternal auspicious desire to the world for the universe's contentment. Far from suffering, sorrow, and illness, through the strength of the spirit of friendship that has come from this one tiny life.

In this passage, the text announces that it will link its discussion of impermanence to a consideration of human ethical action. In the following excerpt, however, the narrator first addresses the issue of time from a broader ontological viewpoint in a conversation with his children. This conversation adopts a question-and-answer format and mode of description that is intended to make the ontological qualities of time more accessible intuitively and affectively:

> After I had explained quite a bit to the children, I indicated,
> "What is the dew? The dew drops are the tears of time."
> Right after that my silver bell resounded sweetly, delighted with life,
> "Why is time crying? What is it unhappy about?"
> I replied, "It looks as though time is crying, because it has to take leave of us and go far, far away in the ripples of the waves of the universal path which never returns. And, a point will come when we will have to take leave of time, going far away to the next world, and we will be in the time dimension of another era that has nothing to do with the present time in this world. The latter point is still very difficult to understand. Let's wait for a day when both of you are older. Then I will explain it to you in detail, which will still involve many steps."
> My daughter's barbet bird voice, still sweetly audible beside me, asked, "You said that time cries because it is sorry about having to take leave and going far away. Where then, does time go?"
> "In explaining the aim of time's path as going far away, I meant that time travels far, far away, child. So all of a sudden, it is as though the lifespan of human beings becomes very short. I cannot explain this path entirely. It is a path that human language cannot reach in its travel. It is at the farthest point of the horizon. And then it even passes beyond to where there is no horizon, even further to the end of the universe. Solitary, passing far beyond to many universes, to the manifold, abundant solar systems, without end. The ancients called it eternity."

The father devises a mode of illustration for the vast dimensions of time and the manner of time's passing. Making vivid the notion of acceleration along an unfathomable temporal vector, the narrative makes plausible both the boundlessness of time and the brevity of human life. The poetic prose piece thereby illustrates the inevitability of loss and change that furnishes the core Buddhist teaching of impermanence. At the same time, it points toward the transcension of impermanence in the timeless state of nirvana. However, at this point, the argument attains additional complexity:

> I told you that time cries because it has to take leave of us and go far away. In addition to crying out of sorrow, sometimes its crying may also be a result of contentment: It is so choked with happiness that it sobs. So the season of the floods in both eyes starts. The reason is that the dew is pleased with having paid respect to the sun. It reflected the pure value of the waves of rays of the sun in seven colors, offering them as a present to the world. The dew always seems sad that it has to suddenly disappear, leave us, not staying to cut the gem of the eye's gleam so that it is impressed with the value of the colors of the rainbow and other beauty. Thus whether it is happy or sorrowful, the dew is like teardrops.

Through his investment of time with emotion, the father is able to develop an unorthodox notion of impermanence. After having highlighted the inevitability of impermanence, the narrator introduces a contrasting vision of the dew's effervescence as desirable. Effectively designating impermanence as productive of beauty, the speaker imbues the concept with a sense that surpasses that of Theravada doctrine.[15] The conversation with the speaker's children continues as follows:

> "Does the dew have a heart and soul, Father?"
> "It does not, child. The dew has no heart. It has no heart or deceptive behavior at all. That I said the dew is happy or sad was because I wanted you to understand easily. If I had chosen to speak in another mode, it would have been much more difficult for you to understand.
> I have the aim for you to be awed by one level of tender feeling first, for you to feel empathy. That is why I invested the dew with human emotion and then spoke according to my own feeling, as if the dew had a heart. All this is because I had already invented a heart for the dew and then wanted to make you feel moved, so you would be impressed. This will slowly become the source of deep understanding of the value of art on higher and higher levels."

While the multivalence of impermanence regarding emotion and beauty was established earlier in the text, this passage links impermanence more closely to a mandate for human ethical action.

A subsequent passage then recaptures the dew's impermanence and integrates the fact of this impermanence into a desirable ontology and into the cyclicality of natural phenomena:

> "As I said, the dew drops are the tears of time. They make us see the impermanence of the path of movement of the Wheel of Time for a moment. The dew serves the sun by reflecting the rays, projecting the glittering rays of the sun to illuminate the sky, reflecting the luminous rainbow brilliantly, gradually dropping down, dissolving, dying; grateful that the sun has the merit to help burn it, destroy it, and disperse it into a sea, so that it becomes clouds. The clouds have the dew as a son, and the dew lets a source of water originate, a stream that then flows to nourish the world. And, in that fleeting second of the lifespan of the dew, it also decorates Mother Earth. Glistening on every blade of grass. In every plant, in every tall forest, it influences the heart of some lives, like mine, seeing this divine treasure. That makes your poor father suddenly a millionaire, seeing and knowing that divine value that is abundant and beyond estimation.
>
> The dew exists only for a second, including the time in which it is beautiful and resplendent before it dissolves, so that human vision will know deeply the value of the beauty of those short golden rays. There is birth as well as duration and cessation, like in the lifespan of human beings. It is very appropriate to compare this lifespan to the teaching of the dew drops. No other comparison would be more expressive."

The second half of the passage finally aligns human life with the cycle of beauty, dissolution, and beneficent transformation that the dew partakes in. At the same time, the dew becomes indicative of nonmaterial value.

What this story outlines is, on the one hand, a Buddhist-inflected eco-poetics for the present and an ontology in which the boundaries between earth and heaven and between human embodiment, text, and nature are permeable. The poet further derives from this ontology an ethical model for artistic and intellectual life.

While the narrative cites as harmful the illusions produced by the *khanda*, its particular conception of impermanence also takes into account the temporalities of human apperception.[16] The concept of impermanence that Angkarn develops in the text thus incorporates the essential belatedness (*Nachträglichkeit*) of perception and feeling into the notion of a beneficial relation to time. Rhetorically, the text signals this consideration of individuals' inability to immediately conform affectively to the implications of impermanence—even if they are intellectually able to recognize its truth—through its developmentalist account of human capacities of spiritual realization, its address to children, and its attempt to provide easily assimilable illustration.

Like many Buddhist texts, "Dew Drops" departs from the demand for immediate detachment or the strict, instant realization of the consequences of impermanence.[17] Instead the reflection on temporality in this prose piece allows for the validity of human attachment—to life, to people, to art, and to activity in the world.

What is more, this incorporation of human perceptive and emotional belatedness does not merely take into account an interim period of adjustment, as many doctrinal texts also do. On the contrary, in the poet's vision, these elements that are not in accord with doctrine become firmly integrated into a desirable, Buddhist-inflected ethics.

Angkarn's Buddhist ontology is remarkable for several reasons. To conceptualize impermanence both as inevitable transience and as productive of lasting beauty and ethical action has implications for the way in which we understand the relation of Buddhist soteriological thought to conventional time.

The reflections of "Dew Drops" are not those of a religious professional; rather, the piece stands out in that it conceives of a lay (or householder's) life that is not merely restricted to merit making and delegating the work of philosophical speculation and action geared toward achieving nirvana to the professionals. Rather, Angkarn's deliberations develop the notion of lay intellectual-artistic access to nibbanic Buddhism.[18]

Angkarn's writing thereby provides for a highly egalitarian model of access to philosophical speculation, spiritual progress, and salvation. Most significantly, his deployment of Buddhist-inflected temporality bridges "the overall *saṃsāra-nirvāṇa* dichotomy, itself predicated on the social dichotomy of layman-monk."[19] Collins invokes this dichotomy to make clear the extent to which Buddhist action and soteriological possibility are radically divided between a layperson's status that, due to its indelible ties to *saṃsāra* (the cycle of transmigration), does not include access to the soteriological path, and a "professional" status—that of the "religious virtuoso"—that allows for access to the path of religious development and the potential transcension of worldly temporality and suffering.[20]

The poet's improvisation on the notion of impermanence allows him to expand the capacity of worldly life to incorporate high-level philosophical-soteriological activity. Sacralizing worldly activity and allowing lay life to partake in *thip*—"the divine," as it does, this model folds nibbanic temporality and opportunity into conventional time.

In the context of modern Thai Buddhist thought, this incorporation of nibbanic into conventional time may be understood to approximate the philosophy of Buddhadasa Bhikkhu, who holds that Buddhism as a religious system can be defined as concerned only with the present life. While not denying the existence of an afterlife, Buddhadasa places possible future lives outside of the focus of his philosophy.[21] According to Buddhadasa, the *paṭiccasamuppāda* is then also restricted only to the present life of a person, and not the past, present, and future lives as traditionally understood.[22] It is thus also in parallel with this philosophy that we can read the close attachment to the world professed in many of Angkarn's poems.

Conclusion

While recapturing for the reader Buddhist philosophical discourses on time's different gradations of substantiality, the poet's work also exceeds these doctrinal notions. Angkarn's conception presents "time as conflict" in a double sense. First, his work oscillates between notions of time as substantial and as insubstantial. Second, where time is portrayed as substantial, it engenders conflict in the sense that it puts the artist, as well as a generalized contemporary human subject, under insurmountable pressure.

While several poems reference the nonentity of time, all texts concerned with the status of subjectivity and with human vocation designate time as the highest reality. These are also the texts that contain the most anguished statements on time and subjectivity. While the mood of "Nimit Nai Sai Rung" is contemplative, the tone of several of the texts surveyed in this study conveys extreme urgency as they speak of the agony of the individual in the face of having limited time at his disposal.

Time in Angkarn's poetry moreover frequently seems to be moving toward an end: the poems regularly predict apocalyptic circumstances.

These teleologies of destruction most frequently culminate the poet's critiques of cultural decline. When read in combination with Angkarn's poems about subjectivity and art, which primarily convey urgency concerning creation in the face of the flux of time, they present an at least partially linear view of time.

In the texts that reflect such anxiety over finitude, time possesses a decided irreversibility. The poet's vision of Ayuthaya—in which all of history culminates in the idealized period of Ayuthayan cultural production (1350–1767)—further underlines the notion of the linearity of time.

While the poet's perspective may in several instances be that of a continuous, linear time, his vision for a desirable cultural modernity distinguishes itself from the "homogeneous, empty time" of national modernities.[23] The poet's conceptualizations of time are designed to disrupt the time of the nation and of capital. His is an effort to resacralize time in order to provide a countervision for the Thai present. While his writing certainly bears universal significance, the chapters that follow will detail the ways in which Angkarn's reflections on time always retain a very located concern with the cultural and historical situation of Thailand in the second half of the twentieth century.

We might then also understand the recurrent apocalyptic predictions and accounts of the end of the world as simply the end of an age, of a *kalpa* or *yuga*, and thereby as part of a Buddhist cyclical concept. Combining terms and images that reference both linearity and cyclicality, the poet exploits the ambivalent valences of time in Buddhist discourse.

The poet thus pursues the negotiation of time as conflict along several strands of argumentation. One function that these debates have in Angkarn's framework of thought is to make the mobility of temporal concepts within classical, canonical speculation available to present-day ethics and aesthetics; another is to address the condensation of temporality and attenuation of human possibility in the Thai present and to develop a panacea for its cultural crises.

Much of Angkarn's writing that personifies time and reflects on the temporal parameters of personhood responds to this notion of the acceleration of time in the modern world. The poet repeatedly diagnoses a rupture that comes to inaugurate a new era. This is figured in the recurrent theme of time waking suddenly. In Angkarn's work, this motif marks the reflection of a turning point in the experience of temporality. Time suddenly seems scarce. The poet designates this occurrence as the origin of (Thai) modernity and attaches to it an imperative to act for the contemporary Thai subject.

While the motif of time awakening signals an era of crisis, the poet is clear that he wants an ideal Thai modernity to break with European Enlightenment logics of the time of modernity. He desires to distinguish a desirable temporality of Thai modernity from hegemonic European conceptions.

Harry Harootunian critiques European conceptualizations of modernity with regard to the hierarchies of temporality that they instituted. He writes, polemically, of the deployment of colonial notions of time:

> The here and now of actual experience, our modernity, is our history, our time, and never theirs. The distancing of expectation from past experiences thus becomes the condition of asserting the difference of our self-valorizing and self-referring modernity and its superiority over both its antecedents and others. But the decision to shift the concept of modernity to the register of an absolute historical present eventually required misrecognizing the apparent contradiction that our time and place is characterized by its unique difference from others.[24]

Rather than to refute such a notion of temporal difference, Angkarn's recuperative agenda aims to resuscitate and preserve qualitative temporal difference. Benedict Anderson has described the time of the nation and of modernity as follows: "What has come to take the place of the mediaeval conception of simultaneity-along-time is, to borrow again from Benjamin, an idea of 'homogeneous, empty time,' in which simultaneity is, as it were, transverse, cross-time, marked not by prefiguring and fulfillment, but by temporal coincidence, and measured by clock and calendar."[25] In opposition to this flattened temporality of the modern nation, Angkarn advocates a temporality that brings modes of "prefiguring and fulfillment" back into the world and human life. Intent on constructing a different kind of modernity, one that sutures the aesthetics and hypothetical experiences of the Thai past to the present, Angkarn thus suggests making use of all facets of temporality available within a Thai cultural context.

During decades that centrally instantiate the homogeneous, empty temporality of the nation, the late 1950s–late 1980s, in which the focus is on development and later global capitalist engagement, Angkarn refurbishes temporality with the dimensions of *saṃsāra-karma-mokṣa*, the three elements that furnish the "conceptual background" of the cosmos in Buddhism.[26] This reconstruction enables the poet to emphasize causality, accountability, and the possibility of transcending the present. *Saṃsāra* provides an additional dimension to the notion of life, even if it is not a desirable dimension. *Karma* is used by Angkarn to figure thoughts about responsibility, and *mokṣa* (release, liberation) heralds the possibility of change and even of deliverance. *Mokṣa* is moreover differentially thought by Angkarn as something that occurs both in relation to religious practice proper as well as within the world.

Finally, in addition to in-depth engagement with Buddhist debates on the dimensions of time, the invocation of these dimensions assumes a rhetorical function in the poet's work. His Buddhist-inflected delineations of temporality serve as a device of amplification: the vast temporal and spatial dimensions referenced by Angkarn's texts lend gravity to his claims, establish a notion of historical rootedness, and enhance the force of the poet's cultural critique.

The poet's at first seemingly contradictory conceptualization of time—as entity and as nonentity, as boundless and as limited—thus serves the expansion of the conceptual resources available to modern Thai literature and other kinds of cultural production both on the levels of content and form.

3

History

The Dream of a Contemporary Ayuthaya: Angkarn Kallayanapong's Poetics of Dissent, Aesthetic Nationalism, and Thai Literary Modernity

This chapter examines historical elements in the constitution of Thai literary modernity in Angkarn Kallayanapong's poetry. Focusing on the poet's adaptations of the classical literary genre of *nirat*, I investigate Angkarn's conservative political dissent as well as his poetic innovation. In this context, temporality appears in the sense of a historical timeline that the poet claims for the Thai past and for which he exploits the affordances of the *nirat* genre. *Nirat* are longform travel poems that bear unique temporal features and structures of feeling and thought. The speaker of the *nirat* links details of the geocultural landscape traversed to contemplation of contexts and persons left behind on the journey. Creating a contemporaneity of past and present, *nirat* feature extended passages of retrospective longing, nostalgia, and cultural comparison. Angkarn avails himself of the structure of the genre and manipulates the time of history to make an idealized past available to an aspirational future-present.

Thematically, Angkarn's poetry is marked by forceful statements against the hybridization of Thai culture that has taken place as a result of globalization. At the same time, he creates a language that is itself exemplary of a global era. Investigating the thematic and even formal preeminence of the Ayuthaya period (1350–1767) in Angkarn's work, I argue that by articulating his intense focus on the notion of Ayuthaya with a heteroglot poetic idiom, Angkarn performs a compelling critique of the cultural present.

While several scholars have analyzed the poet's use of the past, the relation of Angkarn's poetry to its own historical and political context remains unexamined. In this chapter, I therefore set Angkarn's cultural criticism also in relation to the reactionary modernism of the Sarit Thanarat regime during which the poet began to write. I further draw into relation the politics of poetics of the Art for Life poets who are Angkarn's contemporaries. I pay close attention to the poet's prosodic choices and their significance in the struggle to define Thai cultural and political modernity.

The History and Development of *Nirat*

When Angkarn began writing in the late 1950s, he was initially vilified for his transgressions of poetic convention and use of "vulgar" language. At the same time, Angkarn is a poet who is schooled in and vitally draws on traditional poetics. He is the modern poet who uses elements of the *nirat* genre most prolifically and adapts this genre to the purpose of cultural critique.

Suchitra Chongstitvatana was the first to stress the poet's proficiency in integrating elements of the *nirat* genre into his poetry. Examining his adaptations of *nirat* conventions to the exigencies of the present, Suchitra analyzes Angkarn's mobilizations of the *nirat*'s theme of love-longing and deployment of temporality and nature, as well as of the *nirat*'s techniques of punning and transfers of meaning.[1]

Nirat are travelogue poems written in the first person in which the journey itself constitutes the framework and in which the themes of separation, longing, and identity are prominent. *Nirat* poems are characterized by episodes of admiration in which phenomena of the geocultural landscape trigger stream-of-consciousness-like associative thoughts about the person or place the traveler has left behind. The tone of *nirat* is one of lamentation; typically, several verses or even whole sections of *nirat* express sadness or melancholy.

The word *nirat* may have been used as a technical term to classify these poems as a distinct genre of Thai literature since the seventeenth century.[2] In the manual of poetics *Cindamani*, the genre is mentioned as *khlong nirat*, whereby *khlong* refers to the meter in which *nirat* of the time were written.[3] Poems bearing the name *nirat* or those in which the author states the intent of writing a *nirat* are attested even earlier, however, as in *Khlong Hariphunchai*, which is believed to have been composed in the sixteenth century.[4]

In classical *nirat* that originate in the Ayuthaya period, the theme of longing resulting from separation from a lover is predominant. Manas Chitakasem separates *nirat* of this period into two basic types. In the first, the "fundamental formal structure is expressed in terms of time progression," while in the second this structure is expressed in the form of "an imaginary journey derived from literary sources."[5] The two basic types of *nirat* are refined in a third ideal type that Manas terms the "true *nirat*." This third type consists of a "timed personal itinerary" in which the chronological process and the excursional process are combined.[6] This combination of spatial and temporal dimensions is responsible for the affective charge and presentation of subjectivity in the genre. Suchitra formulates the quintessential spatiotemporal framework and mode of operation of the *nirat* as follows: "According to [a] Nirat convention, the main theme of love-longing is conveyed through the themes of time and nature."[7]

What Manas refers to as the "true *nirat*" with its "timed personal itinerary" is exemplified by *Khlong Kamsuan Si Prat*, an Ayuthaya *nirat* from the time of Phra Narai (1656–1688) attributed to the poet Si Prat. Setting out by boat from Ayuthaya to the sea on a journey into exile, the poet begins by praising the splendor of Ayuthaya's temples and palaces. He then describes his relationship with his lover and the sadness he feels upon their separation. Through the techniques of punning and transfer Si Prat relates place-names and details of the geocultural landscape to his lover, and especially to her body. As Manas notes, the explicit sexual references to certain parts of the lover's body in the poem are used to intensify the mood of longing.[8]

Connected to the genre's tone of lamentation is thus a strong psycho-sexual element. Space, time, desire, and the body work together in *nirat* to create a gendered geocultural landscape. Typically, the rhythm of the movement of the journey and the punning create a constant link between the traveler's surroundings and the body of the lover. In *Thawathotsamat*, a *nirat* dated to the time of Phra Narai that presents a journey through the twelve months of the year, the stations of the journey are moments in time, and the events of each month spark a corporeal memory:

> The sixth month arrives with heavenly rains.
> I think of your beautiful blossoms, my love.

This month we used to share our love and happiness.
Till your soft navel felt the pains.
When thunder roars I feel restless with desire,
My heart so painful as if being torn out.
The month brings news of ploughing,
My heart wilts and tears fill my eyes.[9]

During the Rattanakosin period (1782–present), both the popularity and thematic diversity of *nirat* increased.[10] Sunthorn Phu (1786–1855), in particular, the most prominent *nirat* poet of the period, extended *nirat* conventions into new areas of concern.[11] As the kinds of departures or separations diversify in the development of *nirat*, so does the expression of sadness and pain. Thus, in Sunthorn Phu's *Nirat Phu Khao Thong* it is not the separation from lover or home, but the death of King Rama I that the traveler mourns.[12]

JOURNEYS OF IDENTITY

Many *nirat* poems display a sense of anthropological mission and meticulously record the customs of the peoples in the areas traveled through. A focus on collective cultural identity thus also marks the genre, as the observations of other cultures are accompanied by the traveler's reflections on central Siamese or Thai identity. Frequently, poets describe phenomena observed along the way as strange and subsequently classify them as inferior. Such pieces develop oppositions between what is Siamese or Thai and what is not, between the urban and the rural, and between the central and the peripheral. Although the boundaries of territory and sovereignty are frequently indistinct, those of identity remain clear throughout. In *Nirat Nakhon Sawan*, a work likewise attributed to Si Prat or to Si Mahosot, the traveler expresses disdain for some of the rural places through which he travels and states a preference for the city.[13] Thus the traveler in Sunthorn Phu's 1807 *Nirat Mueang Klaeng* makes declarations regarding the superiority of Thai culture and urban life. The speaker of the poem repeatedly makes derisive comments about the rural communities that he encounters. Upon reaching Thap Nang, for instance, he deplores the lack of beautiful women in the village:

Reaching Thap Nang (Woman-Hut), I suddenly feel desolate:
Only farmers' huts are to be seen,

There is no delight in the country women,
They have shabby spots of scurf as though smeared with
    indigo.
The women of the city, even slaves,
Are many times better than these women.
Oh, once having left the city there is no more beauty.
The more I think about it, the worse I feel and miss the city.[14]

This example from *Nirat Mueang Klaeng* also indicates the extent to which *nirat* deploy femininity and the bodies of women to achieve a variety of discursive ends and political goals. The passage quoted thus shows how the construction of central Thai identity is achieved through the objectification of women more generally and over the bodies of 'the other' women, which are here described in derogatory terms.

Nirat frequently describe journeys from the center of power to the periphery. These voyages are often undertaken for military reasons or as part of royal, and later government, expeditions. Thus, *Nirat Nakhon Sawan*, for instance, represents a celebration of royal power and military might. Conversely, Craig Reynolds has shown *Nirat Nongkhai*, a nineteenth-century *nirat* written on a military expedition to the northeast frontier of the Siamese state at Nongkhai, to bear "simultaneous referents in both elite and subaltern mentalities."[15] *Nirat Nongkhai* contains graphic accounts of soldiers' suffering as well as pointed remarks about the misguided military decisions responsible for it.[16] Charges of sedition were leveled against the author of the poem. Reynolds stresses the fact that these charges focused on the transgression of the poetic order, rather than on the critical content of the poem. He thereby highlights the fact of the customary significance of form for the political import of Thai literary works. Reynolds argues that, by virtue of using vulgar language that was understood as signifying an empowerment of the subaltern classes, not only the content but also the very form of *Nirat Nongkhai* constituted a threat to the status of the elite.

Journeys of Emotion

At the same time, *nirat* record journeys of concentrated personal reflection. The scholarly writing about *nirat* describes as particular to the genre the self-conscious subjective identity and emotionality of the *nirat* narrator.[17] In addition to giving rise to considerations of identity, the separations or departures of *nirat* also engender longing, pain, and melancholy. Pain caused by separation from a loved one, from home, or from a certain community is a prominent emotional component of *nirat*.

On his journey, the traveler experiences cultural and emotional displacement so strongly that he therefore calls to mind those things that best reconnect him to home or to the object of his desire, as the scent of a lover's cheek in *Kamsuan Si Prat*, for instance. Classical *nirat* thus chronicle, alongside the journey through physical space, a journey in the mind. As the traveler moves away from home and from the familiar, he undertakes, prior to his actual return, a mental journey back home. In this context, memories of his lover's body frequently seem to provide a stabilizing function and to counter the anxiety produced by the journey through unknown territory.

On the level of language, the meter, rhyme, and punning in *nirat* generate a rhythm that mirrors the movement of the journey. In several poems, the temporality created through the regularity of movement through space is a very linear one. In *nirat* that record actual journeys, this regularity and the organic concreteness of the landscape situate the traveler in an everyday spatiality and temporality. The subjectivity that arises out of these dimensions of time and space is twofold. On the one hand, the speakers frequently travel as subjects in the sense of officials or employees of the court—and later as citizens of the nation-state. On the other hand, the imaginary journey back home or to the lover modifies the *nirat*'s linear temporality, and the travelers' subjectivity manifests also in the introspective, emotional charge that likewise marks the genre.

Contemporary Nirat

The modernity of contemporary *nirat* lies in the fact of their self-reflexivity and consciousness of the history of the genre. In contemporary *nirat* the themes of separation, longing, and identity remain prominent, and movement still plays an important role, but the body disappears as a central referent. *Nirat* now frequently become journeys in history, travels in collective memory, and ways of reflecting on the past. Contemporary *nirat* include Naowarat Pongpaiboon's *Krung Thep Thawarawadi: Jaruek Wai Nai Pi Thi 200 Haeng Krung Rattanakosin* (1986) and Mala Khamjan's *Jao Jan Phom Hom: Nirat Phrathat In Khwaen* (1991).[18] Angkarn Kallayanapong is the modern poet who works most prolifically in and with the *nirat* form, however. *Lamnam Phu Kradueng* (1969) and *Bangkok*

Kaeo Kamsuan Rue Nirat Nakhon Si Thammarat (1978) are long *nirat*, and Angkarn's other works include numerous short *nirat* as well as pieces with *nirat* character.[19] I reference selected passages from his long *nirat*, but focus on the various short *nirat* poems published in *Kawiniphon Khong Angkarn Kallayanapong* (1964), *Bang Bot Jak Suan Kaeo* (1972), and *Panithan Kawi* (1986).[20]

Angkarn began producing a significant body of work during the Sarit Thanarat regime (1958–1963). This regime developed a form of nationalism that emphasized historical roots but was at the same time strongly committed to technological modernization. According to Thak Chaloemtiarana, Sarit's reactionary modernism would serve as the dominant philosophy of governance for decades to come.[21] Sarit's advancement of right-wing ideologies was paralleled by the continued development of Thai socialist thought. Reflections on socialism made their way also into the domain of poetics, beginning with Chit Phumisak's socialist politics of poetics of the late 1950s. These poetics were revived in the Art for Life poetics of the 1970s when the struggle for political freedom took center stage in the national arena.

Angkarn's poetry does not explicitly reference these political and representational contexts. Instead, for Angkarn, all of Thai history culminates in Ayuthaya. For Angkarn, the Ayuthaya period, which lasted from the fourteenth to the eighteenth century, stands for a glorious era in Thai history, but above all denotes artistic achievement and sophistication. This idealized state and period become pivotal in his vision of the nation. In his poems on the past, and in his art and *panithan* (artistic credo or manifesto) poems, this vision emerges with great clarity.[22]

In 1957 Angkarn writes a poem titled "Ayuthaya":

Ayuthaya, your status higher than heaven come down to earth,
The power and merit of the kings of old built
Beautiful *chedis*, palaces of Indra,[23]
Pure gold on the inside and outside.

Luminous fortress of Ayuthaya,
Beautiful gates strong towers.
Ayuthaya, more than a valiant heavenly phenomenon, like
    the regions of the gods,
Very much like heaven to the eye.

O Ayuthaya, excellent place, greater than heaven,
You have fallen, brave soldiers are not to be found here anymore.
Wasting the energy of those expert craftsmen that created you,
Scores of wild animals came to aggravate you, ground you smooth, o great treasure.

Silenced, Phra Sri Sanphet rolls in the soil.
Vultures, packs of dogs, and swarms of crows eat this side of heaven.
From the eyes of an apparition run tears of blood,
Flooding and flowing, caressing the world that has fallen, its city disappeared.

So, pulverized dauntless kingdom, ha ha,
O Ayuthaya, you resemble a burial ground.
Of the great heavenly place is left only the carcass,
Only human blood in this arid world, o deep shame.

O glorious Ayuthaya,
Tears flood the kingdom:
Decayed, fallen apart, suddenly mud,
Like a graveyard ill with mourning.

City of palaces, *stupas*, and castles,
Kingdom that was completely destroyed.
Only residue is left,
The soot and ashes of Thai bones.

Ayuthaya, o great domain,
Hell has come to destroy and burn your era.
Vultures, crows, and dogs are everywhere,
Destroying and eating all of the beloved terrain.

Sorrow for the art,
And magnificent civilization.
The kingdom is finished,
Sadly taking leave of the Thai ancestors.

The precious *stupa, bot, and vihan*,[24]
In pieces, still exceedingly beautiful.
The lotus on the pillar of the lion pedestal,
Everything pitifully destroyed.

Sri Sanphet, the great main hall,
Pulverized, Ratburana Mahathat,
Every temple, palace, and castle
Of the dominion ruined, the Thai spirit destroyed.

The gravel, sand, and soil sob,
The cold ground of the precious city quivers.
The brick and mortar are decaying,
Gradually fading throughout the *kalpas*.[25]

The breast of the earth has tears,
For the burial ground of heaven.
The soul ponders and laments,
Ominously year in year out.

The king, the former great ruler,
Cries loudly with the voice of a ghost.
With a long thundering noise, cheering on for victory,
His horses and elephants and scores of soldiers.

Flutes, gongs, and drums of victory,
Resound forsakenly.
Every tuft of grass suffers,
Sobbing until the end of time.

Angkarn begins "Ayuthaya" with two *khlong* stanzas from Si Prat's seventeenth-century *Kamsuan Si Prat* that celebrate the glory of Ayuthaya and then sets against these three *khlong* stanzas of his own that describe the fall of the city. For the remainder of the poem, he uses a meter called *kap yani* 11.[26] Against a vision in much of the writing of his contemporaries on democratic transformation and a poetics that draws strongly on elements of folk culture, Angkarn tells of the high culture of a grand past and juxtaposes these accounts with dramatic stagings of Ayuthaya's downfall.[27] In so doing, the poet develops a distinctive poetic style marked by its highly Sanskritic lexicon and borrowings from Ayuthaya poetic style.[28]

As Trisilpa Boonkhachorn notes, in Angkarn's writing the *bot chom mueang* of classical *nirat*, the episodes of admiration of the city, are transformed into criticisms of modern life in which "the poet's modern voice ironically denies that nostalgic tradition."[29] Suchitra investigates the innovations that the poet makes with regard to the *nirat*'s convention of love-longing and the figure of the lover. In her examination of Angkarn's long *nirat*, *Lamnam Phu Kradueng* (Kradueng Mountain Song), she notes that this lover emerges as an ambivalent figure. Thus, the poet at times reconfigures the *nirat*'s notion of loss by comparing women to death itself. At other times, he expects his lover also to be an intellectual companion.[30] We can understand Angkarn's first modification of the *nirat*'s figure of the lover—the equation of women with death—to follow Buddhist conventions that closely align femininity with impermanence and use women and their demise as "object lessons" to teach the futility of attachment. Liz Wilson has critiqued the misogyny of this textual and pictorial tradition.[31] The second way in which Angkarn modifies the convention, however, is entirely new and noteworthy for the way in which it positions women as potential actors, if not equal partners, in an intellectual project. Suchitra describes how, rather than follow the *nirat* convention of referring to physical attributes of the lover, the speaker of Angkarn's long *nirat* delineates her intellectual qualities: "Apart from praising her intellect as well as her beauty, the poet expresses his desire to share his intellectual life with her. By all this, they will create an ultimate union with each other, an ever-lasting love which is above and beyond time."[32]

According to Suchitra, the poet modifies the convention of love-longing still further. This additional improvisation on the convention becomes especially important for those poems that critique the poverty of the contemporary cultural imaginary:

> According to the convention, a Nirat poem is essentially a complaint of the poet's sufferings caused by the separation from his loved one. Angkhan followed this convention but his suffering is somehow different. His main lamentation is not so much caused by his inevitable separation from his loved one but by his loneliness and his complete lack of a loved one.[33]

Angkarn thus abstracts from the convention of lamenting the absence of a specific lover to proffer a complaint about the lack of love more broadly. This move is intensified in those poems in which he extends this notion of privation to a general complaint about humanity: "To manipulate the convention of using the theme of love-longing in Nirat the poet not only laments the lack of love for himself alone but also laments the lack of love in all humanity of the present time."[34]

Angkarn's poems about historical cities and eras deploy this modification of the theme of separation to yet another end. While the stations of the journey in Angkarn's city *nirat* are no longer the geocultural landscape of the traditional *nirat*, neither is there any longer a body of a lover—in fact, there is no lover at all in these historically themed poems. Instead, a moment and location in the past take the place of the lost object of desire. In this sense, there is a place that has been left by the traveler of the *nirat*, but there is no longer a home.

Angkarn's "Ayuthaya" blends literary elements of the past and the present. To begin with, the two stanzas from *Kamsuan Si Prat* represent an example of classical Ayuthaya *khlong nirat* from the "Golden Age" of literature during the time of Phra Narai (1656–1688). Si Prat writes of the magnificence of the Ayuthaya of his time, a city at the height of its power and splendor. Significantly, Si Prat is leaving Ayuthaya on a journey into exile. As he does so, he evokes an image of the unearthly beauty and opulence of the city that is "like heaven to the eye."

Following Si Prat's stanzas, Angkarn's lines emphasize the violence of the city's destruction. These stanzas are replete with mockery and pain. The thematic of cultural loss of Angkarn's lines complements the notion of departure into exile of Si Prat's stanzas. The theme of former glory juxtaposed with images of devastation is recurrent in Angkarn's poetic treatment of the old cities. The resultant tension becomes even more poignant in Angkarn's meditation on the loss of Ayuthaya in his 1964 poem "Ayuthaya Wipayok" ("The Perishing of Ayuthaya"):

> Ayuthaya has disappeared all over the sky,
> Has vanished from the heavens.
> It is a burial ground of art
> Of inestimable value,
> Created to give rise to the dream of a
> Divine world,

Only residue, waste is left,
Speaking to the scarcity of human ideals.

O Sri Ayodhya,
You are a charnel ground, defying the buried dream.
Miraculous art of eternity,
Auspicious spirit of the heavens, you have come to be
    submerged in the earth.

Ratchathan Kaeo Palace,[35]
Pulverized you are still winding in agony.
Your tears are flooding and flowing,
Crying the story in painting.

Sri Sanphet, pitiful,
Destroyed your highest beauty.
The Burmese come alive to kill repeatedly,
'Til the extinction of the Thai soul.

A pang of longing for your art flares up,
Great Ratburana Mahathat.
The Thai nation plundered,
Then crushed to pieces under the soles of their feet.

The divine decorative patterns,
Touched by the hands of beasts without ethics.
Dharma broken, basely destroyed, climbed upon,
Finding and killing every soul.

Prang, chedi, bot, and *vihan*,[36]
Those dull beasts took them all apart.
Taking the brick stones and earth,
Devouring everything, brainless scum.

The Patriarch, a yellow lizard,
Under whom the world of the inauspicious prospered.
Deeply hurt in dignity,
Once so high, now only particles of dust.

Ayuthaya, higher than the domain of the heavens,
Now only residue.
Filth of those earthly animals,
Prospering in their power.

The sheen of Chai Wathanaram,
Beautiful like a stratum of the heavens.
That pack of dogs and crows, those gloomy vultures,
Assembling to devour it.

Mahachai, by the disgrace of the animals,
Ruined, utterly destroyed.
The precious city fallen apart, submerged under the earth,
Insulted, meaning the disappearance of the Thais.

The remnants of brick and mortar sobbing,
How can this spirit be revived?
The exhaustion of human values,
In this world, they do not really exist.

The end of the art of Ayuthaya,
Severely disgraced all over the earth and the sky.
Left is only the essence of monkeys possessing
Siam, o shame.

As the speaker travels through the ruins of the old city in "The Perishing of Ayuthaya," he names each devastated site. The techniques of punning and transfer of traditional *nirat*, however, are absent. Instead, each station of the journey is used simultaneously to evoke the glory and devastation of Ayuthaya. Although Angkarn describes several stages of history in his writing—from poems about nature located in an undefined point in the past[37] to the time of the Buddha,[38] and from the periods of the Thai kingdoms up to the present[39]—the poet locates the culmination of Thai history in Ayuthaya. In contrast, all descriptions of Bangkok and all accounts of modern life in Angkarn's poetry will speak of anguished alienation.

When considering Angkarn's treatment of the past in its entirety, his notion of Thai history seems always to culminate in Ayuthaya. Still more significant is the thematic of collective cultural departure from this idealized period. This painful separation from the past becomes the most significant feature of the present in the poet's writing. The complexity of his *nirat* lies in the facts that the various stages of time intersect with different spaces and that the movement through these dimensions is also manifold.

Angkarn retains the technique of contrasting two cultures that is a common feature of traditional *nirat*. Unlike in earlier *nirat*, however, the poet expresses no disdain for features of the local or the peripheral. Angkarn's poetry glorifies the "center" that is Ayuthaya, and his *nirat* move solely through the sites of central Thai power in accordance with a nationalist, hegemonic perspective on Thai history. Nowhere does the poet contrast this center to peripheral cultures. Instead, from the locales of the old cities, there emerges a juxtaposition of two points in time, rather than space, as Angkarn mobilizes the force of the old Thai centers of power for his critique of present-day Bangkok.

What stands out in Angkarn's use of space is that the stations of the journey are not only the individual ruins of Ayuthaya, but include heaven and terrains beyond. The space of the *nirat* now extends into the cosmos. The poet's rhetorical focus on the enormity of time is always accompanied by vast dimensions of space. This entry into the dimension of cosmological space constitutes a further feature that generates the vehemence of his rhetoric. Thus, in the 1962 poem, "Sinlapa Ayuthaya" ("The Art of Ayuthaya"), Ayuthaya, and by extension the Thai nation, is accorded divine status, but at the same time shown to have lost its rightful place in the universe:

> Ayuthaya, like the graveyard of heaven:
> The prosperous divine lotus,
> The *kanok wan* pattern,
> Have fallen from the sky.
> Have decomposed, have been ruined ominously,
> Destroyed, fallen,
> Dissolute and base, every blade of grass,
> Flowing heavily with the tears of Siam.

The geocultural landscapes in many of Angkarn's short *nirat* poems thus appear as sites of destruction. Significantly absent from the desexualized Thai literary present of these particular poems is the body of the lover, which played such an important role in traditional *nirat*. Instead, inanimate objects—the ruins—are invested with something akin to corporeality and merge with the organic. "Ayuthaya Wipayok" and "Sinlapa Ayuthaya" leave the reader with the impression that the cosmos joins in mourning the fall of Ayuthaya. Its destruction, as described in "Sinlapa Ayuthaya," is felt across worlds and eras:

> O Ayuthaya, great place,
> Scattered brokenness, rolling,
> Chewed on and thrown away by vultures, crows, and dogs,
> Completely motionless throughout the three worlds.
>
> The sound of the carcasses of brick and mortar sobbing,
> The ground of the Thai state trembling, solitarily,
> Through each speck of sand and dust,
> Throughout all ages, deliriously.
>
> Hurting the Thais throughout existence,
> Destroyed, embittered, every blade of grass,
> Blood inundates the feet of elephants and horses,
> A burial ground throughout eternity.
>
> The deities, the four guardians of the world,
> Every *wiman*, every precious heavenly plant,
> Cries heavily,
> The earth and the skies trembling with grief.

The cosmos and the sites of the Thai kingdoms replace the landscape of the traditional *nirat*. At the same time, the body of the lover simply disappears, and desire is directed toward the recuperation of an early modern socio-aesthetic order. The theme of longing is employed to describe a collective vision rather than the sphere of the personal. Where his poems critique the present, Thailand itself becomes the alienating, anxiety-provoking foreign territory through which the *nirat* traveler journeyed in traditional *nirat*. Anxiety is no longer produced by travel in the territories under imperial Siam's suzerainty but by what the poet perceives to be the detrimental impact of global culture on Thailand.

Unlike his contemporaries, who often use *nirat* to invoke ideals of social justice or to commemorate the political uprisings of 1973 and 1976, Angkarn's use of the poetic past is directed toward an entirely different purpose.[40] His concern lies neither in the sphere of concrete politics nor in the realm of everyday struggles of identity between the local and the central. Instead, the explicit scene of conflict in his writing lies in struggles over what form Thai cultural modernity is to take.

Art for Life Poetics: Angkarn's Contemporaries

The 1960s–1970s saw the burgeoning of experimental approaches to literary form and the coming into being of what some have called Thai New Wave literature. In Thomas Hudak's estimation, the landscape of modern Thai poetry in these decades is defined as follows:

> Poets such as Prakin Xumsai, writing as Ujjeni (b. 1919), and later Naowarat Pongpaiboon (b. 1940) emphasized nature, love, and emotion along with social crit. The 1960s saw much experimentation with verse forms, incl. free verse (*klǫn plaü*). During this time, the poet-painter Angkarn Kalayanapongse (b. 1926), probably the most respected of contemp. poets, developed his themes and style. Often described as a nature poet, he finds expressions of universal messages in Buddhism, nature, art, and the past. The fluid political climate of the early 1970s revived protest and socialist themes. The student uprising of October 14, 1973; the return to democracy; and the subsequent suppression on October 6, 1976, have provided the themes for much of Thai poetry up to the present. Naowarat Pongpaiboon (b. 1940) has emerged as the most eloquent chronicler of these events. Women's issues, along with moral, political, and social concerns, remain major themes in contemp. poetry.[41]

The writers of the 1960s and 1970s can roughly be divided into three groups: those who use conventional form, especially *klon*, to express new, leftist content such as Naowarat Pongpaiboon; those who use older, traditional forms such as *khlong* and *kap* to express contemporary content like Angkarn and Khomthuan Khanthanu; and, finally, those who reject traditional and conventional forms altogether, such as Chang Sae Tang and others who experiment with free verse or *klon plao* as well as with new genres such as science fiction (Suchat Sawadsri). Chang Sae Tang (or Chang Tang, 1934–1990) is particularly iconic, working—like Angkarn—in both painting and poetry, and often in both mediums at once.[42] Most notably, Tang invented his own concrete poetry to record everyday occurrences.

Angkarn's work has largely been contrasted with the work of the left-leaning Art for Life poets of the 1970s. This is a logical distinction and my own comparison echoes this tradition; however, such a contrast also overlooks lines of convergence in poetic style and content during this period.

Against the progression of Thai right-wing ideologies in the latter half of the twentieth century stood the development of Thai socialist ideology—an ideology also thoroughly worked through in poetics. In the 1950s, the Marxists Chit Phumisak and Atsani Phonlachan launched their attack on *sakdina* decadence as encoded in classical literature.[43] Around the time that Angkarn began to publish regularly, Chit Phumisak wrote *Art for Life, Art for the People* (1957), a polemic in favor of politically committed art.[44] According to Chit, revolutionary art was to be a political weapon against classical Thai *sakdina* culture, which had served the oppressive interests of the ruling classes.

Chit's manifesto objected not only to the content of classical literature but also to the fact of an elite literary language. Regarding poetic lexicon, the language of simple everyday and peasant speech was to replace traditional aristocratic vocabularies. In addition to identifying classical literature as an instrument that maintains the status of the elite, a further feature of Chit's revolutionary aesthetics was its almost obsessive condemnation of the sexual content of that literature. Although Chit argued for revolutionary literature to be socialist in content, he did not believe that the *forms* of classical literature had to be changed. The new literature was to be national in form and socialist in content, and hence a Thai Marxist aesthetics was created.[45]

With the revival in the 1970s of Thai Marxist thought, Art for Life poetics continued to exert a strong influence. In the course of the Art for Life debates, folk elements in Thai poetry came to have the connotation of resistance to unjust governance and social stratification. In their search for progressive Thainess, poets frequently turned to the regional and the rural, sometimes making use of their own cultural roots. On a thematic level, a shift in attention toward the concerns of "the people" occurred. On a formal level, rhythms, elements, and fragments of folk songs were incorporated into Art for Life poetry.[46]

Poetics and the Nation

At stake in the Art for Life poetry of the 1960s and 1970s, especially, is the question of the nation. The 1960s were marked not only by Sarit Thanarat's indigenist nationalism and policy of accelerated development but also by Thailand's security relations with the United States and by the Vietnam War. Benedict Anderson understands Bangkok's tightening of control over the rural population, its expansion of the education system, and the Americanization of the country as characteristics of the 1960s. At the same time, Anderson also ascribes the rise of the middle class and the formation of oppositional political consciousness to American influence. According to him, the political radicalization of Thai students in the United States led to a questioning of policy at home and, finally, to active resistance.[47]

In the mid-1960s, the Communist Party of Thailand began its armed struggle. By 1973 opposition to the government that followed Sarit's, the Thanom Kittikachorn-Praphat Charusathien regime, led to protests and the demand for constitutional rule. The government's violent suppression of these protests in 1973 was followed by a brief period with elements of democratic rule before escalating state violence in 1976 ended this phase.[48]

The cycles of poems that chronicle the events of 1973 and 1976 are suffused with a political vision and idealism that are indicative of how politics and poetry were interlinked during these periods. Poets active at this time include Sujit Wongthet, Naowarat Pongpaiboon, Chiranan Pitpreecha, and Khomthuan Khanthanu. The axis on which the writings of the Art for Life writers and their poetic heirs turn is democratic transformation—as the factor thought to be able to transform the nation into the counternation they envision. Naowarat Pongpaiboon's collection of poems, *Phiang Khwam Khluean Wai* (Mere Movement), is exemplary of this writing.[49] Weighted toward the indigenous meter of *klon*, Naowarat's poems are suffused with the rhythms of folk songs and oral literature. Pieces with titles such as "Mere Movement," "Flute Song Over the Rice Field," "To the Children of the People," and "Krathum Baen" (a migrant worker neighborhood in Bangkok) tap elements of the lives of urban workers as well as the cycle of agriculture and rural festivals to create symbols of "the people" and to partake directly in struggles over national political transformation.[50]

Against this leftist conceptualization of nationhood, Angkarn sets a poetry of heightened cultural consciousness. From the 1950s to the

1980s, his writing appears almost untouched by the particular kind of political consciousness that is so strongly present in the writing of his contemporaries. Even in "Sanam Luang," a station and poem in his long *nirat*, *Bangkok Kaew Kamsuan* (Lament for Beloved Bangkok), from 1978, Angkarn only laments the general decadence of the present. Although Sanam Luang is the place in Bangkok where the uprisings of 1973 and 1976 took place and is virtually synonymous with these events, the poem makes no mention of this.

In contrast to that of his contemporaries, Angkarn's political ideology may thus appear conservative or even reactionary. A distaste for the quotidian, especially for the realm of day-to-day politics, also frequently becomes evident in his work. Instead Angkarn posits ethical absolutes in combination with a primacy of aesthetics. Especially in his artistic manifestos (*panithan*), the poet advances the salutary power of art as a redemptive force. Thus, while in the poetic manifesto "Kawi" ("Poet/ry"), which I will discuss in the next chapter, Naowarat vows to write truth and reflect life in his poetry, Angkarn's manifestos proffer first a pledge to "sacrifice and leave behind life" and later to "forsake even nirvana" in the quest to create redemptive art.[51] In these poems, art becomes a way of making offerings (giving *than*, Thai; *dāna*, Pali) to the world. These pieces attack the rational present from the site of an essentialized past in which, as Suchitra has argued, high art takes the place of religion.[52] It becomes clear that instead of a political order, strictly speaking, Angkarn envisions an order in which aesthetics plays a central role.

In his writing, the present of the nation seems determined by a conventional understanding of Thai history as based on cultural continuity. In what reads as a programmatic call for a return to national cultural essence, one may discern a more totalizing form of the nation than in the writing of his contemporaries. At the same time, however, Angkarn's writing cannot easily be relegated solely to the domain of the nationalist center. For one, the intensity of anxiety over cultural loss in these poems shows the poet as contending with the legitimate question of how a local culture might sustain itself against global forces. What is more, Angkarn's imagination of an ideal present ultimately reaches beyond the confines of the Thai nation-state.

In close connection, Angkarn's poetry plays off against each other the conflicts between an economic system geared toward a maximization of efficiency and a culture that he sees as based on humility. All striving in Angkarn's system is to be directed toward ethical behavior and the creation of art. What sometimes appears as a facile critique of capitalism is a vision that the poet also endeavored to live, to the extent of living in poverty in old age. What is more, his poetry's elevation of Ayuthaya to the highest ideal of a socio-aesthetic order stands in critical opposition to the dominant ethos of governance introduced in the late 1950s.

"Sukhothai" as National Ideology and Style of Governance

From 1958 through 1963, Thailand was governed by the authoritarian regime of Sarit Thanarat, which aimed to revive indigenous models of authority—including that of the premodern patriarchal system of Sukhothai. As Thak Chaloemtiarana writes, "Sarit's regime tried to implement 'traditional' concepts of political leadership seen as approximating Sukhothai paternalism."[53]

Under Sarit, the nation was conceived of as a large family, in which administrative officials were to take the role of heads of the family. Paternalistic leadership was provided by the army and legitimated by the monarch. As David Wyatt writes, under Sarit the king was "restored to the apex of the moral, social, and political order" and first assumed an active role in developmental and national affairs.[54] Political parties and trade unions were abolished and both the *sangha* and the press tightly controlled. Sarit abrogated the constitution and ruled by decree under martial law, arguing that historically the nation had only prospered under authoritarian rule.

Sarit's strict control over all institutions of the state, however, did not extend to the business sector. He further promoted national development through Western-trained technocrats. The hallmark of Sarit's policy thus lay in his emphasis on the indigenous in combination with his adaptation of a foreign body of knowledge into his program of modernization. Sarit can be termed a reactionary modernist in that he combined a vision of large-scale technological development with cultural nostalgia. Assessing the impact of this politician's political philosophy, Thak stresses that "Sarit, more than any other person in the modern period, set the pattern of present-day politics in Thailand."[55]

Angkarn's Ayuthaya

Angkarn produced significant sections of his early work, which holds up Ayuthaya as the highest ideal, during the Sarit Thanarat era. But before I contrast Angkarn's invocation of Ayuthaya with the vision of nation and statehood espoused by the Sarit regime, I want to stress that we cannot attribute intentional differentiation between Ayuthaya and Sukhothai to the poet. Neither can we claim that Angkarn invokes the cosmopolitan character of Ayuthaya from the perspective of contemporary historiography. What then do we make of the fact that Angkarn's work invokes as essentially Thai something that, according to historian David Wyatt, is itself the product of a premodern, or early modern, kind of globalization, a cosmopolitan culture superseding a more Tai and purportedly more homogeneous one?[56] The poet's understanding of Ayuthaya as quintessentially Thai seems to converge with conventional historiography, in that he delineates Ayuthaya as a glorious episode in a continuum of historical Thai kingdoms. However, distinguishing between author intention and the work that the poems perform irrespective of their author's objectives opens up yet other perspectives on the political import of Angkarn's "city" poems.

The historical correlate for the opposition between Sukhothai and Ayuthaya can be found in the fourteenth and fifteenth centuries, when a revived Sukhothai stood against and was eventually superseded by an emergent Ayuthaya. According to Wyatt, Ayuthaya represented a change in the way Tai states organized themselves and marked the transition to a new political and economic order. In contrast to Sukhothai, Ayuthaya emerged as an imperial, highly organized and hierarchized polity that consciously situated itself in a larger world of international relations. Wyatt describes King Ramkhamhaeng as having created an essentially Tai culture as the foundation for his kingdom, while the rulers of the new Tai empire of Ayuthaya made the decision to incorporate "foreign" elements of statecraft into their political programs.[57] The work of Sheldon Pollock adds a further dimension to such claims: Ayuthaya consciously situated itself as part of the large cultural sphere that Pollock terms the "Sanskrit cosmopolis." At least in the first millennium of the Common Era, this Sanskrit cosmopolis extended all the way from "Afghanistan to Java."[58] This broad cultural corridor consisted of polities that, via the adoption of Sanskrit poetics, fashioned themselves as members of a transregional formation that adhered to certain notions of a universal, cosmopolitan political order and kingship.[59] The literature of Ayuthaya is marked by adaptations, frequently via Cambodia, of Sanskrit metrics, tropes, and other poetic forms.[60] In this context, Ayuthaya itself can be understood as an amalgam of South Asian, Khmer, and other "outside" influences.

Angkarn's volume *Kawiniphon* includes not only numerous poems about Ayuthaya, but also two poems referring to the Sukhothai period, named "Sukhothai" (1964) and "Si Sachanalai" (1961). These two poems evince the same nostalgic sensibility and style of invoking the past as Angkarn's Ayuthaya poems. What gives "Sukhothai" a distinct character is its paraphrasing of some of the most famous lines of the Ramkhamhaeng inscription—an inscription that lauds King Ramkhamhaeng's polity (1279–1298) as marked by agricultural plenitude and by its ruler's concern for and just governance of its population.[61] But while the inscription reads, "In the water there are fish, in the fields there is rice," Angkarn's "Sukhothai" laments, "The fields are devoid of rice, the water depleted of fish." This juxtaposition of former abundance with present-day deprivation parallels the poet's mode of complaint in his Ayuthaya poems. Angkarn might thus seem to perceive Sukhothai largely along the same lines as Ayuthaya—as part of a trajectory of Thai historical glory—and not to differentiate the two periods from each other. However, his invocations of Ayuthaya are much more plentiful—both in *Kawiniphon* as well as in his oeuvre as a whole—so that Ayuthaya emerges as the core trope of the poet's understanding of an ideal historical model. Vis-à-vis a deplorable present, his invocations of Ayuthaya take on an oppositional character.

Scholarly inquiry into Ayuthaya as a highly cosmopolitan polity is still a recent development, pioneered by scholars such as Bhawan Ruangsilp and Dhiravat na Pombejra.[62] Dhiravat describes the plural character of Ayuthaya as follows:

> Ayutthaya was a leading Southeast Asian port, an entrepot and trading kingdom which dealt with merchants of many races and religions. As a result, Ayutthaya became a cosmopolitan city where several communities of foreign traders, missionaries, and mercenaries co-existed with the already ethnically diverse (and mixed) local populations. Dialogue and interaction between these groups naturally ensued, taking place within a context of close administrative control by the King of Siam and his officials.[63]

School textbooks, as exemplary of widely disseminated notions of Thai history in the early 1960s, provide an indication of how broad sections of the population were instructed to view Ayuthaya. Rather than put forth a perspective that contrasts sharply with Dhiravat's delineation of Ayuthayan cosmopolitanism, however, these instructional texts do not present as unified a view of the period as expected. A look at the third edition of the *Social Studies Textbook: History*, issued in 1963 by Thailand's Ministry of Education for use in the eighth-grade classroom, furnishes a mixed perspective on the cultural makeup of Ayuthaya: while chapter 9 of the textbook speaks of the lifestyle culture of Ayuthaya as quintessentially Thai and foundational for Thai national character until the present,[64] its authors take care to present the artistic traditions of Ayuthaya as multicultural. They note Portuguese, Dutch, French, and English influences on architecture as well as the adoption of European notions of science and medicine.[65] Chapter 7, "The Flourishing of Ayuthaya," begins with a section titled "Friendly Relations with Western Countries" and notes also the important role of the Japanese in the court and in trade.[66] The *Social Studies Textbook: History* (1964) for the seventh grade likewise speaks of Ayuthayan statecraft as an amalgam of Khmer and Sukhothai elements and describes the customs, art, and religions of the polity as subject to multiple influences, which include Khmer, Indian, Brahmanic, and Buddhist ones.[67] The textbook also mentions trade with a wide range of international counterparts.[68] Thus, while holding on to a notion of historical continuity, these 1960s high school texts acknowledge some of the plural elements of the early modern polity of Ayuthaya.

From the late 1950s on, we can understand Angkarn's poetry to perform the work of counterposing Ayuthaya, with its connotations of sophistication, to the more parochial Bangkok era marked by Sarit Thanarat's model of an indigenist, nationalist technocratic order. While Sukhothai in this context denotes a localized, familial culture, Ayuthaya represents the idealized high-cultural world that Angkarn's poems constantly reference. Citing those elements of Ayuthaya culture that are metropolitan and cosmopolitan—even if solely by virtue of the poetic lexicon that Angkarn deploys—this poetry evokes the image of a more complexly structured culture than that of Sarit's "Bangkok-Sukhothai." At a time when the notion of Sukhothai represents an important element of national ideology, Angkarn's work thus summons the era of Ayuthaya as a period representing a more refined vision of Thainess.

With its acerbic criticism of the globalized cultural present, Angkarn's poetry echoes elements of the longing for cultural autonomy found in Sarit's nationalism. In this the poetry bears the marks of both modernism and an at times reactionary political stance, especially where its nationalist-xenophobic content is concerned. Yet in setting a cultural vision in which Ayuthaya is paramount against Sarit's style of authoritarian paternal leadership à la Ramkhamhaeng, Angkarn's work also strongly opposes the prevailing national ideology of his time.

If the modernity of Angkarn's writing lies not only in the pointed way in which he expresses anguish over the threat of cultural homogenization, his choice of poetic means also bears significance. Thus, with regard to form as well, his poetry constitutes a serious reflection on cultural modernity and the possibilities of representation.

The Politics of Poetics: Prosody and the Past

In aiming to describe what constitutes the modernity of Thai poetry, the concepts of form and content have frequently been mobilized. Many scholars agree that in traditional poetry, form and euphony—as opposed to content—and the emulation of the past masters are paramount.[69] In the study of modern poetry, this theme of form-over-content is understood to be reshaped or even reversed: while certain forms are retained, content now takes precedence and becomes the primary field of contestation. Trisilpa insightfully modifies this binary in the following way: "The transference of poetic values from the musicality of sounds to the emphasis on the unity of sounds and messages guides contemporary poetry to express what really is rather than [the] idealistic or romantic expression."[70]

Prosodic choices can indeed not be divorced from meaning or content. As Barend Jan Terwiel has shown for the Thai context, prosodic innovation was frequently intimately related to changes in governance and social structure.[71] Thai poetics has represented a contested site of discourse since premodern times. For hundreds of years, Thai poetry has thus been a constantly shifting field that engages with elements of South Asian poetics on the level of metrics, lexicon, convention, *rasa*, and genre, as well as content (in the form of plots, motifs, and religious ideas, for instance). Premodern manuals of poetics, such as the *Cindamani*, *Kaphayasarawilasini*, and *Kaphayakantha*, as well as *Tamra Chan Wanaphruet lae Matraphruet* from the Bangkok era, prescribe in detail the lexical and metrical possibilities of poetry.[72] Significant in these manuals of poetics is the introduction of South Asian prosodic means. What results is the indigenization of South Asian poetics and its combination with Thai prosodic conventions.[73] The extension of South Asian poetics by such local prosodic features as rhyme and tonal constraints, in turn, gave rise to poetic possibilities that remained in flux in the centuries that followed.

THE PAST IN PRESENT-DAY POETICS

A distinct feature of contemporary Thai poetry is that, for the most part, it is in meter. Through the use of traditional metrics such as *klon*, *khlong*, *chan*, *kap*, and *rai*, the past is carried over into contemporary poetry. As past transgressions of the poetic order are incorporated into the body of possible poetic forms, the field of poetics diversifies and expands. Thus, Angkarn's own poetry, once condemned on the grounds of its vulgarity and transgression of metrical rules, was subsequently awarded numerous literary prizes and became part of high school curricula. Trisilpa describes contemporary poetry's uses of traditional prosodic forms as "dialogues with the voice of Authority."[74] As Trisilpa further clarifies:

> Contemporary texts demonstrate the admiration of the aesthetics of the past and conserve them by continuing their poetic traditions. But they also debate with the authority of the past and subvert a specific system of beliefs and ideology. In this way the relationship of the present to the hegemonic past is a dialectical relationship. Contemporary texts debate with authority and receive only the aesthetics, but drop political and social authenticating authorities.[75]

Since the 1950s much of Thai poetic discourse has moreover taken the form of explicit contestation in poetic manifestos (*panithan*) rather than of theoretical texts.[76] Even where there is no explicit manifesto, it can be argued that poets invariably participate in the discourse simply through their prosodic innovation.

Angkarn's Poetics

In the domain of prosody, the most remarkable feature of Angkarn's dialog with the past is his combination of divergent strata of language. His discordant use of registers engenders a tension that is evident in much of his writing, but in his early work, it is most marked in his poems about Bangkok. We saw how in "Ayuthaya" Angkarn first quotes two stanzas of admiration passage from a classical source and then sets his own stanzas about the downfall of the city against these, thereby converting the convention of admiration passages into one of admiration *and* deploration. In addition, a jeering, defiant tone pervades his own *khlong* stanzas. The mood conveyed in "Ayuthaya" is one of sadness combined with sarcastic bitterness. However, the poem drops its biting tone in the *kap* stanzas that follow, turning into a more straightforward narration of grief over the destruction of Ayuthaya.

In these *nirat* poems about the past, Angkarn juxtaposes widely divergent registers. Verses 11, 15, and 17 of "Sinlapa Ayuthaya" and verses 1–10 of "Ayuthaya Wipayok" are good examples of this juxtaposition of different strata of language, some of which remains evident in the English translation. In the poems on Ayuthaya, the reader thus reencounters the emotional content of pain of the traditional *nirat*, but finds it modified through variations of the *nirat* convention in tone, mood, imagery, and choice of lexicon.

Bangkok

Angkarn's poems about Bangkok register a formal and thematic shift. For one, the poet's tone becomes venomous and sarcastic. While we can still read these poems as *nirat*, the tone of lamentation of the traditional *nirat* intensifies into what Suchitra has described as a tone of *boriphat*, censure or accusation.[77] A further distinct feature of these poems is that Angkarn transforms the customary emotional content of pain into rage in order to convey the state of crisis that he diagnoses for the Thai present.

One also finds a conflicting juxtaposition of registers in Angkarn's Bangkok poems. But the particular hybridity of these poems no longer reflects the longing for the recovery of a lost ideal of Thai culture. A stanza from "Tuen Thoet Lok Manut" ("Awake, Humanity," *Panithan Kawi*) reads as follows:

> A pity, born to corrupt,
> Waiting, day and night, crazy with coup d'états,
> Extorting the country, that pack of depraved, rabid dogs.

> I condemn the fruits of their doings, as they sink their teeth
> into Thailand.

In "Beng Ngan Bat Sop Jop Phop Trai" ("Excreting Work Eternally Vile") from the 1986 volume *Panithan Kawi*, Angkarn asserts:

> Those vile, diseased cancerous ones,
> Studied in the university of heaven,
> Received the various, miraculous animal degrees.
> Joyfully, the tree lizard received a B.A.
>
> Waking the ghosts of every burial ground,
> Dealing in hashish, superb, splendid opium,
> Worms of the buffalo's stomach, of extraordinary quality,
> Teach a blood-sucking method, gorging on *adharma*.

As early as in the poem "Benjasin" ("Five Precepts") from the 1978 *Bangkok Kaeo Kamsuan*, he makes similar allegations:

> Drinking captivating alcohol, the spirit of Europe, superbly
>   effective.
> Deranged, drunk, like low, base animals,
> All foolish dangers, all vile poisons are there,
> Waiting for the waves of insanity to bury their faces, to rot
>   and burn in hell.

While the message of Angkarn's poems on the present sometimes becomes repetitive or tends toward the fanatical, the energy of challenge that is generated by the juxtaposition of the divergent registers is engaging. A passage in "Benjasin" ("Five Precepts"), *Bangkok Kaeo Kamsuan*, reads as follows:

> Capital city, trendy Bangkok, refuse of the heavens,
> Chameleons, lizards, huge lice are sure to creep there.
> All of a sudden frogs and toads are masters
> Vulgarly moving and flying on and on.

> Fatiguing, this region of the waste of Siam,
> Divine city, domain of gods,
> > out to pursue heaven to feed off.
> Showering with sweat instead of water,
> > pursuing just one thing.
> That thing can be rented, including even the soul.
>
> Divine city with the name of the gods,
> The gods relegated to the earth, persistently avaricious,
> In a pack, inhuman beings crawl, fly together.
> Here the entire soul is sold, can be bought and rented.[78]

And, in an untitled poem in *Panithan Kawi*, Angkarn writes:

> With four faces the god shakes his head, fed up with the
> > earth, three-eyed, turbid green,
> Despising, disdaining the world.
> Base, nuclear fire of the vicious, will destroy the world.
> In the modern age, why is humanity so insane? Crazed with
> > dealing in nuclear material.[79]

The linguistic hybridity of the Bangkok poems differs from that of the Ayuthaya poems. The poet again combines evocative religious concepts and a Sanskritic idiom—a poetic lexicon composed of "classical" Sanskrit-derived terms and loan words, comparable to the function of Latin and Greek terms in European languages—with a lexicon of colloquial Thai words, but these increasingly include curse words, slang, or "vulgar" language. Thus, the first stanza of "Five Precepts" quoted above deploys what was at the time a youth slang term, "ko," for the notion of something trendy. It uses this term to define the Sanskritic *phranakhon*, the royal, capital city. Together, these two terms from divergent strata of language create a notion of irony.

In these critiques of the present, not only the high proportion of neologisms and English words stands out, but also the juxtaposition of Angkarn's characteristic cosmologically infused lexicon with slang, swear words, and neologisms. In the untitled poem from *Panithan Kawi* quoted above, the term "nuclear" marks one such instance that remains legible also in the English translation. These pieces let the reader sense the accelerated pace of industrialization of the 1970s and 1980s in Thailand and the notion of a threatening material and ideological global modernity.[80]

Metrical Choices

In the late 1950s and in the 1960s, when national ideology is expressly modeled on Sukhothai, Angkarn not only writes obsessively about Ayuthaya, but he does so in a genre (*nirat*) and meter (mostly *khlong*) that signifies Ayuthaya. Where metrical choices are concerned, it seems appropriate for Angkarn to prefer *khlong*, an indigenous Thai meter that may reach back to the fourteenth century. This creates a correspondence between the formal elements and the intentional content of his poetry. The complexity of the meter can be understood to parallel the complexity of Ayuthaya culture that Angkarn seeks to invoke. In addition to *khlong*, the poet also uses *kap* extensively. Both *khlong* and *kap* are used for didactic purposes and concur with the didactic tendency in Angkarn's writing.

Khlong is a meter closely associated also with Ayuthaya *nirat*. It is the oldest form of poetry and may have been used for more than six centuries. The oldest work in this meter is *Ongkan Chaeng Nam Khlong Ha* (The Royal Water Oath), from the reign of Ramathibodi I (1350–1369).[81] Due to its tonal and rhyming constraints, *khlong* is believed to be indigenously Thai. Klaus Wenk notes that most literary works from the Ayuthaya period are in *khlong* or *lilit*—the latter of which is a form that is again made up largely of *khlong*. In addition to the meter's usage in *nirat*, *khlong* was also used for didactic literature such as *Phali Son Nong*.[82] Due to its complex rhyming and tonal constraints, *khlong* is considered the most difficult of the indigenous Thai meters.[83]

The other meter that Angkarn uses prolifically, and that can also be brought into close association with Ayuthaya, is *kap*. Trisilpa notes that in the past, *kap* was used as a verse form for narration as well as to compose textbooks in every field. In modern poetry, as Trisilpa writes, it develops from a "soft and smooth rhythm to a concise and powerful prosodic form."[34] She maintains that between 1973 and 1976 *kap yani* was the most popular prosodic form used to compose poems of social consciousness.[85] Angkarn, in contrast, uses the critical-didactic charge of *kap* to lament cultural loss.

Poetic Extremes

Angkarn's poetics signify at once his reverence for a specific artistic and religious tradition as well as a high measure of irreverence for the cultural, intellectual, and bureaucratic establishment of his day. His juxtaposition of divergent registers is frequently aimed against a corrupt bureaucratic elite, responsible in part for the crises that Angkarn's poetry deplores. Furthermore, it is directed against a rigid academic elite. This hostility is evident in the many spiteful passages that mock academic institutions and conventions. What Angkarn advocates instead is an elite culture that is not institutionally based.

Angkarn's strategy in setting Ayuthaya against Bangkok-Sukhothai and in juxtaposing divergent registers serves his larger aim of advocating a desirable cosmopolitanism over and above an undesirable form of globalization. On the level of argument, the poet calls for a return to the culture of Ayuthaya. His deployment of Ayuthaya style in combination with contemporary linguistic elements, however, is somewhat opposed to the intentional content of his writing. It is in this ironic tension between argument and form that the attraction of his poetry lies. On the one hand, Angkarn presents forceful statements about issues of globalization and Thai culture in which, notwithstanding Ayuthaya's multicultural heritage, he calls for a kind of purity; on the other hand, he centrally inhabits an expressly hybridized language. He thus mixes an intentional content that conjures the image of an early modern cosmopolitanism with a poetics reflective of globalization. What results is an experiment in a desirable kind of present-day cosmopolitanism.

Conclusion

Angkarn's poetic journey through national historiography registers as one in which the anxiety of the traditional *nirat* is raised to the level of fear, the object of desire is not recoverable, and temporary cultural dislocation becomes ongoing alienation. With his focus on Ayuthaya, with his allegorical subject that stands for "humanity" rather than "the people," and with the abstract collective—rather than a single lover—that his historically themed *nirat* are addressed to, Angkarn's poems on the past improvise on literary convention to make a bid in the competition over the definition of the Thai cultural present. With the movement away from the parochial toward the cosmopolitan, the poet's vision ultimately transgresses the confines of nation and nationalism. The poet has thus transformed the lamentation of traditional *nirat* into what, with all caveats about its apparent nationalism and xenophobia, we can understand as strident criticism of Thai cultural modernity. In so doing, Angkarn has made high cultural forms, rather than solely those of popular origin, available for effective critiques of the present.

4

Subjectivity

Modern Manifesto:
Poetry as Redemptive-Therapeutic Action in the World

In his 1959 "Pledge of the Poet" ("Panithan Khong Kawi"), Angkarn Kallayanapong famously vows not merely to dedicate himself to the creation of art, but also to sacrifice his life in the course of this artistic-redemptive pursuit:

> I will consent to sacrificing and leaving behind life,
> Hoping for precious things created anew, radiant.
> May the science of poetry be sacred, the highest science.
> Magical like a flower from the crystal forest, falling from the
>   sky, fragrant.

In Thai, Angkarn calls his "Pledge" a *panithan*, a declaration of intent on the part of the poet, or a kind of manifesto. If the twentieth century is the century of the manifesto—that document of political and artistic innovation that seeks to "invite the future" and open up space for new forms, ideologies, and affects—Angkarn is its most prolific exponent in the Thai context.[1] Throughout his books *Kawiniphon* (Poetry, 1964), *Lamnam Phu Kradueng* (Kradueng Mountain Song, 1969), *Bangkok Kaeo Kamsuan* (Lament for Beloved Bangkok, 1978), and *Panithan Kawi* (The Poet's Testament, 1986), at least twenty texts put forth poetic manifestos, or make the nature of poetic dedication their issue.[2]

A manifesto is a quintessentially modernist document. As a piece of writing that seeks to impel change, its mode of address is "hortatory" or imperative.[3] Temporally, it is tied to futurity, 'position[ing] itself between what has been done and what will be done, between the accomplished and the potential, in a radical and energizing division."[4] In the rebellious spirit of a manifesto, Angkarn formulates an extravagant new literary-artistic program and understanding of self for the Thai cultural present in his texts.

A *panithan* constitutes a particular type of poetic-literary manifesto, however. In Angkarn's poetry, the term denotes the concept of the artist's vision of his role and identity.[5] In translations of his work, *panithan* has been rendered as "testament," but further possible translations include "vow, dedication, resolution, or determination." The Royal Institute Dictionary helpfully defines the closely related, Sanskrit-derived *pranithan* as "the establishing of a desire." The *panithan* thus emerges as a kind of manifesto that remains closely connected to author intention as well as bearing residual elements of a religious vow. Rather than point merely to the "handcraftedness" of the manifesto, the term "*panithan*" further denotes the supraworldly—gesturing to dimensions beyond the sphere of the human everyday and to linkages with the divine.[6]

Suchitra Chongstitvatana claims as singular the extraordinary faith in the value of art and aesthetics evident in Angkarn's work and cites the abovementioned 1959 "Pledge of the Poet" as testimony to his dedication. According to her, Angkarn is not the first Thai poet to state his aim in composing poetry explicitly, but his pledge represents a new instantiation of artistic dedication in the field of Thai poetry.[7] In his similarly named 1986 poem, "The Poet's Testament" ("Panithan Kawi"), she finds a further augmentation of the poet's level of dedication—to the degree of founding a "religion of aesthetics."[8]

Like his contemporaries across the globe who produce literary manifestos, Angkarn approaches the vicissitudes of modernity with incisive guidelines for future political and artistic engagement. Unlike his international contemporaries, he is not as concerned with wresting poetry free from its pasts as with revivifying the artistic past, though transforming it in the process. Both in international and national comparison, Angkarn's manifestos diverge from those of his contemporaries in the degree to which they engage Buddhist imaginaries.

I began in chapter 2 to discuss the ways in which Angkarn's work draws on traditions of decentering the self that Buddhist philosophies of impermanence hold available, and at the same time stressed that the poet does not necessarily deploy these in a doctrinal fashion. In this chapter, I argue that the oscillation between doctrinal and nondoctrinal positions regarding the self in Angkarn's oeuvre further illustrates the position of a modern subject that has to negotiate competing forces of individuality and fragmentation.

My analysis builds on discussions in Thai literary criticism of the 1980s and 1990s of indigenous poetics and of Angkarn's work in particular. I dedicate special attention to Suchitra's influential essay, "Kawiniphon Khong Angkarn Kallayanapong: Sasana Haeng Sunthari" (The Poetry of Angkarn Kallayanapong: The Religion of Aesthetics), which I argue pioneered the adaptation of Buddhist thought to literary theory. Both Suchitra and comparative literature scholar Chetana Nagavajara gauge the compatibility with Buddhist doctrine of Angkarn's dedication in his manifestos but come to slightly different conclusions.

Building on the work of these scholars, I investigate how Angkarn's poems concerning humanity in time, the status of the arts, and the self-understanding of the artist are closely interwoven with shifts in notions of subjectivity, as well as with the poet's continually evolving agenda for Thai cultural modernity. In addition to a philosophical analysis, my investigation thus turns the focus to the sociocultural subtexts of the subjectivity that this poetry outlines. What happened in the almost three decades between the "Pledge" and the "Testament" that motivated what Suchitra describes as the intensification of Angkarn's poetic dedication to the point of forsaking personal salvation? What social and political circumstances informed this change? What is the significance of the increasingly heteroglossic character of Angkarn's poetry across these two formulations of intent over almost thirty years? How do the poems' forms relate to their intentional content?

The Pledges

The magnitude of the poet's claims in the "Pledge," his facility with Buddhist cosmology, and the poems' world-traversing imaginary drew considerable attention in Thai literary criticism. "Panithan Khong Kawi" ("The Pledge of the Poet") was first published in 1959 and is included in the poet's 1964 volume *Kawiniphon* (Poetry):

> I take the sky, wrap myself in it against the cold,
> Late at night I eat rays of starlight instead of food.
> Dew glittering under the skies I take for drink,
> Streaming forth poetry from morning until the end of time.

I sacrifice my heart to become an ominous charnel ground,
My spirit goes far away to a dreamland on the side of heaven.
It seeks divine substance in heaven to bring to earth,
Soothes the sand planes, the blades of grass, so that the
    world may know contentment.

Creating poetry to redeem the soul,
In the waves of the stream of time, swift and bold.
In a short time this life won't be.
The heart spews forth rays of divine substance, defiant, until
    heaven and earth crumble.

Let the funeral pyre smolder, burning my body,
Kap poetry is not fragrant with the strength of the heart
    anymore.[9]
Taking birth in whichever world, that world
The spirit will inundate with precious, lustrous divinity,
    letting the essence of the gems of the age rain down.

Words move serenely, give pleasure,
Precious rain from heaven that puts out the heat.
The heart blows far away to dream in other worlds,
This fragrant world reflects the fragrance of the next.

I will consent to sacrificing and leaving behind life,
Hoping for precious things created anew, radiant.
May the science of poetry be sacred, the highest science,
Magical like a flower from the crystal forest, falling from the
    sky, fragrant.

The text "Panithan Kawi" ("The Poet's Testament," *Panithan Kawi*, 1986) contains the proclamation of dedication of the poet twenty-seven years later. In his reformulated manifesto, Angkarn further increases his dedication to the creation of art:

Who would ever dare trade in skies and oceans,
This pure world created by the gods.
At last taking leave of my bodily parts, laying them down
Where the earth and the sky connect.

Subjectivity

We are not the owners of the sky and space,
The elements of the earth, of all the heavens in their entirety.
Humanity never created the sun and the moon,
Not even one grain of sand.

Struggling to take land, brutal, thinking only of killing,
Because of the crazy, cruel thirst dwelling in these skeletons of ghosts.
Forgetting the burial ground, ethics, goodness,
Giving up beneficence, the real value of the soul.

The state of all things in all the parts of this world,
One should realize their divine miraculous value.
Preserving the earth, water, and sky throughout time,
That they may remain in their high divine station, the crystal mansion of nirvana.

Fields, wild forests, woods,
Great rocks thrusting into the heaven of Indra.
Wild animals, tigers, elephants, monkeys,
Ants and insects of different species in the entire universe.

They are like close friends, comrades
Born in the same swift stream of the Wheel of Transmigration,
The worth of their lives inestimable,
Sweet charm of the sky, earth, and stars.

Even if others were free, and flew to the highest point of the horizon,
Taking the moon and stars as a great path,
I ask to love this world forever,
Dedicating my heart to the earth in all my lives and deaths.

I will even not go to nirvana.
I will whirl and swim in the manifold cycles of transmigration,
Translating the meaning of the real value of the many galaxies
Into stanzas of poetry for the universe.

To erase suffering and sorrow in the human world
As much as I can, moving toward an age of bliss and
  contentment.
At that moment I will be blended, pulverized to become
  earth.
I will be a fossil, torturedly existing and observing.

The end of the charm of literary art that life can offer,
Fumbling for divine value as replacement,
Pitiful life, every dusty particle of it,
Great sadness, horrifying even the ashes.

World arid of poetry, earth and sky moving,
I will compose brilliant gems of dignity,
Taking leave of sweet humanity,
Intending to create a universe of the mind.

To be captivated by *kap, klon, khlong,* and *chan*,[10]
To permeate every stratum of the celestial mansions of Indra
  and Brahma,
Creating merit through art for all eternity,
Immeasurably long, immortal, timeless.

In the latter half of the 1986 "Testament," the conceptual shift that has received so much attention in discussions of the poet's work becomes clear: Angkarn has increased his poetic dedication from pledging his life to sacrificing the attainment of nirvana in order to continue to create art for the redemption of the world.

The Religion of Aesthetics: Suchitra Chongstitvatana

The work of Suchitra Chongstitvatana helps us understand the ways in which Angkarn's view of subjectivity and the arts undergoes a surprising change in the 1986 poem "Panithan Kawi." Whereas time is portrayed as absolute, especially in its power as destroyer in prior texts, Angkarn now finds a way out of the intolerable state of being subjected to time. In order to make art eternal, he reverses the ontological status of time and the arts. He now sets the arts as absolute, elevating them to a status above time. As the artist, he forsakes nirvana, his own personal salvation, in order to create redemptive art for the world and thereby to work toward universal salvation. To this end he makes use of the Mahayana Buddhist concept of the Bodhisattva in a unique way.

Suchitra's essay merits detailed review, not only because it represents a pathbreaking study of Angkarn's poetry and its relation to Buddhist doctrine, but also because it sheds light on the temporality of subjectivity in Angkarn's poetry. She argues that the measure of the poet's dedication becomes evident already in his choice of lexicon and definition of poetry as *thip thi sawan*—"divine substance in heaven." She further finds evidence of the extraordinary nature of Angkarn's dedication in his definition of the aim of poetry as redemption of the soul and in the fact that his level of dedication extends to the point of pledging his life. In setting these standards, "it is as though he establishes the status of poetry as a religion and the highest ideal in the poet's own life."[11]

For Suchitra, Angkarn's "Panithan Kawi" ("The Poet's Testament," 1986), which is published in a volume of the same name twenty-seven years after the 1959 "Pledge," represents the augmentation of this attitude. She cites this poem as further proof of her claim that Angkarn establishes poetry as the highest aesthetic, intellectual, and moral value. The augmentation of artistic dedication consists in Angkarn's preparedness in the later poem to forsake even nirvana—his own personal salvation—and in his willingness to go on existing in the form of a "tortured fossil" in order to create redemptive aesthetics (*sunthari*) for the world.

According to Suchitra, in this poem, the speaker's willingness to forsake nirvana—the highest aim of Buddhist spiritual advancement—as well as his belief that creating poetry is *kusonsin* (meritorious art) testify to the close relationship between creating literary art and performing *dhammic* acts (*bamphen thamma*). In Angkarn's *panithan*, poetry and the activity of composing it are accorded a higher status than in any other poet's profession of dedication.[12] Already in 1967, the poem "Lak Chai" (*Kawiniphon*) designates the production of art as "Giving alms to the era all over this stratum of heaven."[13]

In *Lamnam Phu Kradueng*, Suchitra finds further evidence of the notion that in Angkarn's philosophy, human redemption has to proceed through the appreciation and production of aesthetic materials: "Most importantly, the helping to indicate and the pointing out of the way to salvation to humanity has to pass the 'philosophy of beauty' of the poet."[14] The ability to see and understand the beauty of nature is the first step to getting to "heaven."

Beauty, furthermore, shows us the relationship of *dhamma* and nature (*thamma* and *thammachat*): for Angkarn nature represents a force that itself performs *dhammic* acts (*bamphen thamma*). Humanity should therefore learn *dhamma* from nature—that is, learn compassion, contentedness with what one has, love of giving (*dāna*), and forgiveness. In the poet's view, this will lead toward personal development as well as the ability to coexist peacefully with fellow human beings. Nature thus figures as a moral force and as a poetic force in Angkarn's texts.

As far as the status of the poet is concerned, Suchitra claims, Angkarn links *jintanakan*, (artistic) imagination, to *sajjatham*, truth, which in turn leads to *waeo thip*, the "divine shine, or glow," of life. This divine glow aids the poet in his redemptive work.

The poet performs *dhammic* acts by creating literary art. In this context, Suchitra asserts that Angkarn envisages the poet as occupying a role akin to that of a Bodhisattva. The poet's work as Bodhisattva is in turn linked to the love and deep understanding of nature. Nature is accorded a status that Suchitra describes as exempt from the illusory nature (*māyā*) of the world. Rather, nature represents the embodiment of *dhamma* and *khunatham* (goodness): "Therefore the 'beauty' of nature in the view of the poet is not part of the 'illusion' of the world which according to Buddhist precepts changes continually, but it is a manifestation of the '*dhamma*' and of 'goodness' which are instrumental in indicating the way for humanity."[15]

Suchitra further claims that Angkarn's conception of beauty is extraordinary in including not only the beauty of nature and art but also that of "low" things—a highly egalitarian aesthetics. Nature is explicitly accorded creative agency in this context: "Nature has the ability to compose songs of poetry in the beauty of all natural phenomena."[16]

Angkarn's careful, detailed construction of his "religion of aesthetics" also becomes evident in his poetic lexicon. In this context, the word *thip* ("divine") becomes the most important concept: "Angkarn has come to use this word in high concentration in his work; it has become a term particular to Angkarn."[17] *Thip* is inextricably linked to *sunthari*, and its manifold meanings—which Suchitra divides into three groups (one in which *thip* occurs in conjunction with terms that have to do with poetry; another in which it is linked to mood, feeling, and sensory perception; and a third in which it relates to philosophy and religion)—help to elucidate the religion of aesthetics.[18]

In these works, the narrator-poet as an individual has discarded all greed, except for the desire to create. He appears as humble, on the one hand, and as filled with unprecedented professional pride, on the other. Despite his emphasis on the poet's integration into the cosmos and the at times otherworldly quality of his work, Angkarn asserts that "the path leading to heaven is in this (very) world."[19] The poet's attachment to the world also stands in strong contrast to his poetry of censure manifest elsewhere.

Comparing two versions of the poem "Kha Mi Khru Yu Thua Fa" ("I Have Teachers All over the Heavens") in two different editions of *Lamnam Phu Kradueng*, Suchitra concludes that Angkarn's later work shows the development toward a poetry that has become more substantially Buddhist in content.[20]

Proceeding to explain how Angkarn constructs the religion of aesthetics, Suchitra notes that all literary activities including reading are elevated to become religious acts. She finds a parallel to the idea of reading as leading to redemption in the *Traiphum Phra Ruang* and in the *Thet Mahachat* tradition. In the comparison with these early literary works, she defines Angkarn's conceptualization as an extension of the convention.[21] According to Suchitra, the development of literary convention is evident in form as well as content in Angkarn's writing. She notes the symbolism, the didactic method, the *chom nang chom mueang* passages, and the pledge of the poet as responsible for this development.[22] She concludes that Angkarn has added dimension to, played with, and developed convention in all these respects and rejected it in others.

Chetana Nagavajara also attempts to gauge the compatibility with Buddhist doctrine of Angkarn's perspective on the arts: "He does not hesitate to secure for [Buddhism] an ally, namely the arts, or more precisely poetry, which at first enjoys a status almost equal to religion, but which, in his later works, gradually usurps the preeminence of the latter."[23] Assessing the degree of dedication manifest in "Panithan Kawi," Chetana further writes, "The poem is not an outright rejection of Buddhist values; rather it seeks to outdo them."[24] From this, he concludes that

> Angkarn does not content himself with just leaving his work to posterity: his physical death will not mean the cessation of vigilance over his own creation. The process of physical disintegration is but a transformation into "dust" and "fossils" that continue to keep watch on the poet's work. This way of thinking is contrary to Buddhist doctrine and would be considered as impurity (*Kilesa*). Such an attachment can never lead to Nirvana.[25]

Suchitra's and Chetana's assessments are significant in that they inaugurate modes of thinking about Buddhist elements in literature that exceed the question of their conformity to doctrinal maxims. Even though Chetana's essay ends with an evaluation of Angkarn's *panithan* as counterdoctrinal, I also want to draw attention to his initial assessment of the relations of Buddhism and artistic credo in the poet's work. When Chetana writes about Angkarn's early work and first *panithan*, "He does not hesitate to secure for [Buddhism] an ally, namely the arts," Chetana is positioning Buddhism and the arts alongside each other, rather than in opposition. He thus begins to model a way of accommodating Buddhist values with the at times counterdoctrinal ideals put forth in modern literature. This is evident also in Chetana's subsequent assessment: "The poem is not an outright rejection of Buddhist values; rather it seeks to outdo them."

Suchitra's analysis does not dwell on gauging the counterdoctrinality of Angkarn's work, but rather investigates Buddhism as a resource that furnishes frameworks for purposes other than those of religious instruction. This does not mean that she designates the Buddhist elements in his work as having a strictly nonreligious purpose. Rather, her work is able to accommodate doctrinal and nondoctrinal versions of Buddhist thought within one conceptual framework. Already in her 1984 thesis, she writes about Angkarn: "Poetry is his vocation and through his poetical achievements he wishes to free himself from time and mortality." In a subsequent passage, Suchitra integrates the poet's desire for the immortality of the imagination into a Mahayana Buddhist framework: "For him, imagination is timeless and through imagination the 'immortality' in any artistic works is possible. Therefore, the spiritual value of poetry is almost comparable to being a Bodhisattva who helps others to attain enlightenment."[26]

While the creation of art may have been conducive to spiritual advancement in the Thai cultural past, it never reached the status of highest spiritual activity or the ontological status that Angkarn's poetry accords it. In this poetry, artistic products are confidently positioned as substantial, able to outlast the ages, and not subject to impermanence (*anijjang*, Thai; *anicca*, Pali).

Thus, in the 1959 "Pledge of the Poet," the poet's own existence remains subject to transience as he contends with the flow of time the destroyer. The poet's work, on the other hand, is not subject to destruction through time, but will retain eternal meaning:

> Creating poetry to redeem the soul,
> In the waves of the stream of time, swift and bold.

In a short time this life won't be.
The heart spews forth rays of divine substance, defiant, until heaven and earth crumble.

Throughout Angkarn's work, literature achieves the status of an enduring artifact that withstands transience. It represents a stable ontological entity that remains exempt from change. Chetana Nagavajara describes the extent to which Angkarn's work elevates the position of the arts and the role of the poet as follows:

> The poet is ubiquitous and omnipresent. He does not want to wield his influence on earth and on humankind alone; his "universe of the mind" will embrace also heavenly abodes which shall be "imbued with the magic of poetry." Poetry is then omniscient, omnipresent and omnipotent, a very big claim.[27]

This ontological status is not explicitly construed as something that contradicts Buddhist conceptualizations but, according to Chetana, simply transcends them. Regarding the relation between art and temporality in Angkarn's work, I argue that we can understand art as taking the place of the *dhamma* itself, which is *akāliko* (does not possess temporal characteristics) and is not subject to the law of *aniccatā*.[28] In this understanding, *dhamma*, as the universal truth proclaimed by the Buddha, endures forever and is understood even to have preceded the Buddha.

This explication does not solve the problem of the subject's status in time. As the poet creates a comprehensive philosophical framework in which art moves to the center of an ethical-ontological system, this also becomes a panacea for the predicaments of the modern subject.

I understand Chusak Pattarakulvanit and Nopporn Prachakul's short 1996 article, "Thruesadi Wannakam Naeo Deconstruction" (Deconstructionist Literary Theory), to facilitate such a perspective. Chusak and Nopporn's work stands in some contrast to the viewpoints of other Thai literary scholars. These authors suggest that we pay attention to the ways in which a deconstructionist lens of analysis allows us to show how a given piece of literature undermines the seemingly definite meaning that it puts forth on a surface level.

Thus, Chusak and Nopporn contend that Angkarn's poem, "Panithan Kawi," which seems merely to extol the virtues of poetry, in fact simultaneously subverts this proposition. What is more, they argue that in doing so, the poem—which other scholars have understood to formulate a Mahayana Buddhist artistic idealism—draws on a logic of capitalist production. While "Panithan Kawi" seems to set the material and spiritual in opposition, and to elevate the spiritual to a position high above the material, it ultimately foundationally undermines this binary. The poem becomes "merely the offspring or product of the poet" and works toward the poet's eternalization, undoing oppositions of the material and immaterial and complicating notions of Buddhist selfhood.[29]

In what follows, I will track how Angkarn develops his notion of artistic subjectivity and compare his understanding of writerly craft to that of his contemporaries. My argument thereby spins out further the claim about aesthetics-as-religion first made by Suchitra with regard to Angkarn's work and undertakes an analysis of Buddhism and self that builds on Chusak and Nopporn's call for a deconstructive reading of meaning.

(Artistic) Subjectivity

Angkarn's thinking about the arts is evident not only in his *panithan*—it remains central throughout his entire oeuvre. Thus, his poetry consistently stresses the inextricable link between the vocation of the poet, the status of the arts, and a desirable human existence. As early as in "Laeng Wanakhadi" ("Devoid of Literature," 1964), the poet writes:

> Devoid of literature this life is
> As though the auspicious spirit is no longer to be found.
> Without the precious jeweled rainbow—
> Light of the soul in the world.

In the first stanza of the poem, Angkarn establishes literature as indispensable for the world and for human life. In the eighth stanza, he deplores the absence of people who direct their efforts toward creating art and strive for knowledge:

> Devoid of good people, Sri Ayuthaya,
> Born to redeem bold and sacred knowledge,
> Sacrificing, combating fate single-handedly,
> That is more than can be hoped for, a shame.

Almost a decade and a half later, the poet stresses the link that exists between the creation of poetry and the well-being of the world; this idea finds a particularly clear formulation in the 1978 poem "Pakka Thip" ("The Divine Pen," *Bangkok Kaeo Kamsuan*):

> The divine pen draws the heavens and the universe,
> In the essence of literary art, precious thing,
> Raising humanity to its real value, eternally,
> Great, immense future benefit, letting the world reach a supreme age.
>
> Whenever the heart is bright and joyful,
> Presenting *khlong* poetry as tribute, offering it to the world,
> Suffering is alleviated, the gloomy spirit suddenly cheerful,
> Loving, sharing in the pleasure of the heavens, prosperous with the charm of art.
>
> Foolish longing envelops the soul,
> Now cold, then tortured,
> In a life, where is the supreme essence hidden?
> Real warmth would derive from true understanding of the world.
>
> The soul of the world trembles with divine *kap* poetry,
> Prospering in this age, going far ahead to the next world.
> The stars and the moon in the ten directions will be cheered,
> Praising the essence of the powerful Bodhisattva, singing to sleep all of earth and the heavens.
>
> The last dream of calm commands the sky in changing times,
> To delight humanity, all beings,
> Erase the age of evil cruelty,
> Savagely descending into the expanse of hell.
>
> Sacrifice heaven to the world, making a wish,
> Sweet divinity of endless time all over the sky,
> Come to the world for longer, creating the humanity
> Of a new age, supreme and bright, there as a challenge until the *kappa* crumbles.[30]

> That the evil that befalls all beings disappears from the world,
> All true suffering, all sorrows under the sky.
> Mostly humanity gives disease to the world, maliciously—
> Hurry, round up brave strength, kill, wipe out distress.
>
> The stars hang from the luminous sky,
> Surpassing the novel idealism of the age.
> So far, what divine value have you to renounce to the world?
> Put out grief, do away with disease, raise the world higher
>   than heaven.
>
> The *khlong* of Angkarn, precious poet of Siam,
> Are for the distant future,
> The *kap* and *klon* roam divine eternity,[31]
> Introduced into the world so that it may be without grief,
>   hurrying to delight in literary art.

From its first stanza, "Pakka Thip" highlights literature's cosmogenic properties: "the divine pen draws the heavens and the universe." Literature's redemptive potential does not only concern humanity, it extends to the universe. Thus, stanza 5 presents literature as having the ability to "erase the age of evil and cruelty." In stanza 6, literature transports heaven and eternity to earth to create an unprecedented age, and, finally, in stanza 8, the earth is elevated to a higher status than heaven. It is declarations like stanza 9's, however, that stand out most in their vision of the poet's role, and critics have noted the *ahangkan*, or heightened sense of authority and subjective agency, that appears in Angkarn's poetry.[32]

While the status of the arts has been described as incomparably high, transcending the principle of impermanence, the concept of the (art-producing) individual that Angkarn develops analogously accords an extraordinarily high status to subjectivity. In parallel to the contention that art contravenes the principle of *sarvam anityam* (all is impermanent)—seemingly a strong deviation from Buddhist ideas—Angkarn's work thus asserts a strong concept of (the artist's) subjectivity. The question of this subjectivity's concordance with or deviation from Buddhist notions is still more complex than in the case of the arts.

Whereas Theravada Buddhist doctrine puts forth the deathless state of nirvana as an aspirational end of individual human existence, Angkarn allows for no end of the task or existence of the art-creating individual. In his role as Bodhisattva-cum-artist, both Angkarn and a more abstractly envisioned ideal producer of art are charged with the perennial creation of meritorious art. Nowhere is it stated that the duty of this redemptive creator of art will ever be completed. This person's subjectivity thus comes close to permanence. Interpreted in this way, Angkarn's concept of subjectivity is not consistent with the doctrine of *anātmavāda*, the notion that no persistent self exists. Rather, Angkarn's understanding approaches a conception of subjective being as permanent, a notion which Buddhism seeks to invalidate in the intellectual sense and overcome on an experiential plane.

On the one hand, the confident professional pride and strong emphasis on subjectivity evident in Angkarn's conceptualization of the artist's role thus stand in opposition to Buddhist notions. On the other hand, the fact that these activities are to be undertaken for the purpose of creating redemptive art for the world weakens the case stated above. While Angkarn's stance on subjectivity bears a unique stamp, we might argue that it does not necessarily contradict Buddhist notions of subjectivity. Notions of subjectivity moreover remain singularly mobile throughout his work and oscillate between extreme humility and grandeur.

Although Angkarn's poetry proposes a strong concept of subjectivity, it nevertheless does not consistently construe this subjectivity as permanent. In addition to the fact that this subjectivity always stands in the context of the performing of a meritorious act, passages that explicitly label the idea of a self as illusionary and implicitly designate the transcension of the delusion of the self as the ultimate spiritual goal abound in the oeuvre. Thus in "Dew Drops" the poet writes: "That is the stupid, foolish cow, dragging the exceedingly heavy yoke and cart of life with the illusion of the five *khanda*, going on aimlessly."[33] In this piece, Angkarn reminds us that the (illusory) notion of subjectivity is constituted by the strong temporary collocation of the constituent factors of subjective being, the *khanda*. A perspective on the ultimate nonsubstantiality of the self is also strongly manifest in two poems in *Panithan Kawi*, named "Buddhist Spirit" ("Phutharom") and "Awake, Humanity!" ("Tuen Thoet Lok Manut"), in the latter of which the poet writes that "the *anattā* executes the *attā*." Angkarn's oeuvre as a whole can thus be understood to keep opposing notions of subjectivity in tension.

Rather than evaluating it as contravening doctrine per se, we can understand the poet's philosophy to devise a way of folding the nibbanic into the world. Angkarn's concept of forsaking personal salvation, nirvana, in favor of the production of collectively applicable merit, circumvents the difficulty of reconciling the timeless (nirvana) with the temporal—a problem that consistently presents logical difficulties to Buddhist thought.[34] Angkarn thereby proposes a Buddhist ontology and trajectory of subjective being in which the worldly and nibbanic become contemporaneous and are able to coexist.

Fragmented Self, Heteroglossic Text

In addition to investigating Angkarn's poetry from the perspective of its logics of argumentation and authorial intent, it is instructive to relate his formulations of artistic dedication to the Thai political and cultural history of the late 1950s through the 1980s and to considerations of form. I pay attention especially to the heteroglossic nature of his writing—the combination of divergent registers of speech and diverse vocabularies that marks his poetry. The development between Angkarn's two *panithan* spans the decades from the late 1950s–1960s "despotic paternalist" regime of Sarit to the country's mid-1980s manufacturing boom and simultaneous turn toward local intellectual traditions.[35] With regard to Thailand's Southeast Asian neighbors, the late 1980s reflected the turn from Cold War dogma toward market-oriented policies ("battlefields into marketplaces").[36] These decades saw the evolution of the notion of development from a focus on technological upgrading and training to the desire to compete in an expanding world economy and dominate regional markets.

The 1970s were marked by two popular uprisings against military rule in 1973 and 1976. As the previous chapter began to outline, this decade generated a large body of poetic works dedicated to integrating popular forms into deliberations on the human losses of the 1970s, inequality, and enduring democratic aspirations. Much of the poetry written throughout the 1980s remained vitally concerned with the popular uprisings in the 1970s. Thus, the 1989 S.E.A. Write Award honored Chiranan Pitpreecha's *Bai Mai Thi Hai Pai* (The Missing Leaves), a volume of poetry that reflected on the experiences of members of the Communist Party of Thailand who had to flee to remote border areas ("the jungle") after 1976. The most prominent exponent of 1970s political poetry, however, is Naowarat Pongpaiboon (1940–), who received the S.E.A. Write Award for his collection *Phiang Khwam Khluean Wai* (Mere Movement, 1974) in 1980.

Contemporary Poets' Poetics (Panithan)

A look at Naowarat's explicitly formulated statement of artistic intent, or *panithan*, as contained in his poem "Kawi" ("Poet/ry," *Phleng Khlui Phiu*, 1980), and Khomthuan Khanthanu's 1983 poem, "The Writer: A Creator of Art" ("Nak Khien Nak Sang Sinlapa," *Natakam Bon Lan Kwang*), is instructive for understanding the departure that Angkarn's poetry makes from that of his contemporaries. The comparison clarifies not only the difference in intent of the poets, but also elucidates the concepts of self that emerge in poetry in the course of the turbulent decades of the 1970s and 1980s.

While the 1969 collection *Kham Yad* (Word Drops) had focused on making Buddhist thought available to contemporary poetry, the 1974 volume *Phiang Khwam Khluean Wai* (Mere Movement) instantiated Naowarat's poetics of left politics.[37] Christian Bauer stresses the degree to which Naowarat is able to align poetic perfection (a poetry that is "formvollendet") with political content. He characterizes Naowarat's famous poem "Mere Movement" ("Phiang Khwam Khluean Wai") as follows:

> The title poem of *Phiang Khwam Khluean Wai*, that opens the collection reads—superficially, until its last contrapuntal stanza—like the sketch of a provincial idyll: the fluttering of a bird in the sluggish noon heat, the quivering of a leaf in a slight breeze, the rattling of a chain at the gate are all harbingers of a greater movement that, like a tsunami, will sweep up everything.[38]

Bauer is describing Naowarat's ability to let nine stanzas of perfect (*formvollendete*) nature poetry build up to a finale of political resolve. Thus stanzas 9 and 10, the final two stanzas of "Mere Movement," read as follows:

> A promise astir, of nothing evil,
> but of grace, and beauty, taking shape.
> There amid the stillness murky,
> the beginning is begun.
>
> Listen to the temple drums.
> Observe another Holy Day.
> Hear the booming of the guns
> mark the people's battle-cry.[39]

Six years later, Naowarat's poem "Kawi" prescribes that no distinction between *chiwit*, life, and *kawi*, poetry, be made. This close relationship is to enable poetry to depict life authentically, with beauty and power. Read in the context of an oeuvre that became famous for its engagement with leftist political protest in the 1970s, "Kawi's" resolution may be understood as a poetics that strives for truth in relation to social and political realities also. The 1980 poem details the task of the poet as follows:

"Kawi – Poet/ry"[40]

Is the minute of the flower before blossoming,
Dreams that are beginning,
The expertise of the artisan, the creator of words,
The second language of feeling,
The depth of mood in its fragrance,
The heart and soul of truth,
Recollection, remembrance far back.

You are a/the poet.
You have to have beauty and coordination,
Harmony and delight,
A soul that can fathom aesthetic perception.
You have to write life from life,
Create words with rhyme,
Bringing about the meeting of a heart with a heart,
Not limiting the poet/ry only to words.

Six years before Angkarn's 1986 "Testament," Naowarat's *panithan* stresses the bond between human life and aesthetics, but does not extend this credo to the dimension of the universe. Rather, poetry issues from the heart of the poet. Directed toward truth and possessed of a philosophical dimension, Naowarat's poetry's foremost purpose is to "write life from life" and to bring about the meeting of hearts. Suchitra Chongstitvatana first interpreted Naowarat's credo as one in which the intensity of emotion becomes the driving force of poetry.[41] Rather than invoke grandiose cosmic dimensions, Naowarat's pledge prescribes poetic standards in close relation to the (human) qualities of the poet, exhorting him to find sources for poetry in "life" and within human affect. As Suchitra writes,

"This emphasis on human values and efforts corresponds with the poet's 'theory of literature' that the source of literature is human life."[42]

We can understand Naowarat's idealistic pledge to present a more unitary notion of subjectivity than Angkarn's. Even after the turbulent 1970s, Naowarat's work continues to espouse relatively symmetrical correspondences between poetic language, human life, and humanistic idealisms.

In contrast to Naowarat's, Angkarn's testaments are celebrations of the divinity and *anuphap*, or the power and authority, of poetry that elevate it to a level far above the merely affective and human.[43] Angkarn's testaments invoke a poet whose cosmic role is already evocatively captured by the opening lines of the original (1959) "Pledge":

> I take the sky, wrap myself in it against the cold,
> Late at night I eat rays of starlight instead of food.

Artistic production is not only a matter of capturing affect and life in this world; in Angkarn's conception, poetry attains a different dimensionality, crosses borders between lives, and extends across worlds. The "Pledge" also makes reference to a heart, but describes this heart's—as well as poetry's—agency within temporality as follows:

> The heart blows far away to dream in other worlds,
> This fragrant world reflects the fragrance of the next.

The heart here is an ethical-cosmological actor and producer of redemptive art. Poetry is thus always closely aligned with futurity, albeit a supraworldly futurity. In this capacity it is depicted as able to alleviate the sorrows of human beings:

> Words move serenely, give pleasure,
> Precious rain from heaven that puts out the heat.

Expanding the agency of the poet and of poetry, as it does, this perspective lets literary language attain an importance that reaches a cosmic level. It is the "highest science" and bears universal redemptive potential.

The comparison between Naowarat's and Angkarn's *panithan* brings to light the difference in the domain of action in which each poet situates poetry and the creator of art. It clarifies the degree of unity or fragmentation that each poet accords to the notion of a self. Naowarat's "Poet/ry" presents a more coherent unity of self, craft, and intention. Reading the idealistic delineations of "Poet/ry," we get the sense that, given a certain consciousness of its producer, poetic work can be directly effective. In this sense, "Poet/ry" presents the belief in a wholesome notion of self, work, and agency.

A further poem that instantiates the spirit of Art for Life idealism is Khomthuan Khanthanu's (1950–) twenty-five-stanza reflection on the duty of the poet titled "The Writer: A Creator of Art" from 1983.[44] In the concluding stanzas of the poem, Khomthuan sums up the tasks of the poet and of literature as follows:

> The correct task of the writer
> Is to participate, to demand, to respond,
> To humble himself, to dedicate himself as a work ox,
> With a soul committed to resisting the enemy.
>
> Eliminate your frenetic ego,
> Create every thing through the force of collaboration,
> In a literary collective of worthiness,
> There should be no literature of "me" and "you."
>
> Even a hundred thousand rifles raised at you,
> Must lose against the united ends of the pen,
> Even a hundred thousand chains that come to bind,
> Cannot enchain our hearts.
>
> The writer should have freedom,
> Not bend to slavery, indiscriminately,
> Sacrificing a free perspective at the soles of their feet—
> That is the age of dinosaurs, the age of turtles.
>
> When you love being an artist who creates art,
> You have to recognize the victory ahead,
> Truth has to be joined to your pen,
> To be worthy of the value of a People's poet.[45]

Khomthuan's poem is noteworthy for the degree to which it, too, engages Buddhist concepts for the purpose of creating an artistic imaginary. In contrast to Angkarn's, Khomthuan's is an explicitly left imaginary, however. In "The Writer," the poet uses Buddhist conceptualizations to argue for a particular kind of poetology, binding that tradition's espousal of the notion of nonself to a collectively oriented notion of literary production. He further combines the vocabulary of Buddhist philosophy (Pali; Thai, *attā*, "the self") with the lexicon of a left poetics (e.g., *muan chon*, "the People").

Like Naowarat's, Khomthuan's poetry evinces a unity of craft, self, and the collective that differs from that of Angkarn. Across Angkarn's overall oeuvre, both the writerly self and the abstracted collective self of humanity emerge as more conflicted. One may understand this ongoing crisis at the heart of the self to represent the factor that propels this poet's imaginary into the domain of the cosmic.

While the subject of Angkarn's poems reaches levels of unimaginable grandeur and attains a subjectivity of divine, cosmic status, the notion of personhood appears more precarious in other poems. We can thus understand the oscillation between grandeur and diminution that this subject constantly performs also as the working through of the predicaments of modern subjectivity.

Conflictual Senses of Self

Angkarn's poetry is riven with conflicting notions of selfhood. As we saw, on the one hand, these divergent notions of selfhood occupy a function in the logic of the poet's philosophy. On the other hand, the presence of these disparate senses of self throughout the oeuvre points beyond authorial intention, reflecting the discrepancy between the extensive demands for self-sufficiency made of a modern, individualized subject and the simultaneously fragmenting conditions under which this same subject exists. While the notion of an independent individual increasingly takes hold, that same individual is simultaneously exposed to decentering conditions in which individuality means isolation rather than independence, and where precarious economic forms make individual survival precisely impossible. With the advent of neoliberal ideologies in the 1980s, these contradictory demands made of persons escalate further, as we see strong shifts in political ideology from the notion of an obedient citizen to that of a self-propelled entrepreneurial entity. Angkarn's work at this time frequently takes on an alarmist cast, warning of cultural crisis and the devolution of the self. I would argue that the intensifying turn in his work to Buddhism in the

1980s may result from the desire to draw increasingly on that tradition's comprehensive, finely calibrated thought about subjectivity.

In a different historical context, Cynthia Marshall writes: "An emergent sense of the autonomous self, individually operative as never before in the spheres of politics, religion, and commerce, existed in tension with an established popular sense of the self as fluid, unstable and volatile."[46] I do not mean to imply that the sense of an autonomous self is only emergent in 1960s Thailand. Surely such a notion had by that time long been established. Rather, I cite Marshall's work here for its helpful description of a transitional period in which agonistic versions of the self coexist.

"Ku Duang Jai" ("Redeeming the Heart," 1967) represents a relatively early disquisition on the vocation of self and aesthetic life in the poet's work. Already in this work, images of sleeping and awaking establish a dichotomy between the deplorable condition that the poet perceives humanity to inhabit and that which he posits as desirable. But the poem also presents a critique of materialism—as well as of authoritarian governance—thereby integrating its reflection on human vocation into an everyday life defined by sociopolitical challenges:

> Time will come like worms,
> Eviscerating the auspicious spirit, trembling.
> Busy being infatuated, excessively given to enjoyment,
> Unbridled, evil desire will come to kill.
>
> Drunk with riches, self-important with power,
> A real slave of downfall, without aim.
> The shine of life will break and dissolve,
> Shameful, even the effort of breathing wasted.
>
> Awake, rise, and strive for beauty,
> In this world it does exist and brightly so.
> But those things are hidden far away,
> In the expanse of the divinity of awakened knowledge.
>
> Practice truth and beauty,
> Reform your life to bear substance,
> Offer love to the universe,
> For everlasting peace and bliss.

> Redeem the heart to rise as high as the stars,
> Like the shine of great dignity,
> Strive to think, to train the heart,
> In the pure philosophy of release.

Against the background of a 1960s national discourse that was singularly focused on development within the paradigm of a militarized familial nationalism, the poet delineates a countervision of the future-present. The first two stanzas of "Redeeming" address the deplorable condition of humankind, entangled in worldly pursuits. The three stanzas that follow enjoin humanity to follow its real vocation—of striving for spiritual perfection, creating art, and recognizing the value of nature. Rather than only as moral-soteriological exhortation, we can understand "Redeeming" also as an early description of the acceleration of life in the developmentalist era and a reflection of the psychic state of a twentieth-century subject struggling with socioeconomic change, or what Weeks and Maurel describe concisely as "the increasing dominance of economic discourse, economic imperatives and the sense of perpetual crisis, [and] unrelieved urgency this voracious ideological force engenders."[47]

The trope of awakening in "Redeeming" bears the connotation of realization and is part of a soteriological trajectory in Buddhist thought; however, the poet uses this trope also to prompt in his readers awareness of lives mired in consumerism and the quest for status.

The third stanza of the nearly contemporaneous "Laeng Wanakhadi" ("Devoid of Literature," 1964, *Kawiniphon*) further enforces the content of this urgent admonition:

> Offer your still heart to peaceful bliss,
> Write *kap, klon, khlong,* and *chan* poetry to put out the heat.
> Tenaciously pursuing heaven, to offer to the world.
> Fragrant with sorrow, bliss, and suffering, reflecting the real,
>   sacred value of humanity.

For Angkarn, an ethical existence is always an aesthetic endeavor. In these poems, his concept of the poet's *panithan* is frequently embedded in appeals to humanity in general to create art as a way of following its vocation. In the 1960s, this notion of vocation emerges also as a panacea to the pressures under which a modern Thai subject labors. The stanza from "Devoid of Literature" thus calls attention also to the therapeutic value of the production of art—its capacity to "put out the heat."

"Kroen" ("Foreword," 1978) in *Bangkok Kaeo Kamsuan* is a *panithan* in the sense of an explicitly delineated professional ethic. It contains, in the first person, a definition of the duty of the poet and a declaration of faith in his redemptive work. However, we can understand this person also to exemplify the struggles of a modern subject. This subject emerges as a dissatisfied one who constantly pushes beyond the parameters of the present and expands his field of action into the cosmos:

> The dear bright moon shines sadly at nighttime,
> Silver rays pure and bright in the vastness of the heavens,
> The stars glitter, more brilliant than diamonds,
> Tying together the duties of day and night.
>
> The strong sun, lighting up the world with its clear rays,
> Wind fans the fragrant, sweet trees,
> The clouds weave a beautiful rainbow in the sky,
> Dividing the work of those two that rule the *kalpas*.
>
> But the poet is on duty day and night;
> He has to rise and compose *kap* and precious *salok*,[48]
> Or compose for this world of humans,
> Without a day left out, without ceasing.
>
> Minute, thinking that life is so short,
> A pity, the days and nights that have passed and disappeared,
> Tomorrow life might have vanished,
> Dissolving without ashes or particles of dust.
>
> Whatever one does, one does not get time back,
> Come, sweet and dignified precious *kap*,
> I aim to compose all day and night,
> With melancholy and longing.
>
> I will enumerate the excellent elements throughout the universe,
> To sweeten and freshen life in this wondrous age,
> To reform the soul throughout the three worlds,
> To carve out the value of life, dedicate it as *dāna*.

The continent of Himawa, the tributaries of the stream of
  Sindhu,
To the end of each of the most splendid oceans,
I will travel, meeting with events,
Creating eternal work, sowing it in the world and universe.

I will converse even in the language of the dew
With the vast circle of the propitious universe,
Mixing splendid elements into the hearts of people,
Overflowing with nobleness, subduing all dangers.

Conjuring up a heaven for this world,
Stopping to be crazed with war in this age,
Stopping to be crazed by nuclear material, letting go of it,
Altering your heart to become calm and humble.

Then think of creating through marvelous days and nights,
Erase the causes of evil desire, the obscured times,
Invent a new world, stop fearing,
Bliss for every life all over the heavens.

The poem registers the pressures on a modern subject by highlighting the fleetingness of life:

Minute, thinking that life is so short,
A pity, the days and nights that have passed and disappeared,
Tomorrow life might have vanished,
Dissolving without ashes or particles of dust.

Whatever one does, one does not get time back.

"Kroen" moreover makes disparaging references to contemporary political life: "Stopping to be crazed with war in this age / Stopping to be crazed by nuclear material" and exhorts its addressee to "invent a new world." For the project of building this world, "Kroen" relies on cosmological dimensions as additional, refurbished domains into which a constrained self might extend. Drawing on all the resources that a Thai cultural imaginary holds available, the ideal world put forth includes the locales of a Hindu cosmos as well as referencing a Buddhist soteriology.

By the time that Angkarn publishes the volume *Panithan Kawi* in 1986, the theme of the dichotomous conditions of humanity—one that the poet perceives humanity to inhabit at present and one that he envisions as desirable—takes on a more explicitly Buddhist cast. A poem without a title from this volume provides further insight into the relationship between Buddhism, the vocation of humanity, and literature that Angkarn envisions, as well as into the quandaries of the self that his poetry addresses:

> He, whose heart is negligent, killing time,
> As though killing life, making it disappear,
> Lacking brilliant work with eternal value,
> Will die like a rotten dog, meaninglessly.
>
> The current of time, the stream of water,
> Flows steadily, for whom would it wait?
> No things of beauty dwell in the heart,
> New ignorance, old foolish slave.
>
> What are you so greedy for in this world?
> Hurrying to plunder, to extort, stacking the burial ground,
> The brilliant rays of light, are they ever going to be dirty
>   with mud?
> Bitter wisdom holds sweet insight.
>
> That is hell, this is the Lord Buddha,
> Directing attention to questions of *dharma* day and night,
> Rising in darkness to understand the value of time,
> Stretching the value of life to ten thousand years.
>
> Urgently striving to write *kap, klon, khlong,* and *chan* poetry,
> To offer to this miraculous world,
> So that humanity will be immersed in beauty and beneficence
>   and
> The world become heaven forever.

The poem's technique of contrasting cultural dereliction and the minuteness of human life with the desirable life lived in pursuit of ethical, Buddhist work evocatively figures the travails of a contemporary self split into a self-determined one that possesses a substantial degree of agency and another that constantly has to negotiate the threat of both voluntary (soteriological) and involuntary annihilation (due to the law of impermanence). An individualist component is contained in the many admonitions that proper diligence can provide a panacea against the frenzied pace of modern life that shortens time. Weeks and Maurel detect a modernist, Nietzschean impulse in these many invocations of individual will throughout Angkarn's oeuvre.[49]

"Phiang Khru Nueng Ko Muai Samoe Fan" ("In One Instant Dead, like in a Dream," *Panithan Kawi*) evinces a similar consciousness of the paradoxical dimensions of time. When this poem voices the urgent appeal for humanity to become conscious of the pressure of time, it likewise highlights the need of a *dhammic* consciousness, rather than only of human exertion, in the pursuit of creating art:

> The Wheel of Time rolls in in a second, in an instant one is
>   dead like in a dream.
>
> Black cuckoos fly towards the heaven of Indra,
> One *wa* they will sail down to the gods;[50]
> The tree of paradise is fragrant, making me remember far back,
> Opening the sad location of the next world, falling from the
>   world dying.
>
> Coming up in the middle of the expanse of literary art,
> Arriving at the fearful core of life that they tell of,
> Splish, splash, the stream complains,
> How could the core of life be arid, without desire to know
>   the *dhamma* of the Buddha?

In this poem, the dimensions of time and of the cosmos make vivid the aesthetic stakes as well as the capacious possibilities of human beings. But the fact that this mid-1980s poem inserts the human actor more explicitly into a Buddhist cosmological framework can also be understood to respond to a period in which contradictory demands on the self have mounted—conditions that Angkarn now delineates in increasingly heteroglossic terms. By the mid-1980s, the cultural recovery that the poet had been agitating for already had high currency with state agencies and nongovernmental organizations—albeit in formulations that diverged significantly from Angkarn's investment in Thai cultural traditions.[51] Developed in response to globalization, localist ideologies were invoked both by civil society organizations to promote democratic structures of citizenship and, for divergent goals, including authoritarian ones, by a variety of government entities.

What stands out in Angkarn's work is that rather than contain Thai cultural traditions within the confines of the geobody of the nation, the poet's vision exceeds any of the programmatic, and in part policy-supported, initiatives of the 1980s and 1990s that advocate returns to quintessentially Thai forms of life, thought, and exchange. Rather, Angkarn's poetry advocates a resacralization of the world and expansion of the self into the cosmos that surpasses the mundane nation.

In the same volume as "In One Instant," the poem "Wiman Nam Khang" ("Celestial Mansion of Dew," 1986) also depicts the passing of time and the ensuing pressure with reference to Buddhist notions. "Wiman" delineates the poet's characteristic, modified Buddhist framework:

Your rays with their pure charm, much beloved, do not cease.

I would love to take you around the world and the great oceans,
To the edge of the dream,
Before the heavens disappear.
Betrothing you with the value of the luminous sky, most
    beloved, of the beautiful jeweled man.

That overhanging rock jutting out,
Maybe reaching to the supreme stars, gleaming brilliantly,
Or a cluster of trees of paradise, so utterly good,
Or the way of the dimension of eternal dreaming.

There the path of the white elephant, clear and bright,
Some stars the Lord Buddha set up,
Some universes are the divine nirvana,
The waves of the past passing in long *kalpas* and *kappas*.[52]

The fluffy clouds are fragrant like flowers falling,
Demanding thought from the enigmatic world;
Orion ploughs the extremely beautiful field of the sky,
To reap what value of life as harvest?

Late at night the forest dew sobs with sorrow,
Are the tears of the world going to disappear?

> Arrogant humans kill someone, killing the world,
> Consummating this exceedingly evil age.
>
> Not loving and caring for the value of the world,
> They will suffer until heaven ends;
> The era of humanity will end before long,
> Be a witness, swift stream.
>
> As the water is flowing, the time of life is also flowing,
> Leaves are falling, life leaves like a dream;
> Killing life is destroying night and day,
> What work have you to present this world with?

Debating Buddhist temporalities and human creation in the same framework, "Wiman" presents the poet's typical ontological layout. Buddhist impermanence is qualified both by nature's remedial properties and by the antidote that the creation of art offers. Embedding the dilemmas of the age in a Buddhist framework moreover allows for the exploitation of the vast dimensions of cosmological time. "Wiman's" Buddhist focus thus also enables a zooming out and analytical vantage point that is able to assess "this exceedingly evil age" from afar.

The contemporaneous poem "Jiaranai Kaeo Mani Haeng Chiwit" ("Cutting the Crystal Gems of Life," *Panithan Kawi*) reinforces this perspective; however, its focus lies on embedding the poet's vocation even more firmly in a Buddhist context:

> Born to pay debt to the world,
> Owing the auspicious Bodhisattva precious tribute,
> An offering that the world has for humanity,
> Having paid back the price of society, the gem of art sparkles.
>
> Getting up in darkness all the time,
> From short to long, a long life of ten thousand harvests,
> Forcing myself to read and write poetry until dawn,
> The self attuned to the Buddha, luminous, stirring sacred
>   strength.
>
> Closing my eyes in the evening crossing to the moment
>   before dawn,

> From long to short, the life of sorrow decreases to short,
> Ignorance speeds up unbridled worldly desires,
> Falling into the mud, the self stubborn, falling, strength
>   dissolving.

At the same time, "Jiaranai" contains both an account of the failures of the self ("falling, strength dissolving") and an assertion of the self's potency, diligence, and divinity ("attuned to the Buddha"). Transposed into the language of a more rigorous, Buddhist-informed program for the self, we thus find also the individualism of an increasingly capitalist society.

Writing on (early) modern literature, Marshall diagnoses the motif of the shattering of the self as a literary-psychological strategy. She writes: "An aesthetic of shattering or self-negation took hold: it constituted a counterforce to the nascent ethos of individualism."[53] On the one hand, Marshall notes that the shattering of the self also produces pleasure. At the same time, she views the shattering of the self as the recuperation of a previous notion of the self as nonunitary. Her account helps us to understand the degree to which Buddhist notions of nonself might be suited to calibrating struggles of the self in modernity. A cultural imaginary that has access to complex traditions of thinking about the self *as well as* its nonsubstantiality holds sophisticated tools available to take on this task. Thus, we saw in chapter 2 how with his explication of the temporalities of the dew, Angkarn makes Buddhist impermanence available to the notion of something desirable. In these contexts, we can understand the poet to draw on the notion of the discontinuity of the self for different purposes—to produce a counterintuitive notion of time in Buddhism, to delineate a counterdoctrinal notion of pleasure, and to recuperate a dispersed notion of selfhood.

My analysis differs from that of Weeks and Maurel, who investigate the similarity of Angkarn's notion of individual will with a Nietzschean concept. While initially highlighting the similarity between Angkarn and Nietzsche's understandings, the authors conclude that Angkarn's understanding of the individual differs fundamentally from that of the nineteenth-century German philosopher. Their essay ends with the assertion that Buddhist anti-individualism ultimately supersedes modern individualism in the poet's work:

> While Angkarn's aesthetic philosophy may not be devoid of egotism, its determination to situate the human subject *within* a

natural universe makes of it something other than the joyfully willed hubris of the Nietzschean *Übermensch*.

Nor is it insignificant that in "The Eye of Time" the spider on his web is joined by others of his species, implying a natural community. Not only does this suggest a more social orientation, it also unconsciously diminishes the spectre of death as it is attached to the mortal individual. Similarly when Angkarn announces that he will not give up life until he has brought an end to mankind's suffering, it is determined commitment to a communal ideal and not a personal desire to defeat death, that motivates the intended deferral of mortality.[54]

This may be the case in several passages of Angkarn's work; however, I suggest that we do not set Buddhism and individualism in absolute opposition to one another in the context of modern Thailand.[55]

I further argue, by contrast, that Angkarn's work is not geared toward resolving the crises of self, temporality, and vocation conclusively. Neither is it poised to teach a clear Buddhist path of detachment. Rather, it deploys both Buddhist notions of nonself *and* transcends the Buddhist doctrine of the nonsubstantiality of the self. This seemingly internally contradictory stance on selfhood illustrates clearly the quandaries of an age in which subjectivity, collectivity, and world are undergoing significant change.

HETEROGLOSSIC TEXT

The poet works through crises in modern subjectivity also on the level of language. While the pieces in Angkarn's 1964 collection *Kawiniphon*, which contains the 1959 "Pledge," were heterogeneous in lexicon and style—that is, differed from each other—the 1986 *Panithan Kawi* is likely to have been assembled for purposes of submission to the S.E.A. Write Award competition. This may explain its comparatively uniform style of expression.

However, *Panithan Kawi* distinguishes itself in another important regard. Culminating three decades of cultural critique, the poet's 1986 volume evinces the, in part polemical, use of an increasingly hybridized vocabulary. In *The Dialogic Imagination*, Mikhail Bakhtin argues for the foundationally social nature of language and teaches us to see not only content, but also the *forms* of literature as ideologically charged:

> For any individual consciousness living in it, language is not an abstract system of normative forms but rather a concrete heteroglot conception of the world. All words have the "taste" of a profession, a genre, a tendency, a party, a particular work, a particular person, a generation, an age group, the day and hour. Each word tastes of the context and contexts in which it has lived its socially charged life; all words and forms are populated by intentions. Contextual overtones (generic, tendentious, individualistic) are inevitable in the word.[56]

In another passage, Bakhtin clarifies that language, or literary form, can never be regarded as devoid of ideological import: "As a result of the work done by all these stratifying forces in language, there are no 'neutral' words and forms—words and forms that belong to 'no one'; language has been completely *taken over, shot through with intentions and accents.*"[57]

The modification of Angkarn's poetic lexicon in *Panithan Kawi* on the one hand serves the purpose of increasing the potency of the poet's critiques of modernization. But this volume's more cerebral cultural critique and dense disquisitions on Buddhist ethics also point to shifts in the experience of personhood. We already saw that Angkarn's earlier poetry centrally addresses the fragmentations of a modern self; however, his work in the 1980s finds new modes of conceptualizing subjectivity in relation to Thailand's growing integration into the world economy. The changes in form in Angkarn's work of this period can provide insight into the chafing of different social, ontological, and ideological currents. While chapter 5 investigates in more detail the linguistic innovation that Angkarn undertakes and draws his work into transnational comparison, I conclude this chapter's analysis of the *panithan* with an overview of changes in form in the poet's two pledges across the span of three decades.

From Panithan to Panithan / From Pledge to Testament

Not only do Angkarn's poetics merit comparison with those of his contemporaries, but the study of transformations in form between Angkarn's two eponymous *panithan* is also instructive. While the 1959 "Pledge" is written in the shorter *khlong* meter, the 1986 "Testament" uses the longer *klon 8* and is more didactic in tone.

The 1986 "Testament" must be understood to be in conversation with the 1959 "Pledge," yet Angkarn is also trying out something new in the later *panithan*. The poet's deployment of an increasingly hybridized vocabulary not only instantiates an augmentation of critique but also exemplifies an intellectual response to globalization.

Angkarn's poetry begins to draw on English Latinate and Greek terms in the 1960s.[38] What stands out in *Panithan Kawi*, however, is that his poetry now combines terms like the English Latinate, scientific term "fossil" with a more explicitly Buddhist lexicon. With his use of a literary lexicon that becomes increasingly heteroglot in this way, the poet presents a Thai language that is, on the one hand, more and more defined by a technical vocabulary, reflecting the expansion of the institutions and relevance of the sciences, and a society that is experiencing the shift from the national to the global as well as from industrial to finance capital. These are not shifts that Angkarn endorses; rather, his poetry in the late 1980s steps up its prescriptive Buddhist-culturalist rhetoric precisely to counter these developments.

Moving from the paternalism of the Sarit era to the 1980s, Angkarn's later poem is written in a period in which much of the contemporaneous literary writing continues to reflect on struggles for democratic representation. Meanwhile, in official politics, the 1980s see the cooling of fervent Cold War political rhetoric and a liberal turn toward market activity and moderate democratic reform. Distinct from the authoritarian development initiated by Sarit, the mid-1980s political-economic environment is marked by increased entry into global economic activity. The country's manufacturing boom leads to new waves of migration and to pragmatic economic and political liberalization.

While others continue to produce left poetics that reflect the losses of the 1970s and persist in demanding democratic change, Angkarn is frequently criticized for not producing work with this type of political content. However, his poetry presciently formulates a critique of globalization and develops a vocabulary for this purpose, a topic that the next chapter will examine in more detail.

What is more, the augmentation of the poet's commitment to the world in the "Testament" lies not only in his forsaking of nirvana; this more renunciant *panithan* also presents a more detailed account of the physical world—and of the connection of the animal and natural world to *wathasangsan* (*saṃsāra*), or the transmigratory cycle. It thus presents an additional scope for the already expansive ontologies that the poet had previously delineated.

5

Language

Transnational Poetic Modernity:
Linguistic Innovation and Religious Borrowings in the
Work of Paul Celan and Angkarn Kallayanapong

The last two chapters of this book investigate two transnational encounters, deliberating on how we might understand Angkarn Kallayanapong's work in a wider field of global poetry. In the twentieth century, poetry is always a global matter. But how does global connection manifest in a poetic oeuvre that frequently takes a nationalist perspective and whose author explicitly opposes foreign influence?

Angkarn's focus on the temporalities of culture and the losses of modernity in Thailand invites transnational comparison. Throughout his poetic oeuvre, Angkarn mourns a loss that he frequently describes as a distinctly national one. It is Thailand that has lost its rich reservoir of cultural, artistic, and ethical traditions. Lines such as the following abound in the poet's laments over cultural loss:

> "Sinking their teeth into Thailand"
> "The soot and ashes of Thai bones"
> "Sadly taking leave of the Thai ancestors"
> "The Thai spirit destroyed"
> "The bones of the elephants, horses, and Thai soldiers"
> "The ground of the Thai state trembling"
> "Hurting the Thais throughout existence"
> "'Til the extinction of the Thai soul"
> "The Thai nation plundered"
> "Insulted, meaning the disappearance of the Thais"

"The end of renown for Thai craftsmanship" and
"The mortar of the Thai burial ground"

Much of the poet's work distinguishes itself by highlighting a cultural-nationalist stance toward contemporary life. Angkarn's seemingly nationalist outlook nevertheless bears many distinctly transnational elements. For one, a transnational perspective becomes obvious in the antiglobalization stance that we can track throughout the poet's work. Even where its transnational outlook is not explicit, we can detect transnational elements in the poetry and poetic prose that Angkarn publishes from the late 1950s onward. As Chetana Nagavajara writes, we can discern a "deep structure" linking the poet to other poets without Angkarn's necessarily having to "speak foreign languages."[1] Above all, we can identify global political conditions that frame his artistic production and infuse the poet's work with transnational meanings, influences, and implications.

Transnational components are evident also in Angkarn's poetology. The preoccupation with poetology and its manifesto-style publication itself represents a distinctly modern endeavor and finds many correlates during the decades in which Angkarn is most active. A vital element of this poetology is constituted by the poet's linguistic innovation or creation of a new poetic lexicon. The foundational sense of loss that pervades his work likewise finds a corollary in the work of poets across the globe in the second half of the twentieth century. For poets like Angkarn or Paul Celan, it is this sense of loss that necessitates linguistic innovation, albeit in response to highly divergent historical and political circumstances.

The first global encounter, which I outline in this chapter, investigates points of intersection and divergence in the poetologies of Angkarn and Paul Celan. The second encounter, which I pursue in the final chapter of this book, tracks the actual historical intersection of the two twentieth-century poets Angkarn and Allen Ginsberg.

Angkarn Kallayanapong and Paul Celan

Paul Celan (1920–1970) was a Jewish German-language poet born in the multicultural town of Cernăuți (German, Czernowitz) in the province of Bukovina, Rumania (now Ukraine), who survived the Shoah. He committed suicide in 1970. What did he have in common with the Thai poet Angkarn Kallayanapong?

Angkarn and Celan confront radically different historical events and negotiate different poetic traditions in their writing. Like Celan, Angkarn grapples with language after loss—but this loss is of a radically different nature than the devastation of language and world after the Shoah that Celan addresses in his poetry. While the two poets' historical positionings diverge, their poetologies and linguistic innovation can nevertheless be drawn into productive relation.

Shane Weller delineates Celan's immense linguistic innovation through the analysis of the poet's linguistic negativism. Weller describes the general language skepticism of late modernist European poets as "that radical breaking of the contract between word and world." He explains, "Living in the shadow of the historical traumas of totalitarianism, world war, and, above all, the Holocaust, the late modernists concern themselves with the limits of language and with what Beckett terms the 'innommable.'" Weller usefully defines language skepticism as "an engagement that deploys language in such a way as to mark its limits."[2]

Paul Celan's engagement at and with the limits of language yields a novel poetic lexicon, the thorough rethinking of a language tainted by its instrumentality in the Shoah, and a unique poetics. Celan famously proclaimed both his recognition of (the German) language's irreversible transformation after the Shoah as well as the persistence of his faith in this language. In his Meridian speech, Celan speaks of poetry's "starke Neigung zum Verstummen," or its "strong tendency toward falling silent." As he further elaborates, however,

> Das Gedicht behauptet sich am Rande seiner selbst; es ruft und holt sich, um bestehen zu können, unausgesetzt aus seinem Schon-nicht-mehr in sein Immer-noch zurück.
>
> The poem perseveres at its own margins; in order to prevail, it calls and brings itself back, incessantly, from its already no-longer into its still-yet.[3]

As Weller stresses, in Celan's poetic production the notion of the inefficacy—or inadequacy—of language "is to be found not only at the thematic level, however, but also, and indeed above all, in the particular forms of linguistic negativism that characterise his poetry."[4] He further elaborates: "This linguistic negativism is driven by an ethico-aesthetic imperative to memorialise the lost, and to articulate experiences of extremity that are scarcely imaginable."[5] As Weller outlines, Celan's linguistic negativism takes shape in the genesis of a new lexicon for post-Shoah German-language poetics.

An Idiom for the Losses of Modernity

Weller describes the way in which Celan generates a historically appropriate negative poetic lexicon as occurring through "unwording"—the building of a new poetic lexicon primarily through a defamiliarizing morphology of affixes and prefixes that turn words into their opposites, or through modifications that open up new, compelling meaning. In addition, Celan generates formulas of "unsaying," which consist of first making a statement and then negating this same statement in the clause directly following it.[6]

Angkarn's mode of linguistic innovation is not primarily a linguistic negativism and does not only occur on the level of lexicon or through formulas of unsaying. Nevertheless, the loss that Angkarn aims to counter in his poetry is also one of language, representational frameworks, and entire imaginaries. Like Celan, Angkarn is concerned with a radical break within a particular cultural imaginary. This break is one that the poet perceives as having occurred with the onslaught of rationalized life in a capitalist economy. Against this, the poet constructs a reparative postcolonial imaginary that diverges from a European aesthetic modernity but ultimately also exceeds the constraints of a nationalist, nativist imaginary. This theme of his poetry begins long before the 1980s, taking shape in the poetry he produced during the developmentalist era of the Sarit Thanarat government. But in the 1980s, the rationalization of life, work, and human relations takes on a different cast and speed as Thailand begins increasingly to see itself as part of a neoliberal global world.

Rather than primarily undertake the task of new word formation or the syntactic work that Celan performs in his poetry, Angkarn brings about the expansion of a modern Thai poetic vocabulary through the inclusion of new terms and the recontextualization of words. As Suchitra Chongstitvatana outlined in chapter 4 of this book, the poet undertakes a lexical patterning that invests terms (like *thip*; divine, the divine) with new meaning and positions them in new contexts. What is more, he prominently relies on juxtaposition—of the sacred and the profane or vulgar; of registers of language; and of seemingly incommensurable ontologies. This repositioning and rewording has significant implications for the creation of a new poetic language and imaginary.

In contrast to the Art for Life poetry of his contemporaries, Angkarn's work is singularly focused on achieving a universal-nationalist idiom for the Thai present. That is, while his poetry at many points evinces a nationalist agenda, the frameworks drawn from Thai cultural heritage nevertheless elaborate a world of universal extension rather than a parochial national imaginary. It is especially notable that the scale of his perspective differs from that of his contemporaries. While the Art for Life poets focus on the military, authoritarian enemy within and recuperate the lexica of rural and working-class life, Angkarn takes an increasingly global view in the 1950s–1970s—before globalization became a household word in Thailand. More than any other Thai poet at the time, Angkarn thought about the increasing influence of English—when this does not represent as urgent a topic for, say, Naowarat Pongpaiboon. Although Angkarn's work frequently highlights a nationalist-culturalist ethos, his poetry reflects on language change in profound ways. While his poetry incorporates, in sparse but prominent ways, the Greek and Latinate vocabulary of a globalizing era in which the lexica of science and the economy move to the center of policy and public discourse, it also becomes more cerebrally Buddhist in the 1980s.

It is notable that in this respect, too, Angkarn's poetry is more comparable to that of Celan, whose poetry evinces a cosmopolitanism that invokes the pasts and envisions the futures of a world that is closely tied to nature, to the supranational, and to dimensions beyond the everyday.

Although he does not reference this directly, Angkarn is writing the poems collected in *Panithan Kawi* (1986) at the end of an era that sees accelerated engagement with the global. Chris Baker and Pasuk Pongphaichit characterize the 1950s through the 1970s as an era that focused on the building of new national economic institutions under ever-greater US tutelage and streamlined Cold War ideology.[7] The authors then describe the years from 1976 through 1988 as focused on building transnational economic ties. This period increasingly saw Thailand "liaising with the World Bank and other international financial institutions." Baker and Pasuk further argue that, "The period from the early 1980s to early 1990s was the golden age of the Thai technocracy."[8] Since the 1960s, an increasingly technocratic world left its mark on the many coinages in Thai of a vocabulary that described this novel, contemporary life. Angkarn's poems in the 1964 collection *Kawiniphon* feature terms such as "virus," "malaria," and "corruption." In the poems on time in the 1986 volume *Panitnan Kawi*, however, the Greek and Latinate terms of the contemporary world are juxtaposed with a consciously chosen Buddhist vocabulary.

In "The Poet's Testament," we find the poet's preference for continuing to exist in this world as a tortured (Latinate) "fossil," rather than achieving nirvana and escaping the worldly temporalities of suffering. Other poems in the volume, such as "Awake, Humanity!" feature the Latinate terms "corruption," "nuclear," and "serum." "Awake" opens as follows:

> A pity, born to corrupt,
> Waiting, day and night, crazy with coup d'états.

In this stanza, the English Latinate "corruption" is juxtaposed with a vocabulary of ordinary, and in part derisive ("crazy," "crazed"), terms from Thai. The tonal effect and affective charge of the opening of the poem is then one of censure. The poem subsequently segues into a more idealistic-pedagogic mode of Buddhist instruction. In stanza 6, the poet suggests *panya*, wisdom, as a "serum":

> Wisdom, make a serum to inject wisdom,
> Solving all the problems depressing the heart.

Except for the Latin biomedical term, a Sanskritic-Pali lexicon (that includes terms such as "wisdom," "self," "nonself," "poison," "witnesses," "cannibalistic," "danger," and "conscious") dominates the middle part of the poem, before its mood of censure flares up again in stanza 9 with the Latinate word "nuclear":

> Nuclear, inauspicious, vile evil.

A similar tone can be found in the opening of an unnamed three-stanza poem in the same volume that features the word "nuclear" twice:

> With four faces the god shakes his head, fed up with the earth,
>   three-eyed, turbid green,
> Despising, disdaining the world. Base, nuclear fire of the
>   vicious,
> Will destroy the world.
> In the modern age, why is humanity so insane? Crazed with
>   dealing in nuclear material.

Although I have translated it as an adjective above, "nuclear" does not have a clear grammatical designation in the Thai poem. Rather, the term comes to encapsulate the general concept of something supremely vile and could thus perhaps be better translated as "nuclearity."

These terms from modern governance, industry, and medicine are used for their own sake, but a notion like "nuclear," or "nuclearity," also takes on metaphorical meaning and comes to stand in for the characteristics of an undesirable present more broadly. Angkarn's is then always a critique of uneven capitalist development and the cultural change that he associates with it.

Side by side with these Greek and Latinate words, Angkarn's *Panithan Kawi* draws heavily on a Sanskritic-Pali vocabulary as well as a Khmer poetic lexicon. These lexica are composed both of classical literary terms and the new Sanskritic-Pali coinages that abound in modern Thai to provide terms for abstract concepts or scientific-technical elements that define modern life under industrialization and capitalist expansion.

Returning to "The Poet's Testament" and reviewing its core stanzas 8 and 9, we find that the Latinate "fossil" stands in close proximity to a host of Sanskritic-Pali Buddhist and literary terms:

I will even not go to nirvana.
I will whirl and swim in the manifold cycles of transmigration,
Translating the meaning of the real value of the many galaxies
Into stanzas of poetry for the universe.

To erase suffering and sorrow in the human world
As much as I can, moving toward an age of bliss and
    contentment.
At that moment I will be blended, pulverized to become earth.
I will be a fossil, torturedly existing and observing.

Especially stanza 8 is saturated with technical terms from Buddhist ontology and soteriology: *niraphan*, nirvana; *wathasangsan*, the cycle of transmigration; *darajak*, galaxies; and *jakrawan*, universe. Stanza 9 likewise contains a Sanskritic-Pali vocabulary. While the word *thoraman*, tortured, which is in closest proximity to "fossil," is of a more quotidian nature, *yuk kasemsan*, age of contentment, and *thuksok*, suffering and sorrow, likewise carry strong Buddhist overtones. This juxtaposition bears several implications. On the one hand, it can be understood as an updating and validation of Buddhism, infusing it with scientific-biological connotation. On the other hand, the insertion of the poet-narrator's becoming-fossil into a Buddhist cosmology lends gravity and universal importance to this act.

However, there is yet another element of this poem that makes it characteristic of Angkarn's particular worldview. The line that foreshadows "I will be blended, pulverized to be earth" is important, because it stands in for Angkarn's trademark blend of "high" and "low" ontologies—a system in which dust, or a fossil, carries as much redemptive potential as the grandeur of the Buddhist cosmos that he describes. The line "I will be blended, pulverized to be earth" is composed entirely of Thai words and lacks any Sanskritic-Pali components. However, in the poem it is set against a Sanskritic-Pali vocabulary that is commonly associated with high cultural forms. This juxtaposition of lexically diverse elements lends to Angkarn's poetry its powerful criticality, expansive Buddhist *imaginaire*, and redemptive charge.[9]

In this aspect, Angkarn's poetry is also comparable to that of Celan. In his German-language work, Celan's poetic lexicon, too, is suffused with the languages of the multicultural world that he hailed from and variously includes terms from Hebrew, Yiddish, Romance languages, and Greek and Latin.

Both Celan's and Angkarn's poetry turns on a usage of and working through of language that enables the creation of new worlds. Their work records loss while at the same time opening up the view onto new utopian dimensions. Thus, while Angkarn does not primarily promulgate a linguistic negativism or patterns of unwording and unsaying, he does rely on a kind of linguistic innovation that takes the form of rewording and repositioning. Like Celan, the aim of his poetry is to create new worlds that simultaneously reflect great rupture and point beyond a stalled present.

Heteroglossia and Dialogism

The notions of heteroglossia and dialogism offer further ways of conceptualizing the sociopolitical references and significance of Angkarn's poetry. In *The Dialogic Imagination*, Mikhail Bakhtin calls poetic language a fundamentally "monologic" type of language and sets it in opposition to prose:

> The language of poetic genres, when they approach their stylistic limit, often becomes authoritarian, dogmatic and conservative, sealing itself off from the influence of extraliterary social dialects. Therefore such ideas as a special "poetic language," a

"language of the gods," a "priestly language of poetry" and so forth could flourish on poetic soil. It is noteworthy that the poet, should he not accept the literary language, will sooner resort to the artificial creation of a new language specifically for poetry than he will to the exploitation of actual available social dialects. Social languages are filled with specific objects, typical, socially localized and limited, while the artificially created language of poetry must be a directly intentional language, unitary and singular.[10]

In this assessment, poetry emerges as a static language that does not participate in the dynamism of living, socially informed languages. However, Bakhtin continually qualifies his position, for instance in a footnote that weakens the claim of poetry's monologicity:

It goes without saying that we continually advance as typical the extreme to which poetic genres aspire; in concrete examples of poetic works it is possible to find features fundamental to prose, and numerous hybrids of various generic types exist. These are especially widespread in periods of shift in literary poetic languages.[11]

In his essay, "Bakhtin on Poetry," Michael Eskin systematically makes Mikhail Bakhtin's notion of dialogism available also to the interpretation of poetry, rather than only to considerations of the nature and potentialities of prose. While Bakhtin is conventionally understood to relegate poetry to the monologic realm, Eskin presents a different reading of Bakhtin's notion of the possibilities that poetic language holds. He argues that "far from being relegated to the realm of discursive and, by extension, sociopolitical monologicity, poetry may plausibly be construed as the dialogically and sociopolitically exemplary mode of discourse in Bakhtin's writings."[12]

Eskin begins by restating the conventional view regarding Bakhtin's theory of poetry: "Poetry, Bakhtin (ibid.: 109) suggests, is predicated on the 'idea of a unitary and singular language and a unitary and monologically sealed off utterance.'"[13] However, Bakhtin's notion of poetry remains ambiguous and can ultimately be read precisely to furnish the conditions for critical, dialogic expression, as Eskin argues:

> Poetic speech, Bakhtin (1975: 109) suggests, is not simply monologic and authoritative; precisely because it structurally tends toward monologicity, it sets a task before the poet, namely, the task of answerability, thereby announcing its existential, ethical, and sociopolitical significance: the poet "must [*dolzhen*]" become answerable for every element of the act of his poetic utterance.[14]

Taken together with the fact that poetry offers the possibility of a "communal language," the poet's singular position of answerability then creates an unprecedented framework for critical expression.[15] Eskin concludes that Bakhtin "certainly allows for the polyphony of other, prosaicized poetic texts, especially, as he notes, of poetic texts produced in the twentieth century."[16]

The potentiality for critique of Angkarn's poems lies first of all in the fact that the poet has thought long and hard about the structures of Thai poetry. If poetry "structurally tends toward monologicity," the poet's development of traditional metrics, his creation of new poetic lexica, and his juxtaposition of seemingly incommensurate vocabularies, ontologies, and contexts all constitute conscious attempts to modify poetry's structural constraints. My analysis of the heteroglossia of "Testament" above shows that his poetic language is not "sealed off" or "unitary and singular."[17] Contrary to the monologic character of poetry that Bakhtin initially outlines, Angkarn avails himself "of actual available social dialects"—of the terms and vocabularies of his time.[18] This feature of his poetry attests to the fact that the poet writes in a period of "shifts in literary poetic languages" that Bakhtin also recognizes.[19] While Angkarn's poetry evinces a high level of intentionality, it also adapts poetry to include "social languages" that together with his willed creation of a modern Buddhist imaginary create works of art that are imbued with contestatory meaning. Regarding poetry's character as a "communal language," Angkarn is moreover not only integrating aspects of the social languages of the time, he is also forging a language that addresses an aspirational future community.[20]

Another aspect of the potential for critique of Angkarn's work is that his poetry turns on the maximization of inherent elements of Thai grammar, contributing to the obscuring of tense, the indeterminacy of address, and the distribution of agency. According to Suchitra, part of what makes up the modernity of Angkarn's poetry lies in the lexical patterning of his poetry: "Angkhan's flaw of using certain words repeatedly in his poetry is a deliberate device to create a coherent significance in his work. We have seen in chapter 1 how the lexical patterns in the work serve at different levels to create a unity between the main themes and the major symbols of the work. By selecting certain sets of words, the poet can create certain sets of association which help to clarify the meanings of his selected words. These 'lexical patterns' serve, in turn, to lead to the understanding of his work."[21] This statement testifies to the poet's will to wrest poetic language free from its potentially monologic functions. In my estimation, Angkarn's creation of a "willed," idiosyncratic poetic language cannot be severed from the potential for critique that any given piece of literary art might have. Together with the poetry's heteroglossia and unusual deployment of concepts, this creative use of lexical patterning is responsible for the work's superseding of a poetics of sealed utterances and conventional meanings.

If, according to Bakhtin, "each word tastes of the context and contexts in which it has lived its socially charged life," the heteroglossia of Angkarn's work puts together a poetic lexicon that "tastes" of highly diverse contexts.[22] The effect is that this lexicon ultimately breaches the oppositions of divinity and the mundane, cosmology and the worldly, and the vulgar and high-minded. The dialogism of Angkarn's work is thus indicative of the chafing, overlapping, and interacting of divergent ontological strata of the present. This has vital implications for several of the domains that his poetry touches upon, especially those of temporality, ecology, and transnational connection and legibility.

HETEROGENEOUS TEMPORALITIES

The Bakhtinian concern over poetry's "sealed" or open propensities can also be aligned with inquiry into the temporal properties of poetry. Shane Weller attributes a certain temporality to Celan's poetry that becomes central to the "ethico-aesthetic imperative" of his poetics:

> As Celan puts it in a posthumously published prose text: "'Zeitloses' Gedicht: das immer zur Unzeit Gegenwärtige. Das durch Gegenwart als unzeitig empfundene Gezeitigte. Zeitlos = zeitoffen." This temporal openness is very much at one with Celan's concern with his poems reaching an addressee—named,

if at all, as "du"—hence his strong objection to the characterisation of his poetry as "hermetic," that is, sealed. For Celan, the value of a poem lies in no small measure in its remaining "zeitoffen."[23]

The excerpt from Celan's posthumously published notion of a poetology that Weller cites is difficult both in German and in what we might translate it to in English: "'Timeless' poem: that [which] is always present at the inappropriate, or un-time. The timed/that which has been done/made past which is felt as untimely through [its] presence. Timeless = time-open." In this part of his poetology, Celan works hard to create temporal flows and permeabilities that previously remained impossible or unthought. Weller concludes that for Celan, poetry's "ethico-aesthetic imperative must be to do justice both to history and to its own time, while remaining open to the future."[24]

Where it is explicitly voiced, Angkarn's notion of history and temporal mobility does not evince the same openness as Celan's. As I argued in chapter 3, Angkarn's notion of history seems frequently to stagnate around the imagination of the fourteenth-to-eighteenth-century kingdom of Ayuthaya as the high point of Thai cultural achievement. On the other hand, the openness of temporality in his writing comes to the fore in the vast dimensions of Buddhist cosmological time that he recuperates both for the critique of the present and for its redemption. The poet further effects an opening up of temporality when he folds together the seemingly incommensurate temporal systems of worldly and nibbanic time, as outlined in chapter 2. In addition, temporal mobility can be found on the level of lexicon and the juxtaposition of concepts in Angkarn's poetry. Thus, where Weller attributes a temporality of openness to Celan's poetic negativism, we can detect an opening up of meaning and temporality in the abrasions of Angkarn's heteroglossia and the censure that it at times effects. This became obvious in chapter 3's analysis of the "Bangkok" poems.

Yet another kind of temporal openness is evident in Angkarn's work. Angkarn's poetry stands out through a syntax that is frequently without a clearly delineated verb or agent. This is a grammatical feature of Thai, yet the poet maximizes the effect of this language's syntactic openness. This is moreover poetry in a language that does not conjugate verbs. In addition, Angkarn's poetry does not codify tense as precisely as poetry in Thai can. While prose in Thai is by definition more precise in its designation of tense—through the use of particles that mark the relative location in time of the action described—poetry obscures tense and thus allows for additional temporal openness.

The way in which this openness of temporality may translate into English is that many stanzas of Angkarn's poems both appear without a clear subject and may be understood as using continuous forms of the verb. An example for how the continuous form in English may signify an openness with regard to temporality can be found in a stanza from an untitled poem in *Panithan Kawi*:

> That is hell, this is the Lord Buddha,
> Directing attention to questions of *dharma* day and night,
> Rising in darkness to understand the value of time,
> Stretching the value of life out to ten thousand years.[25]

Like Celan, Angkarn is concerned with establishing a particular temporal relation between the past and the future-present. While it is mostly the recuperation of a desirable culture in the past that carries weight in Angkarn's poetry, the temporal architecture of his poetry is not unidirectional or monodimensional. For Celan the past and the German language are tainted. In Angkarn's poetry, it is not the past itself that is terrible; rather, the damaging event that has occurred is one of discontinuity, and his mourning for the loss of access to the past as cultural resource is thus of a different nature.

Amir Eshel attributes a particular temporality and directionality to Celan's poetics when he describes his revivification of poetry as "breath-infused [*atemdurchwachsene*] language in time."[26] Eshel moreover identifies the directionality in Celan's poetry as lying in its rejection of (Heidegger's) monolingual German poetics and countering these with his poetry's consistent address to an other.[27]

Regarding address, we can attribute openness also to Angkarn's poetry, though for rather different reasons. Thus, the frequent omission of a subject or clear designation of agency opens Angkarn's poetry up to multiple notions of address. In other respects, his addressee may well be much more clearly delineated than Celan's, however. While Celan's "thou" remains elusive, no longer reachable, or unaddressable, at least some of Angkarn's poems frequently seem to hail a normative Thai subject or citizen. However, although the poet's mode of address may thus bear simple nationalist inscription in several instances, this impression is superseded by the dimensions of the worlds that this poetry outlines.

In one respect, the poet's work envisions an entirely nontypical addressee of poetry: Angkarn has constructed an epistemology for a human self that is not privileged—a fact that stands in productive tension with the haughty pride and grandiosity of the author evoked by other poems. This has immense implications for a critique of class in Thailand—in the sense of enlarging the pool of those who have traditionally had privileged access to education and the kind of relation to knowledge that the poet proposes. Angkarn democratizes this "traditional" world of access to knowledge and further levels it by juxtaposing high culture with a semiotics of nature and an ontology of "low" things.

A Nondoctrinal Religious Poetry

What does it mean when poets use a religious vocabulary not for the purpose of religious pedagogy strictly speaking, but exploit this vocabulary for other purposes? Searching for a language after the loss of language, Celan frequently turns to the lexica of Judaism and, at times, Christianity. Eshel attributes a religious component also to the temporality of Celan's poetry:

> Attentiveness is the natural piousness of the soul. We have to add . . . the second-long . . . attentiveness experienced [*erlebte*] . . . in the face of darkness (PCTM 61). *Umkehr* thus has both a spatial and a temporal aspect: Like Walter Benjamin's angel of history, who, while blown into the future, is unable to turn his face from the rising piles of historical debris, Celan's *Umkehr* implies a turning toward the historical traces, a search for an adequate idiom for the "darkness."[28]

In this passage, Eshel argues that the poet uses a religious notion to outline a necessary relation to a historical temporality. His reading of Celan's *Umkehr* highlights this author's unwavering commitment to a past that is a *Trümmerhaufen*—a pile of debris, the wreckage of "progress."[29] The angel whose progression into the future is relentless, but whose almost entire attention is on the past, provides for an evocative figuration of a desirable temporality and relation to history (for both Benjamin and for Celan).

Benjamin's work, too, is a good example of mobilizations of religious figurations—such as that of the angel—that reach beyond the domain of the religious strictly speaking, while on the other hand not appearing as anti- or nonreligious.[30] To an even greater degree, Celan's deployment of the religious works largely outside of the confines of the theological. His mobilization of the traditions of Judaism and Christianity for a philosophy of temporality that is adequate to a present after great loss is never doctrinal, nor does it seem primarily to have religious pedagogical intent.[31] The poem "Le Contrescarpe" contains the word *"tekiah"*—Hebrew for the blast of the *shofar* or trumpet—but it appears here in a poem that is not primarily religious themed: "The horn of an aries lifts you—*Tekiah!*—like the sound of a trombone beyond the nights into the day."[32]

Celan's poem "Die Schleuse" ("The Floodgate") contains the Hebrew words *Kaddisch* and *Jiskor*. While these are religious, liturgical terms, and Celan uses them in a poem that invokes a dead sister, he uses them in decidedly nondoctrinal ways.[33] When the poem's speaker states, "To polytheism I lost a word, that sought me: Kaddisch," he leaves the effectiveness and address of his *Kaddisch* in doubt, rather than asserting the certainties of orthodoxy.

In the case of Angkarn, I have suggested that his invocations of Buddhism vitally bear the function of building scale and furnishing the instruments for generating rhetorical force. Like in Angkarn's poetry, religious lexica and framings in Celan's writing also frequently work toward intensification and the expansion of the poetic idiom. However, unlike in Angkarn's work, in Celan's poetry, the invocation of religious motifs also works to question—and at times negate—notions of divinity and redemption. In this context, too, the poet's linguistic negativism is operative. Thus, Weller notes that Celan's poem "Es war Erde in ihnen" ("There Was Earth in Them") includes the line "sie lobten nicht Gott," "they did not praise God." And the "negated subject," *niemand* (no one), which becomes so prominent in Celan's writing, can be understood to represent a further mode of expressing skepticism with regard to religion.[34] The poem "Psalm" in *Die Niemandsrose* contains a similar appeal to a god whose existence one doubts: "Praised art thou, no one."[35]

Although Angkarn does not face the task of recreating "word and world" after the Shoah, he is likewise intent on using the lexica of religion to create a different present and future.[36] Rather than rail against, wrangle with, or outright question divinity, Angkarn tweaks the sacred to perform a different kind of work. Most remarkable about the poet's nondoctrinal deployment of Hinduism and Buddhism is his revision of the temporality of the present. Against the background of the rationalizing, development-oriented decades of the 1950s through the 1980s in which he writes, Angkarn's mobilization of religion may be understood to resacrilize time.

Yet rather than primarily argue for the return of the religious to the world in this poetry, we might focus on the ways in which the poet's rendering of Buddhist dimensions opens up narrow understandings of time. As Angkarn's work reinfuses time with multiple dimensions, readers do not merely imagine themselves to be living in the "empty homogeneous time" of a developing nation under authoritarian governance, they also understand the present and future in this Southeast Asian location to contain yet other possibilities.[37] That it is the dimensions and lexica of religion, especially, that lend such force to the poet's critique is in part found in the fact that Buddhism outlines dimensions of immensity with great precision. Given the association of homogeneous, empty time with Western hegemony and the colonial, the divergent directionalities of time in Angkarn's work make for an inventive postcolonial politics of temporality.[38] At the same time, the poet's intervention consists of his leveling of ontological hierarchies—so much so that an entirely new ontology comes to pass.

Eco-Poetics

Angkarn builds an early critical idiom for discussing environmental issues in the course of constructing his cosmology, critique, and ethics.[39] After all, "The Poet's Testament" begins with a challenge:

> Who would ever dare trade in skies and oceans,
> This pure world created by the gods.
>
> . . .
>
> We are not the owners of the sky and space,
> The elements of the earth, of all the heavens in their entirety.

The frequently rigid, prescriptive Buddhist framing of his 1980s pieces here takes a notable turn toward an eco-aesthetics for the modern world. In this context, the comparison between his two eponymous poetic manifestos, or *panithan*, from 1959 and from 1986 is again instructive. What also distinguishes the later poem's novel soteriology from the 1959 poem is that it contains a more detailed account of the physical world and explicitly connects animals and the natural world to *wathasangsan*

(Pali; Sanskrit, *saṃsāra*), the Wheel of Transmigration, and to an alternate Buddhist notion of redemption.

Throughout his oeuvre, the poet stresses the importance of "low" things, thereby proposing an entirely different ontology that accompanies his focus on high culture. As Suchitra writes of Angkarn's ontology, "Angkhan looks at nature very closely and gives equal value to every element in nature. For him, the stones or earth are as precious as any precious stones. Every natural object is related to every other and all are interdependent."[40] She explains with regard to Angkarn's poem "Lok" ("The World"): "The world does not belong only to the 'superior' but equally to the 'inferior' as well. The poet even emphasizes that the distinction between the two is actually an 'illusion' for the notion of superiority and inferiority ultimately comes from human ignorance."[41]

This has vital implications for an early, progressive perspective on ecology. His 1964 poem "Laeng Wanakhadi" ("Devoid of Literature") begins with the following stanzas:

> Even if comparable to the stars, partners of the sky, months and years,
> At one time one will be a shooting star.
> Do not look down on the earth, trample it,
> This place that hides diamonds of high value for the future.
>
> Foul water caught in a pipe by the roadside,
> May ascend to the sky as rain clouds.
> Though lowly, it aims for supreme results,
> Persevering in brilliant thought, soon ascending to heavenly dimensions.

Thus "Devoid," too, highlights the propensity of all the composite elements of the world to furnish insight. Suchitra further stresses the role of nature as religious teacher in the poet's work, and Chetana Nagavajara highlights the textual, semiotic character of nature in Angkarn's poetry: "He is a semiotician enamoured with the world of signifiers around him to such an extent that he takes the signified for granted."[42] One of Angkarn's poems that delineates these semiotics very clearly is the 1966 "Jaruek Adid," or "Inscription from the Past," from *Kawiniphon*.[43] The poem outlines the following ontology:

This world is like a great library,
Old and new letters can be read from it.
Every leaf has a fun story to tell,
Manifold, under the waters and skies.

The past is inscribed onto the earth,
In the rocks are engraved messages of heaven.
Benevolent Mother Earth,
Teaches everything there is to teach.

The water writes shadows, giving them to the rocks,
Pouring out the manifold precious inscriptions of the world,
To all beings of the Wheel of Transmigration,
As a philosophy of life.

The incomparable value of every particle of earth and sand,
Is as good as bright, pure diamonds.
What value would gems have,
If there were no earth and sand.

Everything is of balanced value,
The scale elevates things to equal height.
The world and the sky give rise to the strength of longing,
The imagination of the soul.

Some places are bright, illuminated by beauty,
Containing the pure, clear language of poetry,
The streams, forests, and waters,
Flavored with divine substance against the stream of age.

Sharpen your vision,
Cull fearless wisdom,
Learn the language of the earth, water, and sky,
Search for contentment.

You will find the meaning of life,
Inscribed into this auspicious spirit,
Use it to create an outlook on life,
That is immortal, winning over death.

> Hold still above time and the minutes,
> Which have such overwhelming power,
> Build up immense sacred strength,
> That makes life worth breathing and not lack meaning.[44]

In "Inscription," the poet presents an ontology of astounding breadth, in which nature is not only animate but also literate—and outlines an ethical and artistic semiotics. As such, nature—like art—acquires the highest ontological status in Angkarn's cosmos.

Angkarn's 1950s work, in which we encounter his forsaking of nirvana in favor of redemptive work on behalf of the world, radicalizes this ontology further. Though the poet continues to draw on traditional cosmology, "low" things are more decisively positioned on an equal ontological plane with "high" things, furnishing a radical democratic ontology. This egalitarian feature of Angkarn's ontology can then also be understood as strong advocacy for an environment exploited by human beings.

After all, in stanzas 9 and 10 of "Testament," the poet-speaker's forsaking of personal salvation is closely connected to the natural world:

> I will even not go to nirvana.
> I will whirl and swim in the manifold cycles of transmigration,
> Translating the meaning of the real value of the many galaxies
> Into stanzas of poetry for the universe.
>
> To erase suffering and sorrow in the human world
> As much as I can, moving toward an age of bliss and contentment.
> At that moment I will be blended, pulverized to become earth.
> I will be a fossil, torturedly existing and observing.

"Testament" then becomes a manifesto not only for art, but also for the environment. Suchitra was the first to note that the image of water in Angkarn's poetry is closely related to the theme of time.[45] In "Testament," what takes on liquid quality is the notion of transmigration; it becomes something that one can swim in (although this is also idiomatic in Thai), while the speaker is pulverized and becomes a fossil. His becoming-fossil and fusion with nature then takes the place of nirvana, the highest goal of Buddhist soteriology. Read together, "Inscription" and "Testament" instantiate an eco-poetics that is mindful of the damage done to the environment, on the one hand, and invests nature with the highest aspects of spiritual-religious meaning, on the other hand. If Angkarn's "Testament" is the poet's most incisive formulation of an alternate Buddhist notion of redemption, then it also performs the poet's strongest advocacy for an 'eco-system' that human beings should respect rather than attempt to subordinate.

Chinese Prose Poetry and the Translocality of Twentieth-Century Literature

There is yet another perspective to be considered when investigating the innovative value of Angkarn's poetry. Much of the poetic innovation of the twentieth century, no matter whether it was initiated by writers who expressly engaged with transnational literatures or not, always included transnational components.

In "Genre Occludes the Creation of Genre: Bing Xin, Tagore, and Prose Poetry," Nick Admussen investigates a particular kind of poetic innovation in Chinese literature that spans the Republican and communist periods and is indebted to multiple processes of translation. Admussen's analysis focuses on prose poetry in Chinese that he argues is "typified by experimentation, generic hybridity, formal lawlessness and a shared mistrust of strict aesthetic categories."[46] Taking the adaptations of Rabindranath Tagore's work into Chinese as his example, Admussen argues that the translations or transpositions of this work by the translator and writer Bing Xin strongly influenced much of the Chinese prose poetry of the twentieth century. The emergence of Chinese prose poetry as a genre was however dependent on a relay of translation: Admussen stresses that "Bing Xin was not translating Tagore's Bengali poetry into Chinese prose; instead, she was translating English prose renditions of Bengali poetry into Chinese prose."[47] The work of Tagore that Bing Xin translated was thus already a work of translation. What is more, Tagore's poetry in Bengali was itself also already the result of processes of translation, as Admussen explains:

> As Chaudhuri puts it, "Tagore's poetry, especially his songs . . . speak of an old world that is lost but is being transformed into something new."[48] The goal is not to wind modernity back to the premodern, but to draw from the premodern—in a way that occasionally satisfies Orientalist notions of the exotic ahis-

torical—in order to create a contemporary, vernacular Bengali poetry that can serve as the basis for a new and independent regional culture.[49]

Admussen is interested in the particular idiom created in Chinese by the multiple levels of translation that occur in the transposition of the Bengali author's work. He stresses the transformation in quality that Rabindranath Tagore's English prose, which was itself a translation from his Bengali poems, brings with it.

Admussen next investigates Bing Xin's translations of Tagore's English-language work and describes the transformation of the valences of the archaic and the modern, vernacular in Chinese prose poetry:

> They do so by working from the assumption that classical Chinese idioms and structures are *not* vernacular—even though they make up a measurable part of daily Chinese speech—and that structures from foreign languages can and should be treated as vernaculars, even when they are archaic or affected.[50]

Thus, a new work of art is created in which elements that previously had a different function in another work—such as antiquated expressions—take on new meaning and functions. I cite Admussen's explanation of the hybrid nature of the genealogy of a poetic form (Chinese prose poetry) as evidence of the at times intangible transnational heritage of national poetries.

In the case of Angkarn, we can argue that, although he may not have read as widely in English or other foreign languages as in Thai, his language and world were by definition suffused with idioms and elements of the transnational. Although he voices his skepticism with regard to *farang* (Western foreigners) and other influences prolifically, Angkarn nevertheless appears as the most globalized of the modern Thai poets. While others have attempted to assert a genealogy regarding conceptual aspects of Angkarn's work—and have asserted Western influence through his teacher Silpa Bhirasri (Corrado Feroci)—no genealogy of translation or the reception of translation of poetic works has been reconstructed for Angkarn thus far.[51] Instead, the transnationality of his poetry is primarily operative in the fact that it leaves us with the keen sense that momentous, transnationally compounded, change is occurring and that he tasks poetry with providing an account of this transformation. At the same time,

Angkarn is the poet who draws so profoundly on the past as a cultural reservoir that he is able to "update" and refunction those seemingly obsolete elements of Thai culture as cosmology. All of a sudden, traditional cosmology comes to have portentous significance also for modern life. Instead of merely hewing to the demands of commercialization and the capitalization of Thailand, Angkarn presents an expansive account of the potential of a Thai-inflected contemporary *imaginaire*. In this he ultimately does not appear as an opponent of modernity at all—on the level of poetic innovation, he is the poet who does not shirk linguistic engagement with the global and instead fully enters this modern domain.

On the level of lexicon and as regards his poetological concerns, the intentional content of his poetry (globalization critique), and even in the reception and circulation of his work, this Thai poet can thus be understood to be influenced by as well as to impact the transnational in myriad ways.

The particular imaginary created by Angkarn also resonated beyond national borders. Although there is a notable dearth of translations of Angkarn's poetry into Western languages, an overlooked case history of translation is the rendition into English of three of Angkarn's poems by the American poet Allen Ginsberg, an encounter that I examine in the following chapter.

6

Politics

One Night in Bangkok: Allen Ginsberg and Angkarn Kallayanapong

When researching translations of Angkarn Kallayanapong's work, one will be astounded to come across three poems that credit the American Beat poet Allen Ginsberg (1926-1997) as the translator. This chapter tracks the remarkable case history of the translation into English of a small number of Angkarn's poems by the American poet. I use this historical coincidence to examine translation in the sense of the ways in which aesthetic trends, political ideology, and Buddhist frameworks of thought—especially as regards writerly vocation—translate across global locations. I thereby investigate the cosmopolitan character of Angkarn's work from a new angle. In this inquiry into his work's cosmopolitanism, Buddhism again plays a central role. Tracking both Ginsberg's and Angkarn's opposition to Cold War American influence in Southeast Asia across vastly different political and geographic fields, my analysis further explores the elasticity of political ideology.

Scholarly work on Cold War ideological convergence addresses cross-bloc ideological continuities, the antidemocratic practices of the United States, and topics such as the global cooptation of critical art through the CIA-funded Congress for Cultural Freedom.[1] By contrast, I am interested in convergences in the work of a radical, queer US poet and an, at first appearance, conservative Thai poet whose main interest lies in the formulation of a revisionary cultural critique. While Thailand and the United States are firmly situated in the same bloc during the Cold War, and Angkarn and Ginsberg produced vehement cultural critiques of their respective countries, Angkarn's poetry emerges as more socially conservative and nationalist. By contrast, Ginsberg's work is famously unpatriotic—consistently posing radical challenges not only to US politics, but also to the very foundations of heteronormative, bourgeois convention.

While Angkarn's and Ginsberg's more discernible political orientations diverge, their work converges around the ways in which they center Buddhism in their poetry and their opposition to US Cold War politics, as well as shared aesthetic concerns. Both create poetic ontologies that reach beyond the quotidian Realpolitik of their times, integrating Buddhism into an everyday world as well as creating radically egalitarian ontologies and intellectual politics. Such an analysis of convergence can ultimately complicate also current, schematic understandings of the ideological contours of the work of Thai writers during the Cold War.

What the Thai and American poet might further have in common is that, rather than being "merely" modernist—like the (in part, co-opted) liberal cultural left in their respective countries—these poets proffer a more radical cultural-political critique. While official Buddhisms were compromised on a large scale during the Cold War in Thailand—a project that included explicit CIA involvement[2]—the two poets under consideration use Buddhist tropes to expand the temporal, lexical, and ontological dimensions of their work, and this is what furnishes the most consequential basis of their critique. In this context, I investigate Mahayana and Vajrayana Buddhism's ability to furnish frameworks for counterpolitical and countercultural thought across these two global locations.

Across the divergent contexts of Thailand and the United States, Mahayana and Vajrayana Buddhist tropes of decentering the self come to represent switch points that function as scaling tools and are able to adjudicate contradictions within the status of subjectivity from the 1950s through the 1980s. In both Ginsberg's and Angkarn's work, we find mobile notions of the self, in which this self inhabits various "high" and "low" statuses and expanded temporalities. It is notions of Bodhisattvahood and *śūnyatā*, especially, that enable this mobility within, and scaling of, time.

The Fact of Translation: The Encounter

When I began to think about the transnational import of Angkarn's work, I recalled having seen a translation by Ginsberg of Angkarn's "Scoop Up the Sea" as early as in the 1980s—a fact I had noted with curiosity, but not given much thought to since. After a more thorough search, I found that translations of Angkarn's poems "The Poet's Testament" (1959), "Scoop

Up the Sea" (1952), and "I Lost You" (1964) all bear Ginsberg's name as translator. How did these two poets, who lived on different continents and inhabited seemingly entirely different linguistic and literary worlds, come to encounter each other? Bill Morgan's comprehensive Ginsberg bibliography records only a single textual connection, listing Ginsberg's contribution of his translation of Angkarn's 1964 poem "Sia Jao" ("I Lost You") to the American journal *International Portland Review* in 1980.[3] The translations of the other two poems are not registered transnationally; both are found only in compilations published in Thailand.[4]

A short passage in the biography of Angkarn written by his daughter, Ormkaew Kallayanapong, records that an actual encounter between the Thai and the American poet took place. Ormkaew, who was born in the 1980s, writes that she was told that Ginsberg came to Thailand and asked to meet with "Thai Beat poets." The public intellectual and longtime supporter of Angkarn, Sulak Sivaraksa, then took Ginsberg to meet Angkarn.[5] This is the only extant record of the two poets actually meeting.

When thinking about what might have attracted Ginsberg to Angkarn's work and what unites their poetological concerns, a number of commonalities stand out. In conjunction with their shared aesthetic concerns and critical focus on a Southeast Asia dominated by US foreign policy in the 1960s and after, both Angkarn and Ginsberg emerge as Cold War poets who develop extensive vocabularies of disaffection with regard to the political present that they live in. In response to the unbearable parameters of their respective historical situations, both rely on making the imaginaries especially of Mahayana Buddhism available to coping with an everyday world in which Buddhism usually does not have—or no longer has—a place.

Tracking Ginsberg's Journey to Southeast Asia

Allen Ginsberg's work and life are much better documented than those of Angkarn. I began to search for Ginsberg's possible connections to Angkarn, Thailand, and Southeast Asia in library databases and on the internet, and ultimately contacted the Stanford University library, which owns the largest collection of Ginsberg's papers. At the Ginsberg Foundation, I contacted Ginsberg's longtime friend and assistant, Peter Hale. In August 2016, Hale found the bibliographic reference to Ginsberg's translation of "I Lost You" for me. In an email, he also confirmed Ginsberg's physical presence in

Thailand in 1963: "Allen stopped through Thailand in May or June 1963 on his way home from India. That's most likely when they [Angkarn and Ginsberg] would have met or made the translations."[6]

Later in August 2016, I received the first of three emails from Tim Noakes, head of Public Services at Stanford Library's Special Collections.[7] He had searched the boxes that might be relevant to Ginsberg's connection with Thailand and found as yet unpublished journal entries of Ginsberg from Southeast Asia, including Thailand, as well as drafts of poems that the poet later went on to publish. It is an exciting find that proves Ginsberg's presence in Bangkok and includes materials that document his impressions of the city and other locations in the region.

The journal begins in Bangkok. The first two pages consist of an entry from May 28, 1963.[8] The next entry from Bangkok consists only of a heading, "May 29—Bankok—The National Museum Sukothai Style." The next, long entry recounts a dream while still in Bangkok. The entry that follows is from Saigon, on May 31–June 1, 1962 [sic; should be 1963] and includes Ginsberg's draft of his poem "Understand That This Is a Dream."[9] Two other Saigon entries are from June 3 and June 5, 1963; that of June 7 is from "Ankor Wat," Cambodia. The last roughly twenty pages of the thirty-five-page scan are taken up by Ginsberg's draft for his poem "Angkor Wat."

Ginsberg's impressions from Bangkok are evocative of a lively city that is transforming under the influence of global Cold War policies and enmeshed in burgeoning wartime economies. The way in which Ginsberg's work brings together mundane and religio-cosmological worlds becomes clear in his delineations of Bangkok, which are jotted down in short phrases without clear verbs or definite subject-verb alignment. This is a mode of expression that he will intensify in his famous poem "Angkor Wat," composed shortly thereafter. The following is Ginsberg's typewritten entry from Bangkok:[10]

Bankok—May 28, '63

Chinese meats red hanging in Shops—Grillwork & old wood—
the river & Dawn Temple across bordered by palmtrees, shanties,
rowboats—Downtown money changers—King Rama VI Statue,
the pedestal at night a park circle of grass, music piped thru
to moderne loudspeaker rock & roll & boys lounging on grass
or the steps of the Statue, in blue pants & lightweight neat

shirts, effeminite or Chinese modern faced in short haircuts black locks & jeans—the motorcycle cab driver—I can get you boy 100 bats—pavilions & sloped azure roofs of Palace Chapels—stone Chinese sages with flowing beards and round ball pop-eyes standing guard at the gates—giant enameled statues—mosaic of old teacups their eyes—tacky Castle & Church—The Siamese Dances in de luxe little theater—a green masked beast I was high slithered his arm in symmetry with the Hero at they battled—one beast danced in Siam—Boxing their yellow boys in red and blue tights scampering around ring surrounded by front seat white haired tourist—Cezanne's dollike card player was there too—snapping pictures & lurching in his seat—kicking the boxers each other on the chin—in the belley—Long walk along arcades of Military main street deserted SEATO avenues across from the tourist office by the Monument to Democracy, wings of Concrete soaring in air, around traffic circle—big motorcycle cabs bumping in and out of bus streets—on long highways thru town, past the Rama Hotel Past Club 99 where soldier-dressed youths wait neatly at the door—clubs with dark interiors seen thru the window—Hotel Silom Thai, the dim light now hurts my eyes to read in, turn on the light and the brown-ness of the room goes a degree lighter brown, the boy went out for Morphia—"plaintive boy crys drift" thru the Bankok Park—a fleshy town, much meat to murch, as Sukyaki Chinese pork or prick suck evening in bed for $2.50 yellow skin smoth & hairless almost pubes like an adolescent Breast pressed to my belly the other evening, first nite I was here asking about my eating viands freely & the ghost sex rising in my loins. And a huge golden Budaha reclining in temple big as a ship.

Ginsberg's account of his brief sojourn in Bangkok is an enmeshed one, replete with religion, drugs, sex, politics, and war. The excerpt's exoticization of Thai male bodies deserves an analysis of its own—as does the self-criticism that pervades Ginsberg's descriptions of his experiences in Southeast Asia. My focus here however lies on the poet's identification of the signs of US imperialism in the region and on the style of his prose. His next stop is Saigon in June and then Siem Reap in Cambodia. His entire journal reflects the atmosphere of an already war-torn region.

Thus, the Bangkok entry references the Southeast Asia Treaty Organization (SEATO), a Cold War military alliance headquartered in Bangkok. Ginsberg describes what is probably Rajdamnern Avenue as a "military avenue" as well as "soldier-dressed youths" queuing at a sex hotel, "Club 99." War is a business everywhere in Southeast Asia, as is visible in 1960s Thailand, the primary ally of the United States in the Vietnam War, which the journal describes so vividly.

Ginsberg's entry is not disapproving of this city in which, as he describes it, religion, drugs, sex, and politics blend. He registers the fact of the availability of "boys" for (little) money—perhaps with some surprise—but later makes use of this service himself. This city with its dense sensual impressions seems rather to interest and appeal to the poet. We know from Ginsberg's larger oeuvre, however, that he was acutely critical of US military action in Thailand and Southeast Asia. This critique of US involvement in Thailand becomes most explicit in his poem "CIA Dope Calypso" from 1972, which exposes that agency's drug politics in Thailand and its vicinity.[11] Ginsberg contributed toward uncovering these connections, and the poem was based on his research in newspaper and policy archives and reveals the names of several of those involved in the CIA's drug enterprise.[12]

This same fact of a Thailand dominated by US foreign policy, military collaboration, and cultural influence is exactly the circumstance that Angkarn's poetry so frequently laments. However, his is not only a political complaint. Rather, Bangkok also more generally exemplifies a condition of urban dissoluteness for the Thai poet. A good example can be found in his complaint about modern Bangkok in "Benjasin"—"Five Precepts":

> Capital city, trendy Bangkok, refuse of the heavens,
> Chameleons, lizards, huge lice are sure to creep there.
> All of a sudden frogs and toads are masters, vulgarly
>   moving and flying on and on.
> Fatiguing, this region of the waste of Siam.[13]

While the two poets' critiques converge around their opposition to US Cold War politics, they also share aesthetic and conceptual concerns. These have mostly to do with the Hindu-Buddhist ontologies that Angkarn and Ginsberg invent for the present. But their work evinces parallels also in syntax and poetic style. The notion of surrealism is frequently used to describe both Angkarn's and Ginsberg's work.[14] What critics mean by this designation is the way in which both poets bring together mundane and religio-cosmological worlds, integrating the supraworldly into scenes of everyday life. We were able to discern some of this quality in the impressions of Bangkok that Ginsberg records in short phrases: his journal entry reads like a list of densely enumerated characteristics of a familiar-exotic location. Thus, even the syntax of the entry gives the reader the impression of a place in which multiple sensory impressions and ontological strata coalesce. In the Bangkok entry, "Chinese meats red," the "Dawn Temple," "rock & roll," "boys," "SEATO," and "a huge golden Budaha" all appear in proximity to one another. The phrases without clear verbs, or definite subject-verb alignment, of Ginsberg's impressions of Bangkok are reminiscent also of the syntax of Angkarn's poetry. This compatibility regarding diction and the centrality of religious-derived imaginaries in the work of both poets may be indicative of global convergences in artistic interest and style from the 1960s onward.

In the decades during which Angkarn and Ginsberg write, the intensified invocation of the religio-cosmological in conjunction with everyday matters is unusual also in Thailand and at first appears jarring to readers. In Angkarn's case, the accusation that his poetry transgresses traditional metrics and uses vulgar language compounds this effect. In the case of Ginsberg's work, it is the poet's irreverence toward conventions of heteronormativity and patriotism that shocks a conservative American public. As Gayathri Prabhu writes, "The resurgence of capitalism in America following the Second World War with its 'all-consuming work ethic, sexual repression, cultural xenophobia, militaristic patriotism, and suburban materialism'[15] brought the accompanying realisation of spiritual bankruptcy' and prompted the Beat poets' forceful interventions.[16]

To counter the trends of a deplorable present, both Ginsberg and Angkarn invented radically egalitarian ontologies. These come to the fore also in the alternative understanding of knowledge and education that they developed. Both poets not only had the experience of seeing their work vilified, they moreover had histories of being expelled from or dropping out of institutions of higher learning (Ginsberg from Columbia University and Angkarn from Silpakorn University). In response to this experience, and as part of their respective alternative worldviews, both create learned cultures that are not dependent on institutions. Angkarn's work, especially, undertakes such a reformulation of knowledge cultures and addresses the question of access to noninstitutionalized learning very explicitly.

Transnational Buddhist Poetic Ontologies

While the previous chapter investigated the ways in which the transnational quality of Angkarn's poetry finds evidence in the composition of his poetic lexicon and in his thematic concerns, the renditions of his poetry into English by the American poet are rare, unexpected instances of this poetry's actual transnational circulation. "Wak Thale" ("Scoop Up the Sea," 1952) is the earliest of Angkarn's poems translated into English by Ginsberg. In an interview, Sulak Sivaraksa confirms that he translated Angkarn's poems on the spot, and Ginsberg then put them in his own language, improvising on Sulak's translation.[17] Ginsberg's translation follows:

> Take seawater Put in a plate Eat it with white rice
> Collect some stars mix with salt for eating
> Watching crabs and shellfish singing pretty
> Insects crawling on two feet flap upward to eat sun and moon
> Wart toads high on gold palanquins fly up to see Heaven
> Smooth frogs going along on the trip while devas hide in coconutshells
> Rain worms make love with girls Sleeping nights with them in the sky
> Millions of cells and amoebas lift their heads and get rich
> The angels are sick of their skies and jump down to earth to eat shit
> Enjoy faeces the taste, They can't find words for it
> Forest creepers and trees talk about deep philosophy
> Sawdust in the dream calculates the weight of shadow
> Those who are afraid to go Heavenly and stay down on earth are acting silly
> As the heavy stuff gets lighter there'll be the greatest drunkenness.[18]

For different reasons, Angkarn and Ginsberg both became disenchanted with an increasingly rationalized, violent present and sought to remedy the dereliction they observed through expansions—and inversions—of the ontological horizons of their worlds. We can see how the intermingling of heaven, feces, forest creepers, philosophy, and wart toads in Angkarn's poem would resonate with Ginsberg's own renditions of the world, which also construct ontologies that combine the religio-mythical with the everyday. According to Jane Augustine, it was from Vajrayana Buddhism that Ginsberg derived his penchant for seeing all things as equal:

> "Worms" with its Biblical ring—"I am a worm and no man"—becomes a favored Ginsberg word along with angel, heaven and soul to express flesh and spirit, rotten messiness and inspired vision as indiscriminately and appreciatively mixed.[19]

This kind of ontology, in which different levels of nature, the cosmos, animals, and human beings merge, is highly compatible with that outlined in Angkarn's work. Augustine details how even Ginsberg's pre-Buddhist 1950 poem "The Terms in Which I Think of Reality" reveals early compatibility with a "Vajrayana view" when it asserts that "the world is a mountain / of shit," but ultimately resolves to build on the dereliction of the world, rather than to turn away from it: "A daring faith is revealed: the poem can take a handful of the world's shit and transform it."[20]

The reversals of "high" and "low" ontologies in Angkarn's poem "Scoop Up the Sea," as angels "jump down to earth to eat shit," are just as much the Thai poet's formulation as they are evocative of the style Ginsberg frequently uses to characterize US postwar life in his poetry. Augustine identifies this tendency already in Ginsberg's 1955–1956 poem "Howl": "In this explosive yet celebratory cry of pain, Ginsberg fuses language, memory and free-associative consciousness of the human realities. He never forgets suffering; it is the basic engine that drives his compassionate protest."[21]

What is more, the syntax of Angkarn's "Scoop Up the Sea," as rendered by Ginsberg, mirrors some of Ginsberg's own stream of consciousness-like writing that is evident in his journal entries as well as in his poetry. Parts of Ginsberg's journal entry from Bangkok read like a list, with longer phrases strewn in that describe distinct actions. In parallel to his rendition of "Scoop Up the Sea," Ginsberg's journal entry also presents an enumeration that relies on continuous forms of the verb in order to transmit immediacy.

While parts of Ginsberg's rendition of "Scoop Up the Sea" bear the impression of a draft, especially in how the stanzas are arranged on the page, S. Sivaraksa and H. Woodward's translation of the poem into English appears more finalized. Like Ginsberg's, this translation is able to convey the blend of worldly and supraworldly elements of Angkarn's poetry to the English-language reader:

Scoop up the sea, pour it in a bowl,
and dine on it and rice,
reach out, gather some stars,
and mix them with salt to eat,
Look at crabs and oysters dancing with joy
and playing nostalgic songs,
or chameleons and galley worms flying
to eat the sun and moon!

A toad climbs on a golden palanquin
and floats around Heaven on a special tour.
He goes together with a bull frog,
and the angels there escape, into the shell of a coconut.

Earthworms woo maids,
the Apsaras who sleep in Heaven,
and every amoeba
sticks up his nose because of his very
high status.

The gods are bored with celestial abodes
so leap down to eat the dung on earth.
This waste matter they praise,
for its taste is most splendid and can't
be described.

Groves of trees and forests
can talk deep philosophy.
Sawdust in its sleep
can calculate the weight of shadows.

Anyone who doesn't go up to Heaven
and remains below on earth is stupid,
for the heavy would be light,
and the world is very, very drunk.[22]

Both renditions of "Scoop Up the Sea" are able to transmit to English-language readers some of the fantasy character, or even psychedelic quality, of Angkarn's poem in Thai—as well as its transnational modernity. In both renditions, the poem features a contemporary vocabulary and addresses issues of transnational, universal concern. Yet it does so with a particular, localized inflection. The translation by Sulak and Woodward even retains the word *apsara* to signal the poem's participation in a Thai-Sanskritic cultural imaginary. This is a term that could just as well appear in a poem by Ginsberg, pointing to the ways in which a Buddhist-Hindu cultural imaginary attains transnational legibility during the latter half of the twentieth century.

The next poem of which Ginsberg produced a partial translation or reformulation is Angkarn's 1959 "Panithan Khong Kawi," which Ginsberg translates as "The Poet's Testament" (and I translate as "The Pledge of the Poet"):[23]

> I wrap the sky around myself
> to keep away the cold
> and eat starlight late at night
> to take the place of rice.
> Dew drops scatter below the sky
> for me to find and drink,
> and out my poems flow
> to greet the morn, to last the age.
> My heart, sacrificed to its grave,
> gains unworldly powers;
> the spirit flies to lands of dreams
> the far side of the sky.
> It seeks divinity in Heaven and brings it back to earth
> to soothe the sand and grass,
> bringing happiness, bringing peace.
> My purpose in composing poems
> is to salvage the soul.[24]

What comes as a surprise in Ginsberg's English rendition of the "Testament" is the relatively conventional way in which the poet formulates this eccentric, multiworld manifesto for poetic creation. In particular, the regularity of the poem's rhythm in English and the conventionality of the syntax stand out. Sounding more subdued than Angkarn's original, it brings a new, more sober tone to the world-inverting original *panithan*, or vow, of Angkarn.

Finally, there is the Ginsbergian rendition of "Sia Jao" ("I Lost You"), which he contributed to the 1980 issue of the *International Portland Review*. How the translation of "Sia Jao" came about is the least fathomable, since

Angkarn only wrote, or published, the poem in 1964, when Ginsberg had already left Thailand:

> A rainbow jewel—it cracked when I lost you.
> Who and what in the world is there to want?
> Not even hoping for the sky, my face
> pressed upon the earth in grief, I eat sand.
>
> From this world to the next, this pain will stay;
> its traces will not dissipate or fade.
> However many lives I'll have to suffer,
> I'll never give my heart to you again.
>
> If you are born in Heaven, I shall request
> to descend to Hell, where I'd rather burn.
> You are the fire and flames, I, only wood.
> You may consume me all, even my soul.
>
> Though those ashes haven't any desire
> for you, nor will they have for evermore,
> if, we chance to meet in a future life
> I'll scoop out my eyes and cast them away.
>
> Dead, I'll go and lie below your footstep.
> Trample on me then, as you would on grass,
> so I shan't forget the gall or bruises
> as long as there's an earth or there's a sky! Oei![25]

Ginsberg's rendering of "Sia Jao" is particularly interesting because it brings the poem into conventional yet beautiful English. It does not render the poem very literally, nor does it attempt to retain its Thainess through reproducing terms in Thai or approximating its context and lexicon through Buddhist terms. However, the conventionality of the poem's English is at the end supplemented by the untranslated Thai exclamation "Oei!," giving the poem a final, quintessentially Thai flavor. The fact that "Sia Jao" also "works" within the framework of its more conventional English rendition suggests that what is most strongly operative in the poem is the usage of cosmology as an intensifier of emotion—a feature of "Sia Jao" that the translation is able to capture, even if it is not able to transmit all nuances of expression and tone.

Angkor Wat: A Political Journey

Returning to Ginsberg's journal account of his trip to Southeast Asia, we read that after his brief sojourn in Bangkok, he makes a stop in Saigon. Here he comes into even closer contact with overt US military action, or at least that is his perception. The poet senses the violent military activities of the United States in the region acutely and, waking up from an anxiety dream in Saigon on June 5, 1963, asks himself: "Am I coward? Nervous stomach in Saigon not wanting to go to helicopter battlefields in rice paddies & watch Chinese bodies be blown apart?"[26] This is his primary association with Vietnam, an association that speaks to his strong and principled opposition to the US war against this country. Two days later, in Angkor Wat, on June 7, 1963, this sense of military devastation is still with Ginsberg as he speaks of a

> foreboding of—what I left behind in dreams of Ganges vegetarian gentleness or cow-stake fires of unseen Mehong [sic] Murder + blister gases of Here all over the High School students on the wireless telephone.
> The streets crowded with fat army cannibals gentle in bars with long haired Chinese ladies & Jazz & sports shirts in window and the jewish correspondents eating Chinese sweet & sour spy meat.[27]

Ginsberg renders the scenes of military intervention as well as military "rest and recreation" in the region with what reads like accuracy, including details of the sonic and visual properties of the scene and the sartorial style of the social actors involved. His Southeast Asia is marked not only by military activity but also by a large new economy—that includes commercial sex—that is attached to the military intervention. US military action in Southeast Asia brings with it not only casualties, but also a pervasive culture of consumption, transacting business, and relating.

The well-known poem that Ginsberg writes during his sojourn in Cambodia, "Angkor Wat," is a long one; in its printed version in the anthology, *Collected Poems, 1947–1997*, it is eighteen pages long.[28] Tony Trigilio understands the language and diction of the poem to exemplify the "poetics of a hybridized American Buddhism" and describes it as prophetic.[29] The prophetic quality of Ginsberg's poem is directly related to the geocultural landscape that he travels through: "Prophetic language in 'Angkor Wat' is primordial, as poetic speech authorized by the Buddhist statuary in the Angkor temple complex."[30] Though set in the premodern cosmopolitan landscape of the temple complexes in Siem Reap, the poem's prophetic import largely relates to the political affairs of the day. As Trigilio further writes, "'Angkor Wat' anticipates the significance of the US war in Vietnam and reconceives the growing military presence there in 1963 as a symptom of imperialism."[31] The poem begins as a drug-saturated trip through Hindu-Buddhist cosmology as Ginsberg sightsees and travels through the edifices of Angkor. However, his consciousness of the war breaks into the account again and again. Helicopters, bullets, spies, US pre-Nixon policy toward China, the murderous imperial imaginary and military actions ("the bodies of the Viet Cong piled on the tank"), and world political figures such as Eisenhower and Sihanouk keep interrupting his narration of the impressions from the temples.[32] "Angkor Wat" skillfully enacts the violence of American military activity in Southeast Asia, prompting the reader to understand this violence as the predominant cultural and political paradigm of the era. Trigilio understands Ginsberg's indictment of US politics as organized by the metaphor of illness and the Buddhist framework that Ginsberg proposes as a redemptive measure: "The sick physical body is a trope for the nationalist illness Ginsberg perceives in the impulse to colonize. In 'Angkor Wat' Ginsberg conceives a samatha-vipassana attentive language for representing the early history of American involvement in Vietnam."[33]

In this poem we can detect also the similarity of Ginsberg's use of Buddhism and language with Angkarn's. Like the Thai poet's, Ginsberg's Buddhist poetics likewise emerge as an oppositional aesthetics in a contemporaneous Cold War context. Trigilio argues that "Ginsberg deployed Buddhism to foreground political questions of agency in a liberatory, neoromanticist discourse."[34] He further understands the intent of Ginsberg's fragmentary, stream-of-consciousness style to be one of systematic political critique: "As a response to the univocal authority of US expansionism, the poem takes shape in disjunctive, collage lines whose multiple voices at times are at cross purposes with each other. Significantly, this collage form voices itself as counterstatements to US policies at the same time that the speaker doubts the authority of his own poetics."[35]

Ginsberg's critique of the US imperial project is consistently paralleled by his inquiry into selfhood, his Buddhist poetics developed in relation to a political and personal challenge. Thus, his critique of Cold War politics always goes hand in hand with a critique of self: "Ginsberg's obsession with the illnesses of his physical body and the American body politic enact narcissism as the nationalist illness that samatha-vipassana might cure."[36]

The scenes of imperial-military violence that Ginsberg details in "Angkor Wat" are largely derived from his awareness of world politics and associative thought, rather than from direct experience. However, the poet's repeated attention to international journalists gathered at the bars in the cities of the war-torn region gives his accounts immediacy, attesting to the iniquity of the war—refuting the denials circulated through right-wing ideology and anticommunist sentiment—as well as marking again and again the fact that the war is *in progress*:

> All the wire services eating sweet and
> sour pork and fresh lichee white-meat
> in sugarwater—
> Discussing the manly truth Gee Fellers—[37]

As in Ginsberg's journal entry, the repeated observation of the presence and activities of journalists in the poems amounts to a secondhand witnessing—as the poet provides testimony of the war economy in all its aspects.

Political Orientations

While Angkarn's and Ginsberg's critiques converge around innovative, oppositional aesthetics and their disaffection with the Cold War in Southeast Asia, their explicit political orientations diverge. As discussed in the previous chapters, Angkarn's critique focuses largely on cultural influences. While the poet was frequently accused of not engaging with 1970s Thai politics, his political orientation remains more complex than what has been alleged. Although he does not address the uprisings and state violence directly in his work of the 1970s, we saw in chapter 4 that he broadly impugns dictators and the violence perpetrated by their regimes in some of his poems of this era.

It may come as a surprise that in a number of his later poems, Angkarn reveals himself as a fervent defender of democratic rights. A poem written for the twenty-fifth anniversary in 1998 of the October 14, 1973, uprising, "Sith Isara Seri Khong Puang Pracharat—Prakat Jetanarom 14 Tula Udomsith Isara" ("The People's Right to Freedom—Statement of Intention 14 October Rights and Freedom") contains such impassioned political expression:[38]

> All humanity, gems of freedom,
> As the sun's majestic beauty in the sky,
> Free, like the Bodhisattva's heart,
> For eternal heavenly peace.
>
> The people, savvy, rise up,
> Awake, demand rights and freedom of the age returned,
> Refuse to submit to dictatorship,
> Democracy rules the land.
>
> A real human needs to rule himself,
> Don't be in fear, under anyone's sole,
> Dictators, bloodthirsty, making tears flow,
> Depraved, inauspicious, accustomed to exploiting Thailand.
>
> The dignity of the People-subjects,
> Powerful unity of civilized disposition,
> When society is just and freedom wins,
> The new society shines with every soul.
>
> The rights and freedom of the People,
> The power to rule oneself, magnificently,
> "Peaceful justice of the People," wonderful throughout time,
> Brave in its justice.
>
> The miraculous rights and freedom,
> Vested in the People, most wonderful,
> Siam's dignity propelled by consciousness,
> *Dharma* leading the world to eternal peace.

Like the Art for Life poets, Angkarn uses the lexica and concepts of democracy in this poem. However, he varies the deployment of this lexicon in significant ways through new compounding: thus *pracharat*—"People-subjects" both points to democratic notions of sovereignty and retains an element that supersedes the mundane plane of secular political action. Although the poet is not a royalist, *rat* in his concoction renders the people beholden to some higher power that is not merely that of the state and participatory democracy. This exalted-democratic conceptualization is further supplemented by a *dhammic* component, a move that we already witnessed in the poem by Khomthuan Khanthanu discussed in chapter 4.

Biographic data again aids in the assessment of the political bent of Angkarn's poetry. The poet's daughter Ormkaew confirms Angkarn's strong democratic inclinations and opposition to the military dictatorships of the 1970s.[39] Sulak Sivaraksa also notes the poet's opposition to the establishment of the day and adds that regarding the violence of October 14, 1973, Angkarn "was on the side of justice; he shaved his head, cried, was very much on the side of the people."[40] In 2003, he is further recorded as taking part in a memorial event for the thirtieth anniversary of the October 1973 massacre.[41] And in 2008 he writes a poem titled "Oh Hok Tula Maha-amahit"—"Oh Brutal Sixth of October," referring to the Thai state's ruthless suppression of the 1976 uprising.[42] Three drawings of Angkarn's titled *Melting Men* from 1976, on exhibition in the National Gallery in Singapore, add further evidence for the notion that the poet was far from indifferent to the events of the two Octobers in the 1970s. A "panegyric" to democracy after Bangkok's "Bloody May" in 1992 completes these impressions.[43]

The three drawings of the *Melting Men*, one of which is featured on the cover of this book, are especially intriguing, because they are dated to 1976. Even without explicit knowledge of author intention, the paintings can be understood to embody the victims of state violence of that year, or to capture a more abstract sense of loss subsequent to the antidemocratic violence of 1973 and 1976. When read together with the "October" poems, we can take the *Melting Men* to point to the poet's serious concern with the state of political repression in Thailand in the 1970s and after.

While we can understand Angkarn and Ginsberg's political concerns to overlap at several points, Angkarn's poetry remains the more socially conservative. For one, sexuality or desire do not appear often in his poems—and when they do appear, they are frequently disparaged, in a doctrinal Buddhist vein, as undesirable "craving." Thus, Angkarn tends to condemn most excesses of personal desire. And, while the Thai poet frequently expresses nationalist sentiments, Ginsberg's work is unpatriotic and poses radical challenges to US politics and bourgeois convention.

Buddhisms

Both poets turned to Buddhism as a system of thought and representation that afforded ways out of the impasses of their respective presents. In both poets' oeuvres, Buddhism enables the expansion of ontological frameworks and, by extension, of the possibilities of aesthetic and political expression. Angkarn was Buddhist almost by default, by virtue of Thailand's deployment of Buddhism as its de facto national religion; yet the poet's heightened attention to Buddhist philosophy was anything but default and represents an unusual engagement with the religion. Angkarn was not only devout, however, but rather struggled with making the precepts and dictates of the religion available to the resolution of quandaries in contemporary Thai life.

Ginsberg had to seek Buddhism out; he became interested in it as another way of expanding experience and knowledge. Gradually he became a dedicated student and practitioner of Buddhism. Erik Mortensen writes of the grounds on which Buddhism became popular in the United States during Ginsberg's lifetime and of the reasons that Ginsberg and Jack Kerouac were attracted to it:

> Kerouac and Ginsberg were at the vanguard of a Beat movement that sought to replace a rigid and materialistic postwar America with a spontaneous, Beat lifestyle. Doubtless, then, that Zen appealed to them as a breath of fresh air in a stultifying 1950s society. But Buddhism offered Kerouac and Ginsberg something more—a completely new relationship to their own selves.[44]

Mortensen further notes the central role that the notion of *śūnyatā*, emptiness, plays in Ginsberg's work:

> The Buddhist stillpoint thus offers Kerouac and Ginsberg a means of jettisoning their smaller, more ego-driven selves in exchange for a conception of self that expands their connection to the universe. Yet how is this stillpoint achieved? The road to "big mind" leads through the notion of emptiness, or what Buddhism terms "sunyata."[45]

This Buddhist concept provided the opportunity to mobilize a very different temporality within the present—one that could break open the apparent unity and validity of the "homogeneous empty time" of Cold War political rationality and its attendant aesthetic imaginaries.⁴⁶ Here Buddhism becomes responsible not merely for ethical-philosophical guidance, but also for providing an expanded vocabulary for cultural critique as well as for achieving shifts in scale and perspective. Mortensen continuously stresses the degree to which the Beat poets' political and cultural critique at the time relied also on a thorough reformulation of the position of the self. He highlights especially the particular way in which Ginsberg was able to inhabit the concept of an "empty" self. Rather than conceive of *śūnyatā* as something outside of the self, he understood emptiness as something integral to subjectivity:

> Buddhist sunyata is not conceived of as another realm standing outside subjectivity that confronts the self with an abyss. Rather, it is an innermost possibility that lies dormant within everyone, waiting for the self to seize it.⁴⁷

In chapter 2 we saw that Angkarn, too, vitally relies on the notion of *śūnyatā* to resolve contradictions regarding the endurance or nonendurance of the self. And in parallel to Mortensen's assertion of *śūnyatā*'s nonexternality to world and self, Angkarn was also shown to fold Buddhist (nibbanic) temporalities into worldly ones and thereby to draw Buddhist soteriological possibility into the reach of laypersons.

A further commonality of Angkarn's and Ginsberg's work is the understanding of their writerly vocation as the work of Bodhisattvas. As Augustine writes,

> Ginsberg took the basic vow of refuge in Buddha, Dharma and Sangha—that is, in the teacher, the teachings and the students, potentially all sentient beings—and the Mahayana bodhisattva vow not to give up working to benefit beings until all are free from suffering and have attained enlightenment.⁴⁸

In terms of the public recognition he received, this quest may have succeeded in Ginsberg's case and estimation. By the time Ginsberg was dying in 1997 he was widely known and, according to Augustine, had "not only changed poetry but the language and life of America itself," a queer, left, entirely irreverent Bodhisattva. In his April 1997 poem "Death & Fame," Ginsberg imagines his own funeral: "Everyone knew they were part of 'History' except the deceased who never knew exactly what was happening even when I was alive (DF 68–70)."[49] Augustine writes, "It is a modest ending to a poem and a life, though he is pleased to see that through poetry he carried out the bodhisattva vow."[50]

For Angkarn, Suchitra notes the centrality of the notion of Bodhisattvahood to his ontological-soteriological framework in which art assumes the status of a religion and the poet that of redeemer. Across two different global locations, Bodhisattvahood thus comes to represent a switch point that is able to subsume and adjudicate contradictions within the status of subjectivity.

In both Ginsberg's and Angkarn's work, we thus find mobile notions of the self, in which the self inhabits various high and low statuses—in Ginsberg's case a mobility rendered also through humor and self-deprecation. In both cases, it is notions of *śūnyatā* and Bodhisattvahood that enable this mobility and these inversions of self and ontology.

In *Phuthatham Nai Kawiniphon Samai Mai* (Buddha Dharma in Modern Thai Poetry), Suchitra Chongstitvatana testifies to the Mahayana influences in the work of a number of Thai poets via the philosophy of Buddhadasa Bhikkhu. Thus, she claims Angkarn Kallayanapong as a poet who is not a disciple of Buddhadasa but is indirectly influenced by this thinker's concept of "nature-as-*dharma*." As Suchitra writes of Buddhadasa, "the concept of nature-as-*dharma* can be said to be an important influence of Buddhadasa Bhikkhu's that is presented clearly in both his prose and poetry."[51] Buddhadasa is also a writer-thinker who explicitly addresses and makes available to Thai Buddhist thought notions of *śūnyatā*.[52]

While Angkarn's work can thus be said to evince parallels with the philosophy of Buddhadasa, Ormkaew attributes Angkarn's stance on the redemptive artistic vocation of the Bodhisattva to multiple sources rather than to the thought of Buddhadasa. She disputes any influence of Buddhadasa's work on her father. Instead she points out how widely read Angkarn was, delving into anything from Indian philosophy to books on Theravada as well as Mahayana Buddhism.[53] I do not want to adjudicate the dispute on the lines of influence in this context. Rather, I am interested in the fact that it is Mahayana-Vajrayana Buddhist notions that attain relevance of such global proportion during the periods in which these two poets write. I want to speculate on why this might be the case and what the notion of *śūnyatā* enabled these poets to express. I conjecture that *śūnyatā* functions as a kind of black box, a notion that enables the poets to entertain philosophical positions that espouse a "both . . . and" rather than only "either. . . or." In this way, *śūnyatā* allows also for a simultaneity of different temporalities.

The Buddhist cosmological dimensions in which Angkarn and Ginsberg challenged themselves to work were not only expansive, but also laid claim to universality. They proved elastic enough to provide frameworks for critique across vast geographic regions (Southeast Asia and the United States), political domains (a leftist, queer radical position and an in-part conservative, nationalist, yet postcolonial and cosmopolitan stance), and historical periods. Thus, Angkarn's cosmological cosmopolitanism is able to encompass everything from critique of Americanization and anti-intellectual tendencies in Thai society to remembrance of the losses of the 1970s and reiteration of *dhammic*-democratic ideals (such as in "Sith Isara Seri Khong Puang Pracharat" ["The People's Right to Freedom"]).

It thus seems as though both in the Southeast Asian and the US contexts of the 1950s–1980s, it was Mahayana and Vajrayana Buddhist elements that provided some of the most capacious frameworks for thinking about the vicissitudes of modernity and furnished conceptual ways out of the confines of societies that were restricted to technocratic developmentalist visions, on the one hand, and narrow moral and political paradigms, on the other. In both cases, Mahayana and Vajrayana Buddhism allowed for the development of frameworks that exceeded the national imaginaries of Thailand and the United States of the time. In the case of Angkarn, his Mahayana-influenced, Buddhist-derived visions of the world moreover remained prescient and broad enough to furnish an idiom that would accommodate a cultural—and at times explicitly political—critique that spanned several eras and was able to address accurately the quandaries of each historical period.

That Angkarn's conceptual framework remains capacious enough to allow for adaptation to new contexts and enable a continuous critique of globalization is also connected to its thematic reliance on temporality. In *What Is a World?*, Pheng Cheah addresses the centrality of temporality to postcolonial literary endeavors. Speaking of the "normative vocation of postcolonial world literature," he writes:

> Here, we encounter the intertwined issues of negotiating with capitalist modernity and opening up homogeneous empty time to heterotemporality as the formal problem of narration and, more specifically, as the crisis of narrating the postcolonial nation in contemporary globalization.[54]

Angkarn's conceptual framework aligns with the ideals for a transformative postcolonial literature outlined by Cheah. The Thai poet has put into practice the injunction that postcolonial writers not position heterotemporality as extraneous to modernity, capitalism, and the nation, but as erupting from within the seemingly homogeneous time stream of our present. This is the ideal that Angkarn's work has enacted for us. On the one hand, the poet has spoken from "inside" capitalist, global modernity. On the other hand, he has situated other temporalities—those of the cosmos, of nature as well as the variegated temporalities of Buddhism—within this very same modernity, attacking, modifying, and opening this problematic modernity up to a horizon beyond itself.

7

Conclusion

Performing a Redemptive Present

Angkarn wields the dimensions of Buddhist temporality with such command that he unsettles the seemingly inevitable forward progress of linear, developmentalist time. As he links the present to premodern and cosmic times, his poetry invokes dimensions that exceed the diminished timescape of the era and ethos that he contests. But the poet does not posit Buddhist time as entirely other to the rationalized temporalities of the present. Rather, he tweaks it to function as a resource for and from within the dispiriting present. Drawing on cultural resources that are distinct from the iniquitous Thai cultural present that he encounters as well as from those of a West that at times looms large in his critique, Angkarn creates a singular framework for modern literary and other artistic pursuits.

Bliss Lim has not only delineated the ways that divergent temporalities persist against the forcible rationalization of time in modernity, but also shown the degree to which heterotemporality contains historically reparative properties. Angkarn's poetry certainly aims for redemptive intercession into the oppressive present; however, the still greater strength of his poetry may lie in its performative cast. His work puts in motion divergent strata of time, makes vivid their chafing, and outlines in great detail the affects produced.

The sorrow, disdain, anger, and anguish in his writing and the ways in which individual struggle is dramatized make palpable the contradictions of a modern Thai existence that the poet identifies as intolerable. Angkarn delineates with clarity the incompatible demands made of persons at a time when economic logics begin to overdetermine all aspects of life. A large part of the criticality of his poetry then lies in its affective charge and the ways it plays out the dilemmas of time, self, and belonging of a complex Southeast Asian modernity.

Ontology

Throughout the poetry and poetic prose in which Angkarn highlights the theme of temporality, he has worked through Buddhist philosophical conceptions of time and made these available to theorizing the Thai present. He undertakes this act of parsing in the performative mode. On the one hand, he conveys great urgency for the fate of the individual and an entire culture that he deems to be on the brink of loss. On the other hand, taking the reader on whirlwind tours through vast dimensions of Buddhist cosmological time, the poet lays out the desirability of a redemptive imaginary. What my analysis showed his poetry to enact is both anxiety and the delineation of a path toward equanimity. We witness how Angkarn's poetry conjures an alternate modernity and seeks to counteract an impoverished present of discontinuity and misguided pursuits. In making Buddhist conceptions of time available to a thorough analysis of the adversities of the present, Angkarn is shown to have developed a type of philosophical speculation that exceeds that of doctrinal Buddhism.

History

Angkarn's work has taken us on a historical journey into the idealized early modern Ayuthaya period. The poet's pièce de résistance is his adaptation of the traditional *nirat* genre, whose conventions of love-longing he both pays homage to and transcends. Thus, he abstracts from the traditional individual lover of the *nirat* and transfers the affective force that is conventionally directed at this individual to a polity and artistic community. For the benefit of humanity in the present, his poetry resurrects an idealized Ayuthaya. The poet invokes notions of awe as he revives its historical sites and elaborates his own passionate attachment to the idea of this kingdom; at the same time, his historical poems play out anger and distaste over its loss. My analysis of his reanimation of Ayuthaya shows how Angkarn's work diverges from a contemporary literary scene that is

Conclusion 167

largely concerned with the modern nation; it also reveals the complexity of the poetic innovation that is this modern Thai poet's legacy. I draw attention to the poet's facility in making critical use of high cultural forms rather than only rural or popular traditions.

Subjectivity

The poet's delineations of the ways that both modern-capitalist and Buddhist temporalities limit and enhance human creativity and conduct are the focus of my analysis of Angkarn's manifestos, or *panithan*. Angkarn's poetological concerns thread through his entire oeuvre, finding especially fierce, compact expression in designated manifesto poems. The intensity of his devotion to the production of art occupied a central position in Thai literary criticism. Through time, Angkarn not only augmented his dedication to the production of art, but the linguistic and philosophical context that he mobilized to underwrite his notion of vocation also changed. The decade in which his poetry became more explicitly Buddhist, the 1980s, was one in which new conditions for subjectivity obtained. As the poet continued to rely on his unique ability to mobilize Buddhist thought for a distressed present, his work dramatized the struggle between the law of impermanence and the subject's desire for personal and artistic continuity. The poems moreover perform the continual crisis that results from a changing socioeconomic landscape. In tone and affect, they veer between notions of grandiosity, commitment to the collective good, and desires that contravene Buddhist orthodox tenets regarding self, time, and world.

Language

Despite its seemingly nationalist bent, Angkarn's work was shown to be distinctly transnational in character. This becomes evident in his preoccupation with poetological questions and the cultural losses of the twentieth century. I locate the performative quality of his work in the divergent lexica that his work brings into conversation. Angkarn expands a classical poetic lexicon to include the terminologies of an increasingly technocratic world; works with the juxtaposition of incommensurate vocabularies; and exploits the inherent grammatical features of Thai. The resultant poetics are immersed in a world defined by the institutions and relevance of science and technology and a society that is experiencing the shift from the national to the global and from industrial to finance capital. Angkarn is critical of this increasingly technocratic context, however. He does not merely accede to these changes passively, but engages these lexica in playful, subversive ways. Conversely, he renders the shift into a global age through a Buddhist and literary lexicon. This is not the invocation of a "traditional" imaginary per se, but rather one that he designs for and flaunts as a vocabulary *of the present*. Only when his poetry steps up its prescriptive Buddhist-culturalist rhetoric in the late 1980s does this strategy lose some of its appeal and appear more dogmatic in content and rigid in form. Angkarn's poems perform discord and anguish but also faith in a redemptive, cosmically infused imaginary. His linguistic innovation creates capacious concepts of temporality and thereby ushers in a present that can accommodate more notions of personhood, collectivity, and culture than those prescribed by an industrialized, capitalist world.

∾

With this dramatization of time in the domains of ontology, history, subjectivity, language, and the political, the poet disrupts the time of the nation and of capital. Angkarn's resacrilization of time is not so much an effort for the sake of the nation as for something that exceeds the modern-day geo-body and polity of Thailand. The desirable temporalities that he charts for Thai modernity are moreover distinct from European conceptions. His recuperative cultural agenda aims to assert difference from Western modernity rather than merely to claim contemporaneity.

Nevertheless, the vision that Angkarn presents is one that possesses relevance beyond the merely local. His poetry's movement away from the parochial "Bangkok" toward the cosmopolitan ideal of "Ayuthaya," especially, enacts an imaginary that eclipses the national. His very focus on the temporalities of culture and the losses of modernity in Thailand represent some of the most distinctly transnational concerns of his work. The paradoxes that Angkarn Kallayanapong stages in his writings from the 1950s until the 1980s present quandaries of a changing Southeast Asian present. But his reflections on the ruptures of this modernity are of global relevance; they are paralleled in other poetries and poetologies that pioneer new forms and integrate multiple levels of translation—such as Chinese prose poetry or the poetries of a Europe devastated by the Shoah. Thus, as much as we may read difference and a distinctly Thai and Buddhist poetics from Angkarn's work, we can always recognize in this Southeast Asian literary cosmopolitanism pressing global cultural and philosophical concerns.

Appendix

Translations of Angkarn Kallayanapong's Work on Time

Kawiniphon (Poetry, 1986 [1964])[1]

Panithan Khong Kawi (Pledge of the Poet, 1959)

I take the sky, wrap myself in it against the cold,
Late at night I eat rays of starlight instead of food.
Dew glittering under the skies I take for drink,
Streaming forth poetry from morning until the end of time.

I sacrifice my heart to become an ominous charnel ground,
My spirit goes far away to a dreamland on the side of heaven.
It seeks divine substance in heaven to bring to earth,
Soothes the sand planes, the blades of grass, so that the
　　world may know contentment.

Creating poetry to redeem the soul,
In the waves of the stream of time, swift and bold.
In a short time this life won't be.
The heart spews forth rays of divine substance, defiant, until
　　heaven and earth crumble.

Let the funeral pyre smolder, burning my body,
Kap poetry is not fragrant with the strength of the heart
　　anymore.[2]
Taking birth in whichever world, that world
The spirit will inundate with precious, lustrous divinity,
　　letting the essence of the gems of the age rain down.

Words move serenely, give pleasure,
Precious rain from heaven that puts out the heat.
The heart blows far away to dream in other worlds,
This fragrant world reflects the fragrance of the next.

I will consent to sacrificing and leaving behind life,
Hoping for precious things created anew, radiant.
May the science of poetry be sacred, the highest science,
Magical like a flower from the crystal forest, falling from the sky, fragrant.

Laeng Wanakhadi (Devoid of Literature, 1964)

Even if comparable to the stars, partners of the sky, months and years,
At one time one will be a shooting star.
Do not look down on the earth, trample it,
This place that hides diamonds of high value for the future.

Foul water caught in a pipe by the roadside,
May ascend to the sky as rain clouds.
Though lowly, it aims for supreme results,
Persevering in brilliant thought, soon ascending to heavenly dimensions.

Offer your still heart to peaceful bliss,
Write *kap, klon, khlong,* and *chan* poetry to put out the heat.
Tenaciously pursuing heaven, to offer to the world.
Fragrant with sorrow, bliss, and suffering, reflecting the real, sacred value of humanity.

Devoid of literature this life is
As though the auspicious spirit is no longer to be found.
Without the precious jeweled rainbow—
Light of the soul in the world.

Buying status and riches,
Flooding and feeding the charnel ground.
There to support the sky and the earth,
Desiring to restrain death.

Not understanding the earth and the sky,
Not knowing the real value of all things,
Bits and pieces of knowledge, stupidity, and intoxication,
Drifting toward death with the worthlessness of defeat.

Disgraceful for the soul,
Until indeterminate eternity, trembling,
Blind, without a vision to lead the heart,
Preposterous, in reality minute and transient.

Devoid of good people, Sri Ayuthaya,
Born to redeem bold and sacred knowledge,
Sacrificing, combating fate single-handedly,
That is more than can be hoped for, a shame.

AYUTHAYA (1957)

Ayuthaya, your status higher than heaven come down to earth,
The power and merit of the kings of old built
Beautiful *chedis*, palaces of Indra,[3]
Pure gold on the inside and outside.

Luminous fortress of Ayuthaya,
Beautiful gates, strong towers.
Ayuthaya, more than a valiant heavenly phenomenon, like the regions of the gods,
Very much like heaven to the eye.

O Ayuthaya, excellent place, greater than heaven.
You have fallen, brave soldiers are not to be found here anymore.
Wasting the energy of those expert craftsmen that created you,
Scores of wild animals came to aggravate you, ground you smooth, o great treasure.

Silenced, Phra Sri Sanphet rolls in the soil.[4]
Vultures, packs of dogs, and swarms of crows eat this side of heaven.

From the eyes of an apparition run tears of blood,
Flooding and flowing, caressing the world that has fallen, its
   city disappeared.

So, pulverized dauntless kingdom, ha ha,
O Ayuthaya, you resemble a burial ground.
Of the great heavenly place is left only the carcass,
Only human blood in this arid world, o deep shame.

O glorious Ayuthaya,
Tears flood the kingdom:
Decayed, fallen apart, suddenly mud,
Like a graveyard ill with mourning.

City of palaces, *stupas*, and castles,
Kingdom that was completely destroyed.
Only residue is left,
The soot and ashes of Thai bones.

Ayuthaya, o great domain,
Hell has come to destroy and burn your era.
Vultures, crows, and dogs are everywhere,
Destroying and eating all of the beloved terrain.

Sorrow for the art,
And magnificent civilization.
The kingdom is finished,
Sadly taking leave of the Thai ancestors.

The precious *stupa*, *bot*, and *vihan*,[5]
In pieces, still exceedingly beautiful.
The lotus on the pillar of the lion pedestal,
Everything pitifully destroyed.

Sri Sanphet, the great main hall,
Pulverized, Ratburana Mahathat,
Every temple, palace, and castle,
Of the dominion ruined, the Thai spirit destroyed.

The gravel, sand, and soil sob,
The cold ground of the precious city quivers.
The brick and mortar are decaying,
Gradually fading throughout the *kalpas*.[6]

The breast of the earth has tears,
For the burial ground of heaven.
The soul ponders and laments
Ominously year in year out.

The king, the former great ruler,
Cries loudly with the voice of a ghost.
With a long thundering noise, cheering on for victory,
His horses and elephants and scores of soldiers.

Flutes, gongs, and drums of victory,
Resound forsakenly.
Every tuft of grass suffers,
Sobbing until the end of time.

Sinlapa Ayuthaya (The Art of Ayuthaya, 1962)

Ayuthaya, like the graveyard of heaven:
The prosperous divine lotus,
The *kanok wan* pattern,[7]
Have fallen from the sky.
Have decomposed, have been ruined ominously,
Destroyed, fallen,
Dissolute and base, every blade of grass,
Flowing heavily with the tears of Siam.

O Ayuthaya, precious kingdom,
Your great sovereignty now fallen, burnt,
The castles and palaces suddenly
Like burial grounds and funeral pyres.

Phra Sri Sanphet has toppled,
Sunken into the fires of hell, severely destructive.

The precious *stupa*, the *bot* and Wihan Rachathan
Have collapsed to the sandy ground.

The voices of brave bones,
The leftover ashes still crying.
Scores of vultures, crows, and dogs
Tear into them repeatedly, bruising the soul.

The great former king,
Stamping his foot, letting the four directions tremble.
Many brave soldiers, elephants, and horses,
Eager, hastening to fight, resounding noisily, all over.

Nothing to be seen on the ground,
Nothing to be heard in the world.
The universe at the time of twilight
Is completely dark in all ten directions.

The precious forts and walls,
The place of worship compelling the heavens to dream,
Prosperous divinity of the *khruea wan* pattern,
In fear, trembling as though about to die.

Ayuthaya, devoid of top soldiers,
Blood floods the country pitifully.
Sri Sanphet, dwelling of Rama,
Mahathat Ratburana, dissolving.

The great Buddha statue,
The *bot*, the Wihan Chai, burnt down.
Brick and mortar, as though they can speak,
Every grain of sand in unending pain.

Lost are the strength and reputation of Ayuthaya,
Its courage is no more.
Bruised in the soul are
You, ancestors of a time far away.

Seven generations of scum killing, wiping out bloodily,
The bones of the elephants, horses, and soldiers of the Thai.

Most extreme sorrow.
Those who are without humanity are truly base and evil.

Art, of inestimable value,
The crazy beasts destroyed, threw away.
The bar of the lion foot pedestal,
Everything, the treasure of the nation is destroyed.

Golden stupas, chedis of victory,
Suparna, mythical bird, pulling back the Nagaraja,
The golden divine pattern,
Drops from heaven, chiseling divine designs.

A hundred tastes of fragrant flowers,
Flowers of heaven, sweet in the ten directions,
Sa Kaeo and Suan Luang distant, all dried out,
Disgraced.

I tremble with longing for the art,
The civilization of high dignity,
The kingdom now pulverized,
Sadly taking leave of the Thai ancestors.

O Ayuthaya, great place,
Scattered brokenness, rolling,
Chewed on and thrown away by vultures, crows, and dogs,
Completely motionless throughout the three worlds.

The sound of the carcasses of brick and mortar sobbing,
The ground of the Thai state trembling, solitarily,
In each speck of sand and dust,
Throughout all ages, deliriously.

Hurting the Thais throughout existence,
Destroyed, embittered, every blade of grass,
Blood inundates the feet of elephants and horses,
A burial ground throughout eternity.

The deities, the four guardians of the world,
Every *wiman*, every precious heavenly plant,

Cries heavily,
The earth and the skies trembling with grief.

The thundering noise of the brave spirit,
Of hundreds of thousands of soldiers, elephants, horses,
Beating gongs and drums of victory,
Resonant, making the earth tremble.

Solitary universe,
To the end of the expanse of water, skies and earth,
In pain, unconscious,
Every grain of sand, to all eternity.

Ayuthaya Wipayok (The Perishing of Ayuthaya)

Ayuthaya has disappeared all over the sky,
Has vanished from the heavens.
It is a burial ground of art
Of inestimable value,
Created to give rise to the dream of a
Divine world,
Only residue, waste is left,
Speaking to the scarcity of human ideals.

O Sri Ayodhya,
You are a charnel ground, defying the buried dream.
Miraculous art of eternity,
Auspicious spirit of the heavens, you have come to be
　　submerged in the earth.

Ratchathan Kaeo Palace,[8]
Pulverized you are still winding in agony.
Your tears are flooding and flowing,
Crying the story in painting.

Sri Sanphet, pitiful,
Destroyed your highest beauty.
The Burmese come alive to kill repeatedly,
'Til the extinction of the Thai soul.

A pang of longing for your art flares up,
Great Ratburana Mahathat.
The Thai nation plundered,
Then crushed to pieces under the soles of their feet.

The divine decorative patterns,
Touched by the hands of beasts without ethics.
Dharma broken, basely destroyed, climbed upon
Finding and killing every soul.

Prang, chedi, bot, and *vihan,*⁹
Those dull beasts took them all apart.
Taking the brick stones and earth,
Devouring everything, brainless scum.

The Patriarch, a yellow lizard,
Under whom the world of the inauspicious prospered.
Deeply hurt in dignity,
Once so high, now only particles of dust.

Ayuthaya, higher than the domain of the heavens,
Now only residue.
Filth of those earthly animals,
Prospering in their power.

The sheen of Chai Wathanaram,
Beautiful like a stratum of the heavens.
That pack of dogs and crows, those gloomy vultures,
Assembling to devour it.

Mahachai, by the disgrace of the animals,
Ruined, utterly destroyed.
The precious city fallen apart, submerged under the earth,
Insulted, meaning the disappearance of the Thais.

The remnants of brick and mortar sobbing,
How can this spirit be revived?
The exhaustion of human values,
In this world, they do not really exist.

The end of the art of Ayuthaya,
Severely disgraced all over the earth and the sky.
Left is only the essence of monkeys possessing
Siam, o shame.

Si Sachanalai (1961)

O Si Sachanalai
Victorious city, Phra Ruang was your lord,
Back then many hundred harvests ago,
Like a stratum of heaven that strayed to earth.

At this time the *jedi* beckons to the *wihan*,
Like a funeral pyre, burial ground of art
Demons playing the *phin*,[10]
Vaguely hearing the sound of the shell, the bronze gong.

Solitary galaxy,
To the end of the great vast universe,
The sound of tortured sobbing,
From the ancient place of worship.

At night the moon and the stars sparkle,
The wind blows through the precious, mysterious forest,
Pleasantly fragrant,
Beautiful auspicious pond, Uthayan Kaeo Gardens.

The jeweled peacock cries out perched on
A divine pattern, fragrant flower of heaven,
Long at the center of Wat Nang Phaya,
The end of renown for Thai craftsmanship.

O Kaeng Luang, branch of Yom,
River grief-stricken, crying, flowing wearily.
Chalieng has fallen, crumbled
In time, swift and empty.

Chang Lom, the *stupa* of the relic,
Resonant, echoing like the voice of a lion,

Its lumps of laterite stones set in motion,
All things crazy with suffering.

Phra Jedi Jed Thaeo,
There as a sign to delight the heavens.
The remains of the
Kings of the Phra Ruang dynasty lie in the sand and earth.

Seeing the pillar of beloved Pathip Thien
Of the stone city, I am stunned:
The space in front of Sri Mahapho lies scattered,
Shamed in all ten directions of the horizon eternally.

Great Phra Patimakon,
Precious *bot* calling out the victory of the gods,
Gold *wihan*, residence of sandal,
Section of the mound of the Diamond Dam, forlorn and wretched.

That is deserted Suwanna Khiri,
Next to Phanom Phleung Wannawat,
The *wihan* with the serpent king stairway
Destroyed, silent, pitifully demolished.

The sound of the remnants of brick and stone sobbing,
Tonight they carry a magic spell.
Rahu suddenly takes hold of the moon, obstructing it,
Dark, dense clouds, the sorrow of the heavens.

Fragrant is the precious Wihan Mondop,
The incline, the edge of the forest, the great mountains,
Phra Patimakon Chai
Falls, scattering among the earth and sand.

Pathum pond, Phra Sri mountain,
The earth cries heartbreakingly.
Art of supreme value, dissolved,
Its spirit weeping pitifully.

Phra Sri Ratana Mahathat,
Sending forth a mat of lustrous rays, shaking the earth,
Fragrant with lanterns, incense, candles; victory
Of the solitary universe throughout the heavens and earth.

At this point, time dissolved,
Everything was destroyed, completely ruined,
O Chalieng, akin to the city of Indra,
Submerged in the earth, sorrowful.

Oven of bowls, water goblets, delicious,
Exceedingly beautiful big and small plated patterns,
The mortar of the Thai burial ground,
Trembling, overcome with sorrow.

The *thap saming khla* snake, the jackal,[11]
Moving to and fro in the middle of the dead city,
Over every precipice jutting out,
Over steep rocks and crevices, lamenting.

The deities, the four guardians of the world,
Every *viman*, precious plant, the heavens
Are crying pitifully—
The spirit of the precious city expired.

PHI PHUNG TAI (SHOOTING STAR)

In the burial ground of the gods,
Among the stars in heaven,
A soul is mumbling to itself,
Dreaming of the world uneasily.

I take the sky as a blanket,
Take wind for food, dejectedly,
Roaming about hazardously, without aim,
Reaching the next world of divine mood.

Forgetting my body on earth,
Long until every strand of hair is decomposed,

The light of the eyes blends into mud;
Covered by mud, I go under, become hard soil.

At this time, my heart
Has turned into a rock in a stream.
One day that rock will crack,
The stream of water eating away until it falls apart.

Who would there be in this world,
To mourn a stone?
They are used only to trampling on stones.
A pang of longing stirs the soul.

Glittering light going out,
A shooting star, trembling,
Disappearing into endless time,
Ending hopelessly, solitarily.

Kalajak (The Wheel of Time, 1960)

That night the Wheel of Time moved about, fatigued, stiff and sore. It fell over, fell into deep sleep, and dreamt: Snails, worms, insects, and tiny microorganisms came to challenge time to a race. So time woke up the clock, in order to have it as a witness and then accepted the audacious challenge immediately. The snails, worms, insects, and microorganisms started to creep along.

Time accelerated to a very fast pace, surpassing everyone else. Until it came to a certain territory into which no one had ever passed before. There were steep rocks, reaching far up into the distance. Some stars touched upon the surface of these rocks when they came by. They burst apart and came down as crystal gems. Touching upon a waterfall, they wove a sparkling rainbow.

The wind carried different kinds of flowers, whirling intense fragrance. The gaze of the divine eye of Time came to see this and was fascinated by the oblivious state of mind of nature. Until it got lost, touching upon the face of the rocks, tumbling over and falling unconscious.

In the middle of the night, a wild animal of bizarre form, leaning out arrogantly from a precipice on the high rocks, looked like it was going to claw the sparkling stars but, jerking at them with its short nails, it did not reach. The bamboo of the forest reached out its branches to show off to the starlight. A poisonous *thap saming khla* snake unraveled, coiling away from the dew. At the time, it was extremely cold, serene, and solitary. The vast expanse of the rocks and the forest all seemed to be fast asleep. When Time awoke, it could see that at the end of the expanse of the universe, the snails, worms, insects, and microorganisms were crawling toward the Path of the White Elephant. They were eating the stars, leaving them full of holes. Time became worked up and extremely worried. So it hurried to make the Wheel of Time continue on its journey.

But the worms and the snails had wings and had already flown there. Time had only gotten to the moon. It thought, I am really slow. This sound moved in a ripple, scattering across the whole horizon. It could be heard on each and every star. At that time, all the stars cried and moaned: We are hurt. We have been tortured for eons. You have just arrived. Why are you so late? Do you not see the disgusting worms, crawling along, gnawing on and eating the stars? We are already full of holes. They are about to fly to other solar systems to eat the moon and the stars there. So, you are still lingering? Why are you not hurrying resolutely to put an end to that vileness?

Time listened to this, apologized, remaining motionless with overwhelming sorrow for a moment. Then it told the clock about its sadness. All the clocks joined in crying until a stream of manifold Time flowed rapidly.

So Time created desire in the form of a golden Chinese junk, taking honesty for captain, endowed with goods, and with spears, swords, and guns as weapons.

At that time, one big disgusting worm, which was slow and therefore the last one in that caravan of creeping animals, was just about to gnaw at the full moon of the sixth month. The golden Chinese junk of Time gave the promise to fight at the same time as charging and lighting the divine guns. Discharging the poisonous arrows and the spears and swords all at once like heavy rainfall, until only fine powder was left of that weird worm, which was blown away and fell down to the lowly planet below as the substance of evil.

Time woke up startled, not satisfied with its nightmare. From then on, Time never slept again, even if the cosmos was sleeping deeply. For a long time that can only be counted in eons, the Wheel of Time remained awake, like a watchman guarding the night and the day in the midst of eternity, which has no limit throughout all of time.

Phlapphlueng (Lily, 1947)

The first *kalpa* was still sleeping; one day later the sun went out and fell down. Saturn crashed into the moon. A great meteor storm came blowing along to destroy the world. The gods allowed the earth, the blades of grass, the microorganisms, and all the things in the world to be able to speak, and they laughed and cried.

Thus, the earth asked the forest fire, You are burning all the plants in the forest, why did you spare only the cluster of lilies in the middle of the fire? Silent for a moment, the flame began to cry. O Earth, in the olden times when there was not yet a ring around Saturn, there was a man with colorful eyes in the night who roamed about until he died and came back to life as a flame. The lily was formerly his mother. When I could remember, even though I was a flame, I myself wanted to be extinguished until only charred pieces of dust and particles were left, rather than know that I was going to burn something I loved.

I would rather be soot and ashes than a flame burning its beloved. Until the skies and time go to pieces, I will not forget love. I will speak until the end of my tongue becomes a charnel ground, burying my heart myself. The earth and the various plants spoke to each other for the last time, and then their speech was put out, dumb throughout all of time.

Sia Jao (Losing You, 1964)

> Losing you is like a brilliant gem cracking.
> Whatever I had hoped for in this world,
> My hopelessness now reaches the sky,
> Lying face down on the ground eating sand.
>
> I will hurt, remembering to the next world,
> The cruel traces of sorrow will never fade,
> Not minding how many skies I am born, how many times I
>   sorrowfully die,
> I cannot expect to receive your love.
>
> If you are born in heaven,
> I ask to burn, down at the end of the world.
> If you are fire, I am wood,
> Letting you destroy my soul completely.

Even the particles of dust are not compassionate,
Forgetting until the world crumbles.
If in any life I meet you,
I will be so tortured that I will tear out my eyes.

Dying I want to be under the soles of your feet,
So that you can trample on me for fun, like on blades of
    grass.
I will remember the myriad poisons of pain,
Until the end of the world.

Om (1952)

Om, making a wish for the next life,
My small self asks to love, destitute,
Dumb, deaf, and blind,
To be a tree stump, a rain worm, a millipede.

I want to know nothing of the beauty of the world
And the heavens.
Unknowing, stupid, crazier than anyone,
My heart coarse like the surface of the earth.

Let my remains fall into the sand,
Scattering and disappearing,
For vultures, dogs, and crows to feed on.
Hear my words, o Gods.

Ku Duang Jai (Redeeming the Heart, 1967)

All over the world there are eyes,
Watching closely from the sky,
Watching for the golden minute,
Of every single person on earth.

Desiring something in a life,
Or having a vile, dissolute heart, empty,
Doing this and that according to habit,
Eating only the residue of life.

Today, do you have a perspective?
Create a heart that attains divinity, sacred and bold,
Building up the shine of crystal jewels for wisdom,
For the value of the eternal soul.

Time will come like worms,
Eviscerating the auspicious spirit, trembling.
Busy being infatuated, excessively given to enjoyment,
Unbridled, evil desire will come to kill.

Drunk with riches, self-important with power,
A real slave of downfall, without aim.
The shine of life will break and dissolve,
Shameful, even the effort of breathing wasted.

Awake, rise, and strive for beauty,
In this world it does exist and brightly so.
But those things are hidden far away,
In the expanse of the divinity of awakened knowledge.

Practice truth and beauty,
Reform your life to bear substance,
Offer love to the universe,
For everlasting peace and bliss.

Redeem the heart to rise as high as the stars,
Like the shine of great dignity,
Strive to think, to train the heart,
In the pure philosophy of release.

LAK CHAI (THE GROUNDS OF ACCOMPLISHMENT, 1967)

Thought is like the sky,
Wisdom like a sparkling star,
Eternal work is precious,
The shine of divine gems bestowed on the earth.

Philosophy is a wellspring of strength,
Immense sacred value in the art of letters,

Supreme without end,
Redeeming the soul beyond the time of death.

Greater than the sky and the air,
Is the power of purpose,
Holding up the value of life
As the basis of the universe.

The eye is the radiant sun,
Luminous, beautiful vision,
The highest knowledge of the time,
The real essence of the world.

Texts are the places of the world,
Study so that everything becomes entirely illuminated,
Even though dead stones do not move,
They still come running to confer.

What is the self?
Know it all, the horizon and the green mountains,
See the self clearly,
Setting out to look all over the land of the heart.

And then teach the auspicious spirit,
To become deeply affected, cheerful.
Life invents the grounds of accomplishment,
Giving alms to the era all over this stratum of heaven.

Clenching the hand, clenching magic power,
Raising the life of the world above that of heaven,
Time is crystal rings, silver and gold,
Every minute of it.

JARUEK ADID (INSCRIPTION FROM THE PAST, 1966)

This world is like a great library,
Old and new letters can be read from it.
Every leaf has a fun story to tell,
Manifold, under the waters and skies.

The past is inscribed onto the earth,
In the rocks are engraved messages of heaven.
Benevolent Mother Earth,
Teaches everything there is to teach.

The water writes shadows, giving them to the rocks,
Pouring out the manifold precious inscriptions of the world,
To all beings of the Wheel of Transmigration,
As a philosophy of life.

The incomparable value of every particle of earth and sand,
Is as good as bright, pure diamonds.
What value would gems have,
If there were no earth and sand.

Everything is of balanced value,
The scale elevates things to equal height.
The world and the sky give rise to the strength of longing,
The imagination of the soul.

Some places are bright, illuminated by beauty,
Containing the pure, clear language of poetry,
The streams, forests, and waters,
Flavored with divine substance against the stream of age.

Sharpen your vision,
Cull fearless wisdom,
Learn the language of the earth, water, and sky,
Search for contentment.

You will find the meaning of life,
Inscribed into this auspicious spirit,
Use it to create an outlook on life,
That is immortal, winning over death.

Hold still above time and the minutes,
Which have such overwhelming power,
Build up immense sacred strength,
That makes life worth breathing and not lack meaning.

Lamnam Phu Kradueng (Kradueng Mountain Song, 1969)

Wela Khue Chiwa (Time Is Life)

Heaven has given us Time,
Like a lord of heavenly status.
Every single minute is life,
Destroying time is destroying oneself.

Does this existence have ideals,
Or is the heart evil, dissolute, without aim?
Worse yet, scores of lowly creatures,
Are carelessly enmeshed in the refuse of worldly entanglement.

One day, feel deeply about something,
Cut a newer gem of wisdom.
All over the earth there is no taste of divine efflorescence
As food for the soul.

The Wheel of Time will approach slowly,
Abducting life and executing it.
Should one merely eat, sleep, reproduce to one's heart's content
Before the end of this life, before death?

Greedy, infatuated, insatiable, crazy for wealth,
The spirit, sorrowful, disintegrates.
The glow of life adverse diminishes,
Lacking dignity, the glow of the heart is lost.

Awake, arise and seek value,
Traces of the way of the great Bodhisattva.
Render the value of your life to the world,
Offer it for everlasting miraculous happiness.

Revolutionize the view of philosophy,
So that the world be pure like heaven.
Have loving kindness and pity, don't kill one another,
Turn the flow of blood into the planting of flowers.

Salvage the heart to the height of the incomparable stars,
Like glimpses of great dignity.
Immortal, far above the turning of the Wheel of
    Transmigration,
Sacred new power, brave knowledge of discursive thinking.

Clearly perceive the entire value of earth, water, sky,
Long until the day of the *kalpa*'s end,
For contentedness throughout time eternal,
For the universe's calm, to erase suffering and peril.

Kala Khue Arai (What Is Time?)

Time, a rapid powerful current, what is it?
Why is it great, all over the skies?
Outside the world there is no time,
Deceptive humans, slaves to evil time.

The great heart is above time,
Beats the clock to death.
If the heart does not hold still, but moves hurriedly,
It will fall into the crevice and whirl in the stream of time.

Forget, erase, give up the nights, days, months, and years.
Do not let them attain too great an importance,
Like the sun in the universe,
Whose life is without nights or days.

That we call them day, night, morning, evening,
Is because we see the radiant beams of heaven.
The great sun in its reality,
Is bright all day and has no night.

In the world time alone is master,
Uses broken-hearted, bitter humanity as its slave.
Hurry and waken your wisdom,
Force yourself to fight for redeeming freedom, abandon the
    poison of time.

Love work, intent on working like a god day and night,
Wake from the dream, pledge with a brave heart to
Distill eternal ideals,
As powerful, divine weapons.

Defeat and destroy time,
So that it has no power, great poison,
So that only the heart matters,
Blissful and cheerful always.

Stop to have dealings with anything in the world,
Erase greed, wrath, infatuation entirely.
Forget the poisonous clock, relinquish it,
Could one ever catch up with the stream of time?

Stay in one place, year by year,
Having power over aging with its ominous power,
The soul is like the essence of jewels,
Gleaming, shining brilliantly.

Striving for high, pure splendid things,
Above all the demonic stains of greed.
At that moment greed will instantly dissolve,
Time lessen its poison and become motionless.

Su Krasae Chara (Against the Stream of Aging)

O Rainbow, have you ever been sad,
Or old? I have never seen it.
Like the sun which never cools.
Seeing the sun low does not mean it has fallen.

The sun is high up, beyond sight.
The horizon deceives, o World!
The time of the sun never goes down,
Throughout twenty-four hours.

The universe combats time's endlessness,
Brave for the timeless ages to come.

The human race may presently become extinct,
But Time will always be paired with the earth.

Why should the heart tremble in fear,
Leading the defiled world to utter sadness?
I, floating higher than the clouds fly,
Am used to grazing the spectrum of the stars.

Taking the mountains, streams, forests, and oceans,
As divine medicine, a tribute to heaven,
The manifold diverse precepts of all of eternal nature,
Come like magnets with the power of a miraculous, sacred
    heart.

Draw joyful, peaceful elements,
Every small and great particle of the world
Combining into the profound unity of the heart,
Which is always new, never subject to aging.

Like the sun in the evening and morning,
Never old, in the moment before dawn, bright,
Differing from decaying excrement,
Always gloomy, throughout time.

Excrement compares to the human race,
Lacking a perspective, great and vast moral precepts;
Stuffy, cramped in a coconut shell, worthless throughout time,
Face down on the hard soil, elements of gold and silver.

If looking at the precious plants they do not see their green
    value,
Souls desolate and full of dread,
Age thus comes in to take control,
Is master over all of life, the mind and heart.

Or one knows how to combat the current of aging,
Awed by the great power divine,
Erasing, letting the holy power of the inner core crumble,
Hurrying to amend, becoming attentive to the divine.

Bangkok Kaeo Kamsuan rue Nirat Nakhon Si Thammarat
(Lament for Beloved Bangkok / Nirat Nakhon Si Thammarat, 1978)

Kroen (Foreword)

The dear bright moon shines sadly at nighttime,
Silver rays pure and bright in the vastness of the heavens,
The stars glitter, more brilliant than diamonds,
Tying together the duties of day and night.

The strong sun, lighting up the world with its clear rays,
Wind fans the fragrant, sweet trees,
The clouds weave a beautiful rainbow in the sky,
Dividing the work of those two that rule the *kalpas*.

But the poet is on duty day and night;
He has to rise and compose *kap* and precious *salok*,[12]
Or compose for this world of humans,
Without a day left out, without ceasing.

Minute, thinking that life is so short,
A pity, the days and nights that have passed and disappeared,
Tomorrow life might have vanished,
Dissolving without ashes or particles of dust.

Whatever one does, one does not get time back,
Come, sweet and dignified precious *kap*,
I aim to compose all day and night,
With melancholy and longing.

I will enumerate the excellent elements throughout the universe,
To sweeten and freshen life in this wondrous age,
To reform the soul throughout the three worlds,
To carve out the value of life, dedicate it as *dāna*.[13]

The continent of Himawa, the tributaries of the stream of Sindhu,
To the end of each of the most splendid oceans,
I will travel, meeting with events,
Creating eternal work, sowing it in the world and universe.

I will converse even in the language of the dew
With the vast circle of the propitious universe,
Mixing splendid elements into the hearts of people,
Overflowing with nobleness, subduing all dangers.

Conjuring up a heaven for this world,
Stopping to be crazed with war in this age,
Stopping to be crazed by nuclear material, letting go of it,
Altering your heart to become calm and humble.

Then think of creating through marvelous days and nights,
Erase the causes of evil desire, the obscured times,
Invent a new world, stop fearing,
Bliss for every life all over the heavens.

PAKKA THIP (THE DIVINE PEN)

The divine pen draws the heavens and the universe,
In the essence of literary art, precious thing,
Raising humanity to its real value, eternally,
Great, immense future benefit, letting the world reach a
    supreme age

Whenever the heart is bright and joyful,
Presenting *khlong* poetry as tribute, offering it to the world,
Suffering is alleviated, the gloomy spirit suddenly cheerful,
Loving, sharing in the pleasure of the heavens, prosperous
    with the charm of art.

Foolish longing envelops the soul,
Now cold, then tortured,
In a life, where is the supreme essence hidden?
Real warmth would derive from true understanding of the
    world.

The soul of the world trembles with divine *kap* poetry,
Prospering in this age, going far ahead to the next world.
The stars and the moon in the ten directions will be
    cheered,

> Praising the essence of the powerful Bodhisattva, singing to sleep all of earth and the heavens.
>
> The last dream of calm commands the sky in changing times,
> To delight humanity, all beings,
> Erase the age of evil cruelty,
> Savagely descending into the expanse of hell.
>
> Sacrifice heaven to the world, making a wish,
> Sweet divinity of endless time all over the sky,
> Come to the world for longer, creating the humanity
> Of a new age, supreme and bright, there as a challenge until the *kappa* crumbles.[14]
>
> That the evil that befalls all beings disappears from the world,
> All true suffering, all sorrows under the sky.
> Mostly humanity gives disease to the world, maliciously—
> Hurry, round up brave strength, kill, wipe out distress.
>
> The stars hang from the luminous sky,
> Surpassing the novel idealism of the age.
> So far, what divine value have you to renounce to the world?
> Put out grief, do away with disease, raise the world higher than heaven.
>
> The *khlong* of Angkarn, precious poet of Siam,
> Are for the distant future,
> The *kap* and *klon* roam divine eternity,[15]
> Introduced into the world so that it may be without grief, hurrying to delight in literary art.

Panithan Kawi (The Poet's Testament, 1986)

Phutharom (Buddhist Spirit)

> I would like to wrap myself in the wind, the sky, and the great ocean,

In a second, a hundred years of human lifetime become
   empty, nothing.
The coffin helps to let go, o soul,
When the world is in turmoil, heaven leaves us the cemetery
   of the universe.

Taking sky and earth as a home,
The brilliant stars and the rays of the moon as torches,
Misty clouds drop down as a blanket,
Enveloping wisdom, singing to sleep the sky.

Crazy possessions all over the sky and universe,
Throw them away, bestow good fortune on the burial ground.
The soul abandons the remains of grief, that hidden
   cemetery,
Forgetting to wake up in the next existence, weary of
   transmigration.

Ever since the sun illuminated the sky,
The golden clock was not time watching the world.
Slavelike humanity, don't be vile, be still.
Attain the core of brave heroic truth, sharp discursive thinking.

Assume a brave and miraculous attitude,
The heart sparkling with the strength of merit,
Buddhist *dhamma* illuminating the spirit.
Place the universe under the sole of voidness.

In a Buddhist spirit, for the instance that an elephant shakes
   his ears,
A snake sticks out its tongue, contemplating this immense value,
Making merit to expel preposterous, shameful arrogance,
Contempt toward others that rots the soul.

PANITHAN KAWI (THE POET'S TESTAMENT)

Who would ever dare trade in skies and oceans,
This pure world created by the gods.
At last taking leave of my bodily parts, laying them down
Where the earth and the sky connect.

We are not the owners of the sky and space,
The elements of the earth, of all the heavens in their entirety.
Humanity never created the sun and the moon,
Not even one grain of sand.

Struggling to take land, brutal, thinking only of killing,
Because of the crazy, cruel thirst dwelling in these skeletons of ghosts.
Forgetting the burial ground, ethics, goodness,
Giving up beneficence, the real value of the soul.

The state of all things in all the parts of this world,
One should realize their divine miraculous value.
Preserving the earth, water, and sky throughout time,
That they may remain in their high divine station, the crystal mansion of nirvana.

Fields, wild forests, woods,
Great rocks thrusting into the heaven of Indra.
Wild animals, tigers, elephants, monkeys,
Ants and insects of different species in the entire universe.

They are like close friends, comrades
Born in the same swift stream of the Wheel of Transmigration,
The worth of their lives inestimable,
Sweet charm of the sky, earth, and stars.

Even if others were free, and flew to the highest point of the horizon,
Taking the moon and stars as a great path,
I ask to love this world forever,
Dedicating my heart to the earth in all my lives and deaths.

I will even not go to nirvana.
I will whirl and swim in the manifold cycles of transmigration,
Translating the meaning of the real value of the many galaxies
Into stanzas of poetry for the universe.

To erase suffering and sorrow in the human world
As much as I can, moving toward an age of bliss and
 contentment.
At that moment I will be blended, pulverized to become earth.
I will be a fossil, torturedly existing and observing.

The end of the charm of literary art that life can offer,
Fumbling for divine value as replacement,
Pitiful life, every dusty particle of it,
Great sadness horrifying even the ashes.

World arid of poetry, earth and sky moving,
I will compose brilliant gems of dignity,
Taking leave of sweet humanity,
Intending to create a universe of the mind.

To be captivated by *kap, klon, khlong,* and *chan*,[16]
To permeate every stratum of the celestial mansions of Indra
 and Brahma,
Creating merit through art for all eternity,
Immeasurably long, immortal, timeless.

Tuen Thoet Lok Manut (Awake, Humanity)

A pity, born to corrupt,
Waiting, day and night, crazy with coup d'états,
Extorting the country, that pack of depraved, rabid dogs.
I condemn the fruits of their doings, as they sink their teeth
 into Thailand.

Is the sky wide like the heart of humanity,
Or narrow, a coconut shell with the world inside it?
All over the earth everyone's disease of greed
Lays claim to everything within the confines of the sky.

Humanity is small and lowly, like animals.
That is the emperor laying claim to the burial ground,
 ridiculous,

Endeavoring to carve his heroism onto the mountains,
Ensnaring the heart of the people, slaves throughout time.

River branch in the forest, whirling, crouching to watch for whom?
Hurry to cut the jeweled value of the age, strange poison,
The grains of sand, manifold like witnesses,
The *anattā* executes the *attā*.[17]

War leads humanity toward loss, and the victors are also:
Manifold humanity.
Cannibalistic age, more danger than one could flee from,
How many worlds have to be destroyed until you stop fighting?

Be conscious, reflect, every heart of every citizen,
Like slaves, fast asleep, not waking, startled.
Wisdom, make a serum to inject wisdom,
Solving all the problems depressing the heart.

Power, sacred and superb, of the Lord Buddha,
Night and day teaching the mind to think of reforming the age.
Force of merit, divine strength of the Three Gems,
Gild the heart to preserve truth.

Fast, hurry to revolutionize the might of the self,
Deeply awed by excellent, supreme victory.
Peaceful bliss, invading to fight the worlds and hells concealed in darkness,
Lead the age to divinity in all ten directions.

Nuclear, inauspicious, vile evil.
Peaceful bliss, superb, praiseworthy
If the side of peaceful bliss wins then it is all too sure:
The world will proceed to a place higher than eternal heaven.

UNNAMED, P. 39

With four faces the god shakes his head, fed up with the earth, three-eyed, turbid green,

Despising, disdaining the world.
Base, nuclear fire of the vicious, will destroy the world.
In the modern age, why is humanity so insane? Crazed with
    dealing in nuclear material.

Authority of *dharma*, stable in all the universe:
All of humanity knowing the value of heaven,
So that everything will prosper until it becomes divine,
Resembling the bright life of a future Buddha,[18] the
    beginning of a supreme age.

With a free heart like the shore of the sky, the universe,
    enclosing the essence of ancient eternity,
Keeping every supreme new essence.
Come to direct your efforts to creating, pleasing the world
    with a blissful age.

Jiaranai Kaeo Mani Haeng Chiwit (Cutting the Crystal Gems of Life)

If life were arid, empty of ethics,
I would lie down to die, disappear not to be remembered,
An ant, a termite that meets with its fate, meaninglessly,
The world does not know of its burning, its great
    misfortune.

Empathy flows from the sky as streams of rain,
Clouds from the heavenly city, dropping down to earth,
Friendship and happiness of all people all over the world,
Sorrow quickly disappears in advance, strong and bold,
    offering auspiciousness.

Born to pay debt to the world,
Owing the auspicious Bodhisattva precious tribute,
An offering that the world has for humanity,
Having paid back the price of society, the gem of art sparkles.

Getting up in darkness all the time,
From short to long, a long life of ten thousand harvests,
Forcing myself to read and write poetry until dawn,

The self attuned to the Buddha, luminous, stirring sacred strength.

Closing my eyes in the evening crossing to the moment before dawn,
From long to short, the life of sorrow decreases to short,
Ignorance speeds up unbridled worldly desires,
Falling into the mud, the self stubborn, falling, strength dissolving.

Unnamed, p. 75

He, whose heart is negligent, killing time,
As though killing life, making it disappear,
Lacking brilliant work with eternal value,
Will die like a rotten dog, meaninglessly.

The current of time, the stream of water,
Flows steadily, for whom would it wait?
No things of beauty dwell in the heart,
New ignorance, old foolish slave.

What are you so greedy for in this world?
Hurrying to plunder, to extort, stacking the burial ground,
The brilliant rays of light, are they ever going to be dirty with mud?
Bitter wisdom holds sweet insight.

That is hell, this is the Lord Buddha,
Directing attention to questions of *dharma* day and night,
Rising in darkness to understand the value of time,
Stretching the value of life to ten thousand years.

Urgently striving to write *kap, klon, khlong,* and *chan* poetry,
To offer to this miraculous world,
So that humanity will be immersed in beauty and beneficence and
The world become heaven forever.

Wiman Nam Khang (Celestial Mansion of Dew)

The celestial mansion of dew is made up of elements of
  dreams,
Taking this stratum of heaven as a crystal dwelling,
A lantern brilliantly radiant,
The shine of the rainbow, radiance of the jeweled row of stars.

The beach of soft fine sand is like a bed,
The pillows of logs are soft pillows of heaven,
The stream flows over the rocks, earth and sand:
Fairies singing one to sleep, consolingly.

Reaching for the golden sickle of the moon in sleep:
Beloved one, shine of the age,
Sweet one, with your soft caress,
Your rays with their pure charm, much beloved, do not
  cease.

I would love to take you around the world and the great
  oceans,
To the edge of the dream,
Before the heavens disappear.
Betrothing you with the value of the luminous sky, most
  beloved, of the beautiful jeweled man.

That overhanging rock jutting out,
Maybe reaching to the supreme stars, gleaming brilliantly,
Or a cluster of trees of paradise, so utterly good,
Or the way of the dimension of eternal dreaming.

There the path of the white elephant, clear and bright,
Some stars the Lord Buddha set up,
Some universes are the divine nirvana,
The waves of the past passing in long *kalpas* and *kappas*.[19]

The fluffy clouds are fragrant like flowers falling,
Demanding thought from the enigmatic world;

Orion ploughs the extremely beautiful field of the sky,
To reap what value of life as harvest?

Late at night the forest dew sobs with sorrow,
Are the tears of the world going to disappear?
Arrogant humans kill someone, killing the world,
Consummating this exceedingly evil age.

Not loving and caring for the value of the world,
They will suffer until heaven ends;
The era of humanity will end before long,
Be a witness, swift stream.

As the water is flowing, the time of life is also flowing,
Leaves are falling, life leaves like a dream;
Killing life is destroying night and day,
What work have you to present this world with?

PHIANG KHRU NUENG KO MUAI SAMOE FAN (IN ONE INSTANT DEAD, LIKE IN A DREAM)

The sea invented waves dancing at the shore of dreams,
In the expanse of the sky the moon shines bright,
The mysterious earth, divine and great,
Spreads precious beauty, disseminating rays of sacred charm.

Longing to swim the arduous expanse of the intermediate heavens,
Suddenly sprinkled with resplendent stars,
Intending to see the spirit of the dear world with its eternal worth,
Scolding myself, haughty fire-fly.

Birds of dawn with beautiful voices, solitary and sweet,
Aquatic weeds, lotuses blossom tenderly,
Various forests of fragrant flowers delight the heart;
The Wheel of Time rolls in in a second, in an instant one is dead like in a dream.

Black cuckoos fly towards the heaven of Indra,
One *wa* they will sail down to the gods;[20]
The tree of paradise is fragrant, making me remember far back,
Opening the sad location of the next world, falling from the world dying.

Coming up in the middle of the expanse of literary art,
Arriving at the fearful core of life that they tell of,
Splish, splash, the stream complains,
How could the core of life be arid, without desire to know the *dhamma* of the Buddha?

Yad Nam Khang Khue Namta Khong Wela (Dew Drops Are the Tears of Time, 1987)

NIMIT NA SAI RUNG (*NIMITTA* IN THE RAINBOW)

The time of night is sleeping in the silk curtain of the powdery particles of clear air. Dripping black, laced with dark blue particles of fiber. That crystal room is the vastness of the earth; it is of an even smooth surface extending to the outermost reaches of the forests, mountains, and streams, completing a circle vaster than the horizon.

Almost having reached the time of early morning, golden rays of light begin to travel toward the earth. The fine mist shrouding the high mountains gives rise to a luminous rainbow. In the divinely colored stripes of the rainbow appears a sign more complex and miraculous than a hundred dreams, as if made by heaven. The shadow of that dream is intricate, hidden, so that one drifts into dreaming. Imagination.

The day arises. A snail inches onto the rainbow in slow movements, with the rays of light of morning. The snail crawls down from the rainbow's arch, and stops to drink of the dew on the blades of grass and flower petals, and asks the drops of dew: Who painted the design on the shawl of Mother Earth during the night? He probably kept painting without sleep.

The dew drops answer: We are the artists.

During the tranquil night we let the drops fall down from the leaves, falling and touching the delicate tissue of the earth, sand, and forest. Wherever our paintbrush came down strongly, the ground gave in in deep fissures. Wherever it touched only lightly, the cracks are shallow. All through the night the dew did not sleep, carefully painting the dots in confusing tracks, in circles ending in a flowing stream, astonishing in its beauty. Straight, a stream of pure nature. We thus suppose ourselves to be crystal artists and paint the pattern of dew on the silk shawl of Mother Earth. So you find it beautiful?

Yes, very beautiful. It makes me see the power of the miraculous charm of the world.

Look at this wildflower there, blooming. A pity only that humanity is foolish, without wisdom, only thinking of killing and destroying the world.

Look at them, they are polluting the air. Great black refuse. Repulsive. Even though they use the air to breathe, have life because of the pure air. But they do not stop to defile, dirty lizards, *preta* out of hell. Until the air will be foul all through the land.

Look at them, they are killing the forests, destroying the streams every moment, without meaning. Only greed, infatuated with heaps of wealth, pitiful. The trees help to purify the air, a gift to humanity all over the world. But they readily destroy the trees, ungrateful humans, don't know the value of anything, only good at making bombs for destruction. For destroying the world. Pain and sadness. As if that was not enough, they are crazy about war. Biting each other like wild animals. Pitiful. Look, it is not even morning, yet they are already honking the horns of their cars noisily. Even wild animals, herds of elephants do not scream as crazily as the car horns. Cluttered with dirty sounds, painful, deafening, liver-burning, exceedingly evil.

The dawn is also saddened and in low spirits, angry at the moment before dawn, which is a bit too dark. No silvery or gold rays like the moment before dawn has on other days. Are you that bitter? Are you that stubborn like them also, dawn? You are acting like you are imitating humans who, if you have silver, consider you a younger sibling and, if you have gold, an older. What good is that? Any moment before dawn that is somewhat impoverished, that is gloomy without gold and silver rays, you should not look down upon, driving it away from the day. That is hurrying, short-sighted, very disgraceful. You should not be hasty, impatient. Do not hurry too much. All the goodness and beauty will disappear. Look, all those other ten and hundred thousands on earth, still sleeping. Except for crazy humanity, greedy, infatuated with money, raving about heaps of gold.

Look, the clock is still asleep, talking in sleep, delirious until a flower has sprung up on the hour and minute hands. Time is fragrant with the scent of pollen dust of the flower. It is probably a dream, not anything real.

It is truth. But everyone in this world who does not comprehend clearly is still in doubt, calling it by a new name: a dream. Should we wake time?, the dawn asks. The snail answers: Do not wake her. Would it not be better to allow my speed to take me ahead of time a hundred years?

Time, very content, mostly goes astray until the golden minute, for which one should be awake and which one should seek, study the core of life, then practice blooming, producing divine results in the world. Mother Earth will not have to be sad about having wasted her mother's milk. Whether time is asleep or awake, do not worry. Do your work, purpose of your life duty, every minute. Time is so great that we cannot conceive of it, cannot limit it, cannot perceive it. It is something profound and great.

Even though time is a void thing. In itself it does not consist of anything. But in this not consisting of anything, which is *śūnya*, all things in the cosmos and the solar systems of other worlds are constituent parts of time in their entirety. It seems a huge dimension, beyond estimation, encompassing profound meaning, extending to all things as the highest unity.

Above the multi-layered dimension of voidness that is *śūnya*, it is a powerful entity. It is possible to say that it has a self and possible to say that it has not. It is the highest purpose, entirely free in its non-attachment or in its attachment that seems to be non-attachment. Speaking honestly and perfectly so that humans mock it. Time always looks as though sleeping, but in that deep sleep it could turn out to be real awakening.

The snail crawled slowly. Not knowing the poison of time. Until it crawled up to death and decayed. But time does not decay. Does not have the trace of a smile, but always looks like it is smiling. The flowers are still in bloom, the streams still flowing, the birds still singing like always.

The only thing that has changed is the snail, which came into being again as a human. And was infatuated with itself for being so civilized, puffed-up and self-important, the most wonderful being. Without stopping to reflect, to compare itself with anything.

Blind, caught in its praise that it was the most excellent being in the world throughout all of time. Alas!

Yad Nam Khang Khue Namta Khong Wela
(Dew Drops Are the Tears of Time)

Sometimes past the time of night I arise; after defecating, brushing my teeth, washing my face, washing myself until I'm clean, I go outside to breathe in the fresh air. I raise my eyes to see the sky and the stars, manifold constellations abundant on the Path of the White Elephant. Radiant, transparent, bitterly cold in the firmament; the elements of the earth, refreshingly sweet with beauty at a time when all of humanity is still sleeping. The drops of dew sparkle brilliantly, as if they had received the blessing of the dawn, glistening with rays of yellow gold and pure silver. Solitary in the expanse of the heavens, evoking feelings of divine solitude and nostalgia, there in the distant sky.

In the southern direction of the goddess of the sun, the flowing silver rays of the sadness of the moon are becoming weaker, drift and change position. Following the wish to take leave of night, which is about to disappear secretly.

The wind god blows gently, sprinkling fragrance. Perfume of the soft pollen of all flowers, sweetly fragrant, clean, given to the god of wind to carry with him. Instantly I breathe in the sweet fragrant perfume, taking time to think how deeply impressed I am with that fragrance of the flowers which is scattered by the wind, traveling to different directions. Hardly anyone could be persuaded to discolor it so that it becomes odorous. But we human beings, how can we do it?

The flowers will definitely not break off friendship, splitting their heart in two. One part of my heart is dedicated to the resplendent sun which is bright, supreme and sacred. Beautiful like pure gold mixed with flashing gems in all colors of the rainbow blending, the results a present offered to this world. Another part of my heart is sorrowful because of the moon, he with the tender rays, which will be mistreated by the strong power of the sun, until the dear moon can be seen only as a foggy mist, taking leave, disappearing.

Looking at the resplendent rays of the sun and then turning to fix my gaze on the moon, all of a sudden I am undecided. Until the rising of the sun in the early morning, fiercely burning, when the koel bird cries out and then flies away. In the course of time, the further the time of my life span passes, the more I feel this worry and longing. I cannot force myself to decide whether I want to really love the sun or the moon, the creators of days and nights which have a kind of secret charm, deep in the dimension of the soul, radiant long throughout time.

Suddenly there is the strength of the divine rays. Far in the distance, almost imperceptibly, silver rays start to glitter brightly—shiny divine rays, sending out brilliant sparks. The flowers, precious plants, and grasses glisten with drops of diamond dew. The earth is wide, the sky is high and distant. Carried along by the wind a swarm of bees flies past, humming, seeking the pollen of flowers, buzzing steadily. The sound of birds parts the sky; calling their friends, reminding them to go search for food. Two fly past. As soon as they have called out "kwaek, kwaek," they turn back to traverse the forest and get another friend. Together they make up three lives. They fly one after the other into the distance across the wide plain to a big pond far from the city.

O birds, you are so diligent. You are really dedicated to work, so very serious about life. Hatching your eggs, raising your young. You are intent on doing this until your young with their weak wings become courageous, their legs strong. You fly with collective strength, together in the flock. You never induce each other to dally away time self-indulgently like your fellow beings, that herd of animals called the human race. The bees are also diligently leaving their nest in the early morning flying toward the pollen of the plants. There is no mutiny, no deception. There is not one bee that would put nettle or cowhage into its own hive or at least mix a little *boraphet* into the honey.[21] The whole race of the bees has never done an evil thing like that. But humanity has collected bad and ugly things in its soul.

In the communal life of the bees there is never any trick or deception, such as taking poison and dissolving it in the honey or taking a special part of the honey to mix it with poison to execute the being who comes to plunder, snatching great benefit from you. Honest toward oneself and the collective, that is, for the most part, the society of the bees, those supreme beings. We esteem them to be one of the incomparable kinds of animals in the world, because they never destroy the world like the human race. But humans are always ready to kill one another. Only a look that does not suit one, it does not even have to be that they are dismantling each other's benefits. Especially in humanity nowadays, there is only impoliteness, vulgarity, and wickedness. They are full of the evil elements of all the venom dwelling in their souls. The bees, these special animals, have never used dirty excrement for deception. This very special quality should be guarded and preserved to teach humanity throughout time.

Every day in the early morning I, Father, take both of my children to greet the dew. Sometimes I talk about the special quality of these things and explain for both my daughter and my son to hear. For a new kind of inspiration, until both children are delighted, motivated, and interested in the different qualities of nature.

I will usually point out the changing, uncertain states of the diamonds of dew drops which are touched by rays of sunlight from the moment before dawn until the rising of the sun in the early morning. I want my children to know that this being touched of the dew by the brilliant rays of the sun is a divine treasure that the sun has given to the world, as complete with beauty and different ethical teachings as anyone could imagine. To what degree can one develop consciousness? One will have no point at which one can stop searching, because one will think on and on. Until one becomes similar to the ripples of waves in the ocean, made up of miraculous elements. At that point, one will compile inspiring qualities, think of, dream of, and create miraculous elements for one's intellect, reaching divinity, able to discern auspicious desire. Knowing clarion reason from beginning to end, one will be able to create work of high auspiciousness from this inspiration. One will be able to think of and produce miraculously beautiful things, giving eternal auspicious desire to the world for the universe's contentment. Far from suffering, sorrow, and illness, through the strength of the spirit of friendship that has come from this one tiny life.

I teach my two children, Hurry to get away from the defiling sound of the radio, vulgar evil waste, without any good. If you stay near it you will be perplexed, in a bad mood, idiotic all morning. Most of humanity is still asleep. In the middle of the field in the suburbs of the capital, the grass is resplendent with drops of shiny diamonds. The dew sparkles but hardly anyone is interested. I speak of real value indirectly, as well as with inspiration, to give rise to creative thinking, manifest in supreme nights and days, so that the children will listen and understand clearly.

I take myself to be fortunate for having this perspective, seeing the excellent value of the earth and the sky which is immeasurable. Born with this tie, this infatuation and love for nature, it is ingrained in my deepest instincts. Elements of excellence are even blended into my soul, without anyone to teach me. The reason is that I have had this conduct for many lives already. Therefore I have a splendid mind that is as though informed by a superb star, making it understand these secret dimensions profoundly, knowing the value of the sky and earth, the end of the universe, even interested in other planets as well. Seeing this absolutely superb value. Not stopping to think, falling silent, tumbling over and falling asleep. I am still astounded by the superb value of the human world and that of other worlds. Taking this novel marveling to store in the bank of my soul, persevering, practicing, studying, hurrying to know about reaching precious art, not taking note of anything else, I teach myself with every breath.

If we have the training and upbringing to attain supreme consciousness, if our vision is superb with beauty, we will see the divine treasure around us. Wherever we go, there are only perspectives, only dreams that are creative, rich with feelings that move the heart with the supreme value of the unending universe that never ceases. Precious thought can create and produce all things. I want to stress again, that in this world there is immeasurably divine treasure in immense amounts. It surpasses that which our vision and consciousness are able to wish or search for in its supreme value. Hold on to its true core to forge it into precious results that will shine throughout the era.

Look, the divine sun weaves golden rays, luminous in a rainbow of seven colors. Seldom is there a planet in the abundant solar system that has value like this world. Children, look there, the most supreme sun is stopping its divine rays. Touching upon, reflecting crystals of dew until there are brilliantly shining rays of gleaming diamonds, luminous and glittering. It is like having a precious mentor, a teacher of auspicious spirit who transforms this supreme value of life into something that makes clear insight arise in all the young children. Knowing clearly until they are able to teach themselves, how to learn and practice until the sparks of life glitter very beautifully in this manner.

After I had explained quite a bit to the children, I indicated,

"What is the dew? The dew drops are the tears of time."

Right after that my silver bell resounded sweetly, delighted with life,

"Why is time crying? What is it unhappy about?"

I replied, "It looks as though time is crying, because it has to take leave of us and go far, far away in the ripples of the waves of the universal path which never returns. And, a point will come when we will have to take leave of time, going far away to the next world, and we will be in the time dimension of another era that has nothing to do with the present time in this world. The latter point is still very difficult to understand. Let's wait for a day when both of you are older. Then I will explain it to you in detail, which will still involve many steps."

My daughter's barbet bird voice, still sweetly audible beside me, asked, "You said that time cries because it is sorry about having to take leave and going far away. Where then, does time go?"

"In explaining the aim of time's path as going far away, I meant that time travels far, far away, child. So all of a sudden, it is as though the lifespan of human beings becomes very short. I cannot explain this path entirely. It is a path that human language cannot reach in its travel. It is at the farthest point of the horizon. And then it even passes beyond to where there is no horizon, even further to the end of the universe. Solitary, passing far beyond to many universes, to the manifold, abundant solar systems, without end. The ancients called it eternity."

"I told you that time cries because it has to take leave of us and go far away. In addition to crying out of sorrow, sometimes its crying may also be a result of contentment: It is so choked with happiness that it sobs. So the season of the floods in both eyes starts. The reason is that the dew is pleased with having paid respect to the sun. It reflected the pure value of the waves of rays of the sun in seven colors, offering them as a present to the world. The dew always seems sad that it has to suddenly disappear, leave us, not staying to cut the gem of the eye's gleam so that it is impressed with the value of the colors of the rainbow and other beauty. Thus whether it is happy or sorrowful, the dew is like teardrops."

"Does the dew have a heart and soul, Father?"

"It does not, child. The dew has no heart. It has no heart or deceptive behavior at all. That I said the dew is happy or sad was because I wanted you to understand easily. If I had chosen to speak in another mode, it would have been much more difficult for you to understand.

I have the aim for you to be awed by one level of tender feeling first, for you to feel empathy. That is why I invested the dew with human emotion and then spoke according to my own feeling, as if the dew had a heart. All this is because I had already invented a heart for the dew and then wanted to make you feel moved, so you would be impressed. This will slowly become the source of deep understanding of the value of art on higher and higher levels."

The ancestors in the olden times before your grandparents understood this feeling very well. In the *Anirut Kham Chan* they said,

> Look at the fragile *thuai*, golden and beautiful[22]
> In the hands of heavenly women
> Divine, holding it up
> Beautiful, radiant is the body of the golden swan
> Holding the *wan thong* pattern in its beak
> As if flying away.

Seeing the beautiful fragile *thuai* plated with pure gold, brilliant, like Apsaras of Indra in the heavens, supremely beautiful; holding up the piece of architecture in the form of a swan, radiant with beauty, holding the golden *kanok wan* pattern, looking like he will take it and fly away.

But if you asked someone else, not me, Father, but for instance a scientist, about what the dew is, he would answer straight from the textbook: H_2O. And he would explain it from its origin until its dissolution and disappearance. But in everything he would be referring specifically and precisely only to water and that is that. It would be a short, curt, and ordinary answer without feeling. I want you children to think like artists, like literary scholars. The deeper your thoughts go, the better. Or practice until you know the eternal laws of the Lord Buddha. And then, even more miraculously, go on to think in the *dharma* transcending the world. I will summarize once more:

If you think about dew diffusely and shallowly in the sense of ordinary truth according to science, that is too much of the truth. That amounts to dullness, is all too precise. Dew is the many particles of steam which run together in fine particles to form drops of dew. That is all. Or, at the most, they would speak of clouds, of temperature, the atmosphere that lets dew originate. But it all comes down to water, H_2O. I do not see anything there that could move you. I do not want you children to think dully straightforward, precise in this manner. Instead I want you to compare the dew with the movement of things that are alive, in a way that will allow you to be moved. This is the starting point of the path that will take you to the world of art and literature.

As I said, the dew drops are the tears of time. They make us see the impermanence of the path of movement of the Wheel of Time for a moment. The dew serves the sun by reflecting the rays, projecting the glittering rays of the sun to illuminate the sky, reflecting the luminous rainbow brilliantly, gradually dropping down, dissolving, dying; grateful that the sun has the merit to help burn it, destroy it, and disperse it into a sea, so that it becomes clouds. The clouds have the dew as a son, and the dew lets a source of water originate, a stream that then flows to nourish the world. And, in that fleeting second of the lifespan of the dew, it also decorates Mother Earth. Glistening on every blade of grass. In every plant, in every tall forest, it influences the heart of some lives, like mine, seeing this divine treasure. That makes your poor father suddenly a millionaire, seeing and knowing that divine value that is abundant and beyond estimation.

The dew exists only for a second, including the time in which it is beautiful and resplendent before it dissolves, so that human vision will know deeply the value of the beauty of those short golden rays. There is birth as well as duration and cessation, like in the lifespan of human beings. It is very appropriate to compare this lifespan to the teaching of the dew drops. No other comparison would be more expressive.

The first stage in which the majesty of steam collects to form drops of water is like initial birth, like childhood in human life. Reflecting the full beauty of the glittering rays of the sun, comparable to the excitement and wonder of the first years. Marveling at the value of things around oneself without end, never abating. Not knowing of decline, aging, and the cessation of all things. At the age of young men and women, bright and beautiful, excessively given to the enjoyment of the taste of life. Then, having passed obstacles, having made various experiences, including those of having a spouse and of work, life is likely to become quieter, more solemn. And then, when life becomes quiet and modest, respectful toward the value of all the things learned in the first years, one will assemble supreme data in order to think creatively and investigatively, conducting oneself with more and more intelligence. Because intelligence can be called the supreme core which will give rise to the great civilization of humanity.

The different information of a vision that perceives clearly and profoundly the supreme value of the nature of this world and others is comparable to precious riches and money, rings and gems that I put into a divine trust. It is the property of my own soul. When I have collected a great amount, I will most probably take it out, distribute it, and use it so that essential benefit arises for the world.

I will not yet speak to you of old age, which is comparable to the dew drops falling down and then breaking, dissolving. Also, old age is the time of dusk of life with the curtain closing for the end. Dissolving and taking leave just as the drops of dew dissolve, take leave and disappear. Human life as well perishes, goes out like the drops of dew dissolve.

I will speak of old age, teach you about it, when both of you children are fully grown up; I will compare age in the world of human life with the drops of dew, which are the chapter of dusk in life. This is too full of sorrow for the innocent lives of you two small children, because it will worry you, make you grave and gloomy. Cut by the blade of truth, a wound might develop. But where I am concerned, my age at this point is comparable to the fall of afternoon and evening. Soon I will take leave of you two children and disappear. Like the time when the sun almost falls down to the ground. The reason is that human life is destined to disappear like the setting sun, permanently leaving behind only the language of tears in the drops of dew, for you children to contemplate and direct your attention to, in the way that I perceived it and explained it to you many times. I taught you about several ethical precepts, all with caring attachment born of deep love, which you will pass on to my grandchildren. Never forget the caring attachment of the love that I have for you both, so that you may pass it on compassionately. The bond of love that I am passing on to the time of your lifespan and to that of my grandchildren and great-grandchildren throughout time: I never want this love, this compassion and care in our line of blood to dry up, never want its flow to stop. And every time that you think of your father, I want you to think of your mother also. Because both of your parents represent the unity of that same love. Your mother endured a lot of hardship and tiredness because of both of you. Especially when giving birth to the girl child, she almost had to exchange her life for that of the child's.

Anytime in the future when you observe and realize the real value of nature in the universe, including the divine results of the immortal work of the Buddha, not even leaving aside the supreme fruits of the work of those other humans with extraordinary ability, at that point, children, you will see traces of the tears of your father, that are full of love and longing for you in taking leave of both of you small children. At the point when the time of dusk in life has arrived, your father will take leave, depart to the next world and disappear. Please look, children, we human beings, if we know how to think and know how to improve our intellect, will be called people who are given to thinking. For such people, even a single drop of dew will give rise to fascination, to different perspectives and ideas. As though having a teacher who knows how to teach you very well.

I already said the dew is like the tears of time, great time. Time is vast, enormous, and without boundaries. It is the incalculable of the inconceivable. Thinking about it, you never finish: it is able to embrace the innumerable, unending universes. Nowhere is there a horizon of time where it will end. Even though it extends to millions and millions of years until it is called eternity, as I already mentioned, the mechanism of the Wheel of Time passes by rapidly, as if it had wings to fly away like a bird soaring toward the sky. The dew compares to the tears of time, as I said, counting from the time of morning, that is, before the moment before dawn, to that time of morning when the sun is bright in the early day, which is fresh and pleasant with the pure air.

The dew seems to be content and cheerful like the tears of the common man who is happy, welling up in the sockets of the eyes. As if they were going to pour out his contentment as a stream of happiness which should flow forever in its manifoldness.

Content with what, children?

Content that this world is starting to have an extremely bright sun: the sun gradually sends out rays across the whole vastness of the earth, giving supreme value to the world. From the moment before dawn, it starts to scatter crystal flakes of flowing silver, reflecting silver and golden rays unto the world below. Any human being that profoundly knows the value of the heart is rich, immediately becomes a millionaire. Because all these divine treasures fill the whole heart, enough to make one a full human being.

How can this be? It is truth for those who practice and study the eternal *dhamma* of the Lord Buddha and modern learning, which discovered real value, like an endowment counting several tens of tens of millions of riches and gold, in the inconceivability of nature's wealth. Then a meritorious spirit will arise which is pleased with tranquility, with calm, trying to find the core of real humanity. One will surely have to raise the level of one's spirit above that of being an outright slave of the economy. As well as realizing that human life is full of flaws, not perfect. One will have to look for real value elsewhere in order for life to be complete. And there is much splendid value and divine value to be found.

Why should life be repetitious, doing work like frying noodles for a living until you die? Or why should you sell rice, or do monotonous work in a bank, never changing your way of life? During all of life never being independent. Becoming an absolute slave of life. Money in the system of the modern economy buys the time of life entirely. Even when one is going to rest in the coffin, one cannot close one's eyes to die, because one is worrying about different activities, never getting enough. Until the spirit is forgotten, thrown away, in a place where it should not be.

One will clearly realize, being born as a common person is already too much; in addition, we are repetitious and monotonous in life, lacking the thinking of humankind, the supreme beings. Not being able to make our thinking move on, not in line with other thinkers of the same era. This way you have to have a repetitious and monotonous life until you die. Like being born to fry noodles, for instance. That is trivial, empty like a *nang rom* oyster that builds a thick and solid shell like a fortification, a wall. In the end, its co-inhabitants of the world, all those various Ph.D. holders, will squeeze lemon on it and eat it raw. It is tasty to their tongues, but the oyster's life ends without meaning. In a hundred lives, no pearl will be found. And even if one found a pearl, it would be like doctors squeezing lemon on it all the same. Dying for nothing. Or they will look at it in the manner of a scale insect. Building a shell like a fortification. Eating, sleeping, reproducing happily in the fortress that it thinks is as strong as it can possibly be. In the end, its co-inhabitants of the world lift up the shell and cook it to make color for dying fabric. Wasting who knows how many foolish generations.

Therefore conscious knowledge, the precious reflection of humankind, should be able to develop, having the power of thought that does not stand still, does not stop, coming to a standstill repeatedly in the same place, backing up one's own thinking to look back; then again directing one's attention to the future, focusing on what is ahead, on the different paths of life. Elevating our intellect until supremely high. Vast, until having a third eye, able to see to the limits of sight. It will have the power to transcend the causes of ordinary life. It does not fall to be a slave, face down on the soil until the end of life. Thinking something, it can be thought about with freedom. Having a perspective that sees the value of the intellect as supreme, one will be reborn in one's quality of humanity that is supreme, transcending the standstill as already mentioned. When seeing the real value of the planet earth and the universe, one will not stand still, be crazed, sluggishly holding onto the value of silver and gold, which are ordinary minerals and elements. They are only special in that gold resembles the rays of the divine sun in some moments. But it is only the color that is exceedingly, supremely beautiful. For instance, some mornings the dear sun creates an atmosphere of gold gleaming purely. Even the rocks far away all turn into rocks of gold, including even the rocks of the divine forest and other jewels taking the place of all the rays of the stars in the solar system. Reflecting brightness as if diamonds had taken the place of the dew. Good and special in the divinely colored perspective of the universe.

But the minerals silver and gold really attained power in coming to have value in an economic sense. And have turned into a wicked enemy of humankind. Replacing ignorance, obstructing the view of humanity, making it think narrowly. Hurt, with greed and desire going in a single direction. The face sticking to the ground like a reptile's: Hurrying to lower one's face looking for food, not knowing how to look up to search for other, ethical precepts in the world. Gold, from the economic point of view, may have poison, may destroy the soul of humanity, making it dissolve, go to pieces, be utterly ruined, as though bereft of a soul, like a mummified corpse. Like a ghost of a corpse not yet burned that can walk. While alive, as though delirious in sleep, not knowing how to wake up and see the real value of life. One will die repeatedly in one's deaths. Ensnared twofold. Wasting the value of being a supreme being for nothing. Not being born once.

With the silver and gold rays glittering purely, the sun reflects divine value onto the world, the worth of which cannot be estimated. Coincidentally these values are not the same as the value of gold in the economic sense that humanity clings to. Therefore they seem like something without value, something that one can just trample on. But the golden rays are never defiled. They have shone onto the earth for ten millions of millions of *kalpas* without becoming old; they are still always new and come back brand new each minute the gaze of humanity falls on them. You do not have to wash them with detergent, nevertheless they are clean. In addition they have rays of warmth hidden away in a miraculous way: the element of divine fire they sacrifice as warmth to the human world, which would otherwise be cold, amasses a lot of merit.

There are some groups of people, like scientists for instance, which have to show an interest, have to care. But for the most part humans are devoid of interest and care. If the sun were a slave of humanity like earth, it would already be rotten at this time. Hardly anyone is interested in the real value of the divine golden rays. Except for the gods, those highest beings. And a tiny insignificant father like me, who honors the miraculous real value of the universe and every single thing in nature. I see the profound divine value until all of my heart is full to the point of almost overflowing, richer than a millionaire's.

But humanity for the most part is not interested, has no tranquility. Its heart is not calm. It is taken up in ordinariness, which becomes lowliness after a while.

I do not want my children to feel and think like most people. I want you to think with your own inventiveness. But at this time you are still innocent, lacking teachers who really have knowledge. You are still young, new to the world. I therefore must point things out to both of you who can just barely walk, still innocent, by writing in prose. Waiting for you to grow up and be educated so that you can read, reviewing the words that your father explained for you to clearly understand forever. And then build on them with your own thinking that diligently directs its attention to critical examination and to learning from the Lord Buddha, the highest being. You will see the value of the future at the time that you will have sons and daughters; continuing your line of blood, you will probably have to think of your father, just as I am thinking of you now, my children. Like grasping a wheel and a cart rolling toward one. Or the long and short hands of a clock which will always circle back to the hour of the life of you two—that is, the early morning, the rising of the sun, like you are just now being explained and being taught to look at the golden rays. And time will gradually go by, becoming late morning, midday, afternoon and evening until finally reaching the time of dusk.

Children, do not forget, please remember well. If you forget time wastefully, if you throw time away, it is like throwing away the real value of life. If you do not think and practice your intellect, study and learn like philosophers, then you will be wasting the value of your life senselessly. Even if reborn for so many hundreds of lives, you will be wasting them. Or like the cart that rolls toward you as mentioned, completing the same old circle of the old stupid cow, that has an extremely heavy life yoke. Dragging the yoke along with extreme difficulty, never asking oneself what goal there might be. Never and nowhere. In addition, having a master that is ignorance. Darkness, blindness, not knowing what dictates its existence. That is the stupid, foolish cow, dragging the exceedingly heavy yoke and cart of life with the illusion of the five *khanda*, going on aimlessly. It is to be taken pity on.

This morning you saw the monks on their rounds for alms. I taught you to pay respect to the monks each time you meet them. In the old times, it was taught like this. When both of you are grown up and have gotten an education to the utmost extent, hurry to humble your heart to the Lord Buddha or the Three Gems immediately. You cannot delay this or hesitate, for the reason that human life in the present is without substance to the utmost extent already. You will have to humble yourself to the Three Gems, practicing and studying the Buddha, the *Dhamma*, and the *Sangha* in great detail. You will be able to enhance your special powers as well as your power of natural insight. Taking all Three Gems into your soul. This will make the stupid, foolish cow see the end of the path. So it can drag the yoke and the cart of life on with contentment, having a perspective, that is not one of a stupid cow which was once deaf, dumb, and blind with ignorance, dragging the extremely heavy yoke and cart of life without a destination at the end of the path and dying senselessly.

As far as this morning goes, let us go home, children. When evening falls, I will take you to see the rays of the sun disappear from the horizon, to look at all the birds and crows in their nests, all the plants drying and wilting and some that part and bloom, sending out a fragrant perfume, smelling sweetly, scattering in the wind, and to look at the new lives which just begin at the time of dusk; they are manifold.

As for this morning, you already saw the ethical precepts of the drops of dew. Let's return home to eat now. At this time your mother will already have prepared food for you and be waiting." So all three lives walked along together.

The life of the father was in the middle with the son on the right side and the daughter on the left. All three lives walked with each other, to another one that was waiting, and then together they made up four lives, harmonizing in one unity with the force of attraction and loving care.

Kawi Sri Ayuthaya[23]

SITH ISARA SERI KHONG PUANG PRACHARAT—PRAKAT JETANAROM 14 TULA UDOMSITH ISARA ("THE PEOPLE'S RIGHT TO FREEDOM—STATEMENT OF INTENTION 14 OCTOBER RIGHTS AND FREEDOM")

All humanity, gems of freedom,
As the sun's majestic beauty in the sky,
Free, like the Bodhisattva's heart,
For eternal heavenly peace.

The people, savvy, rise up,
Awake, demand rights and freedom of the age returned,
Refuse to submit to dictatorship,
Democracy rules the land.

A real human needs to rule himself,
Don't be in fear, under anyone's sole,
Dictators, bloodthirsty, making tears flow,
Depraved, inauspicious, accustomed to exploiting Thailand.

The dignity of the People-subjects,
Powerful unity of civilized disposition,
When society is just and freedom wins,
The new society shines with every soul.

The rights and freedom of the People.
The power to rule oneself, magnificently,
"Peaceful justice of the People," wonderful throughout time,
Brave in its justice.

The miraculous rights and freedom,
Vested in the People, most wonderful,
Siam's dignity propelled by consciousness,
Dharma leading the world to eternal peace.

Notes

Chapter 1

1. Marc Weeks and Frederic Maurel also discuss the centrality of time in Angkarn's oeuvre in "Voyages across the Web of Time: Angkarn, Nietzsche and Temporal Colonization," comparing Angkarn's to Nietzsche's concept of temporality.

2. Christian Bauer, "Angkarn Kalyanapong: Das lyrische Werk" (Angkarn Kalyanapong: The Poetic Oeuvre), entry, *Kindlers Literatur Lexikon*, Stuttgart: J. B. Metzler, http://www.kll-online.de. My translation.

3. On Thailand's semicoloniality, see Lysa Hong, "Invisible Semicolony: The Postcolonial Condition and Royal National History in Thailand," and Tamara Loos, *Subject Siam: Family, Law, and Colonial Modernity in Thailand*. On colonial modernity and the ways in which the colonial extends beyond the boundaries of colonized territories proper, see Tani Barlow, "Debates over Colonial Modernity in East Asia and Another Alternative" and "Advertising Ephemera and the Angel of History."

4. From the poetic prose piece "Nimit Nai Sai Rung"—"*Nimitta* in the Rainbow," *Yad Nam Khang Khue Namta Khong Wela (Dew Drops Are the Tears of Time)*.

5. I have translated *arom* here as "spirit," but it could also be translated as "mood."

6. Suchitra Chongstitvatana, "Kawiniphon Khong Angkarn Kallayanapong: Sasana Haeng Sunthari" (The Poetry of Angkarn Kallayanapong: The Religion of Aesthetics).

7. Marc Weeks and Frederic Maurel, "Voyages across the Web of Time."

8. Dipesh Chakrabarty, "The Time of History and the Times of Gods," 35.

9. All quotes from Bliss Cua Lim, *Translating Time: Cinema, the Fantastic, and Temporal Critique*, 11.

10. Pheng Cheah, *What Is a World? On Postcolonial Literature as World Literature*, 192.

11. Pheng Cheah, *What Is a World?*, 194.
12. Pheng Cheah, *What Is a World?*, 195.
13. Pheng Cheah, *What Is a World?*, 207.
14. Marc Weeks and Frederique Maurel note the poet's antiforeign inclination in "Voyages across the Web of Time," 327.
15. Interview by author with Ormkaew Kallayanapong, December 9, 2016. See also Chetana Nagavajara on the transnational connections of Angkarn's work in Ruenruethai Sajjaphan, ed., *80 Pi Angkarn Kallayanapong* (80 Years of Angkarn Kallayanapong), 77–79.
16. Ruenruethai Sajjaphan, ed., *80 Pi Angkarn Kallayanapong*, 121.
17. I use the masculine pronoun here very consciously, as Angkarn largely envisions a male producer of art—or himself—as the poet.
18. Suchitra Chongstitvatana, "On the Formation of Thai Poetical Convention and Thai Concepts of Poets and Poetry," in "The Nature of Modern Thai Poetry Considered with Reference to the Works of Angkhan Kalayanaphong, Naowarat Phongphaibun and Suchit Wongthet," 246–96.
19. Suchitra Chongstitvatana, "The Nature of Modern Thai Poetry," 281.
20. Suchitra Chongstitvatana, "The Nature of Modern Thai Poetry," 284.
21. Suchitra Chongstitvatana, "The Nature of Modern Thai Poetry," 284.
22. Trisilpa Boonkhachorn, "Intertextuality in Thai Literary and Social Contexts: A Study of Contemporary Poets," 124–25. Trisilpa further explains, "During a time when poetry is not the dominant genre in literary circles, poets without patronage hardly survive in the material world, yet are brave enough to declare their poet's manifestos. The status of poetry is still divine and eternal beyond history and time, yet it comes down to earth to serve social needs" (125).
23. See Chris Baker and Pasuk Pongphaichit, "Ideologies, 1940s to 1970s," in *A History of Thailand*, 167–98.
24. Chris Baker and Pasuk Pongphaichit, *A History of Thailand*, 147.
25. Chris Baker and Pasuk Pongphaichit, *A History of Thailand*, 147.
26. Chris Baker and Pasuk Pongphaichit, *A History of Thailand*, 148.
27. Chris Baker and Pasuk Pongphaichit, *A History of Thailand*, 149.
28. Chris Baker and Pasuk Pongphaichit, *A History of Thailand*, 150.
29. Thongchai Winichakul, *Siam Mapped: A History of the Geo-Body of a Nation*; Baker and Pasuk, see section on "Extending the Nation-State," in *A History of Thailand*, 170–74.
30. Chris Baker and Pasuk Pongphaichit, *A History of Thailand*, 171.
31. Chris Baker and Pasuk Pongphaichit, "Monarchy Resurgent," in *A History of Thailand*, 174–78.
32. Chris Baker and Pasuk Pongphaichit, *A History of Thailand*, 199
33. Chris Baker and Pasuk Pongphaichit, *A History of Thailand*, 199.

34. See, for instance, Tyrell Haberkorn, *Revolution Interrupted: Farmers, Students, Law, and Violence in Northern Thailand*.
35. Marc Weeks and Frederic Maurel, "Voyages across the Web of Time," 327.
36. Chris Baker and Pasuk Pongpaichit, *A History of Thailand*, 203.
37. Chris Baker and Pasuk Pongpaichit, *A History of Thailand*, 201, 221.
38. Chris Baker and Pasuk Pongpaichit, *A History of Thailand*, 199.
39. Chris Baker and Pasuk Pongpaichit, *A History of Thailand*, 233.
40. Chris Baker and Pasuk Pongpaichit, *A History of Thailand*, 233–34.
41. Some of the luminaries of a Buddhist studies that investigated the relation of Buddhism to statecraft include Stanley Tambiah, *World Conqueror and World Renouncer: A Study of Buddhism and Polity in Thailand against a Historical Background*; Charles Keyes, *Thailand: Buddhist Kingdom as Modern Nation-State*; and Christine Gray, "Thailand: The Soteriological State in the 1970s."
42. Richard Gombrich, *Theravada Buddhism. A Social History from Ancient Benares to Modern Colombo*; Donald K. Swearer, *The Buddhist World of Southeast Asia*.
43. Justin McDaniel, *The Lovelorn Ghost and the Magical Monk: Practicing Buddhism in Modern Thailand*.
44. See especially Trisilpa Boonkhachorn, "Intertextuality in Thai Literary and Social Contexts," 233–57. Other major works on Angkarn's oeuvre include Dhanate Vespada, "Lila Nai Ngan Roi Kaeo Khong Angkhan Kalayanapong" (Style in Angkhan Kalayanapong's Poetical Prose), a 400-page master's thesis.
45. Earlier works include, for instance, Herbert Phillips's *Modern Thai Literature: With an Ethnographic Interpretation*, as well as a significant body of work in German by Klaus Rosenberg and Klaus Wenk.
46. I translate the title of this poem as "Pledge of the Poet" (rather than "Testament"). This pertains to both no. 3 and no. 4 of the translations listed here.
47. Anjali Nerlekar writes about the Bombay poets in *Bombay Modern: Arun Kolatkar and Bilingual Literary Culture*. On the Bengali Hungryalist poets' influence on and politicization of Ginsberg, see Steven Belletto, "The Beat Generation Meets the Hungry Generation: U.S.—Calcutta Networks and the 1960s 'Revolt of the Personal.'"
48. Christian Bauer, "Angkarn Kalyanapong: Das lyrische Werk" (Angkarn Kalyanapong: The Poetic Oeuvre).
49. Christian Bauer, "Naowarat Pongpaiboon beīyan gwām gleīān¹ hway" (Naowarat Pongpaiboon: Mere Movement!).
50. Some of the difference in outlook between Angkarn and his Art for Life colleagues may moreover be attributed to age: during the events in the 1970s, Angkarn was no longer a student, but was approaching his 50s.
51. Interview by author with Ormkaew Kallayanapong, December 9, 2016.
52. Stuart Hall, "Notes on Deconstructing 'the Popular,'" 453.

53. Christian Bauer, "Angkarn Kalyanapong: Das lyrische Werk" (Angkarn Kalyanapong: The Poetic Oeuvre).

54. Ruenruethai Sajjaphan, ed., *80 Pi Angkarn Kallayanapong* (80 Years of Angkarn Kallayanapong), 145.

55. Anuk Pitukthanin, personal communication, May 26, 2017.

56. Interview by author with Ormkaew Kallayanapong, December 9, 2016.

57. Interview by author with Ormkaew Kallayanapong, December 9, 2016.

58. Angkarn Kallayanapong, *Kawi Sri Ayuthaya* (Poet of Ayuthaya), 8.

59. Interview by author with Ormkaew Kallayanapong, December 9, 2016.

Chapter 2

1. We can understand *nimit/nimitta* (Thai, Pali) here to mean a sign or even an image. For *nimitta*, Rhys Davids and Stede's *Pali-English Dictionary* lists the definitions "sign, omen, portent, prognostication" as well as "outward appearance, attribute, phenomenon (opp. essence)," but also "mental reflex, image." *Pali English Dictionary*, comp. Thomas Williams Rhys Davids and William Stede, s.v. *nimitta*.

2. Suchitra Chongstitvatana discusses the poet's "religion of aesthetics" in her 1987 essay "Kawiniphon Khong Angkarn Kallayanapong" (The Poetry of Angkarn Kallayanapong), which the next chapter reviews in detail. See also Chetana Nagavajara, "Art in Place of Nirvana: Western Aesthetics and the Poetry of Angkarn Kalayanaphong."

3. See Anindita Niyogi Balslev, *A Study of Time in Indian Philosophy*.

4. Suchitra argues that "the poet's awareness of the destructive nature of time does not prevent him from perceiving time as the creator of the beauty in nature" (47). Suchitra writes more about time in "The Nature of Modern Thai Poetry," 47–49.

5. See Hari Shankar Prasad, "The Concept of Time in Pali Buddhism."

6. Steven Collins, *Selfless Persons*, 21–22.

7. See Steven Collins, *Selfless Persons*, 55. A further definition Collins provides is in "'conditioned things' (*saṃkhāra*—that is, all things produced by *karma*)" (82). He also notes, "It is a mental category ('name' as opposed to 'form') and is thus normally translated 'mental formations'" (202).

8. Steven Collins, *Selfless Persons*, 202.

9. Steven Collins details the significance of the *paṭiccasamuppāda* with regard to the notion of *anattā*, nonself, on pp. 103–10 of *Selfless Persons*.

10. Steven Collins, *Selfless Persons*, 204.

11. Steven Collins, *Selfless Persons*, 262.

12. Steven Collins, *Selfless Persons*, 82.

13. In Angkarn's work, this term denotes the autonomy and authority of the artist; in Theravada Buddhism, it is used as a term that, according to Collins, describes the ways in which the illusion of a persistent self is constituted (Steven Collins, *Selfless Persons*, 100–103).

14. Suchitra Chongstitvatana, "The Nature of Modern Thai Poetry," 46.

15. We might understand this as an instance in which "the poet's awareness of the destructive nature of time does not prevent him from perceiving time as the creator of the beauty in nature." Suchitra Chongstitvatana, "The Nature of Modern Thai Poetry," 47.

16. The section of the text that addresses the *khanda* directly reads, "That is the stupid, foolish cow, dragging the exceedingly heavy yoke and cart of life with the illusion of the five *khanda*, going on aimlessly."

17. While Liz Wilson describes a temporary deferral of detachment before ultimate spiritual resolution in Buddhist hagiographies, Justin McDaniel describes more pervasive counterdoctrinal qualities in contemporary Thai Buddhism. See Wilson, *Charming Cadavers: Horrific Figurations of the Feminine in Indian Buddhist Hagiographic Literature*, 86, and McDaniel, *The Lovelorn Ghost and the Magical Monk*.

18. Melford Spiro makes a distinction between nibbanic and kammatic Buddhism, while later work by A. Thomas Kirsch, Pattana Kitiarsa, and B. J. Terwiel attempts to bridge this divide. See Melford E. Spiro, *Buddhism and Society: A Great Tradition and Its Burmese Vicissitudes*; A. Thomas Kirsch, "Complexity in the Thai Religious System: An Interpretation"; Pattana Kitiarsa, "Beyond Syncretism: Hybridization of Popular Religion in Contemporary Thailand"; and B. J. Terwiel, *Monks and Magic: Revisiting a Classic Study of Religious Ceremonies in Thailand*.

19. Steven Collins, *Selfless Persons*, 262.

20. Steven Collins, *Selfless Persons*, 262.

21. See Jackson, "Buddhadāsa on Rebirth and Paṭiccasamuppāda," 101–27.

22. Steven Collins, *Selfless Persons*, 203–4.

23. Benedict Anderson, *Imagined Communities*, 24.

24. Harry Harootunian, "Remembering the Historical Present,' 483.

25. Benedict Anderson, *Imagined Communities*, 24.

26. Steven Collins, *Selfless Persons*, 201.

Chapter 3

1. Suchitra Chongstitvatana investigates the poet's development of *nirat* convention in the chapter "Convention and Modernity in Modern Thai Poetry: A Study of Angkhan Kalayanaphong's *Lamnam Phu Kradueng*," 8–69, in "The Nature of Modern Thai Poetry."

2. In addition to designating this genre of poetry, the word *nirat* (which derives from Sanskrit *nir* + *āśā* meaning "without hope" or "without desire") is generally used to mean "separation," "to leave," "to be separated from." Manas Chitakasem notes that it also means "to be without something which is dearly desired." Manas Chitakasem, "The Emergence and Development of the Nirat Genre

in Thai Poetry," 138. The *Pojananukrom Chabab Rachabandithayasathan* defines the term as "a) leaving, roaming about, to be without; b) being without hope, desire." Rachabandithayasathan, *Pojananukrom Chabab Rachabandithayasathan* (Royal Institute Dictionary), s.v. *nirat*. In this chapter, I use *nirat*, as in Thai, for both the singular and the plural of the word.

Paul Schweisguth defines *nirat* as follows: "*Nirat* est un mot d'origine sanscrite qui signifie 'séparation, bannissement'; au Siam il sert à designer une pièce destinée à chanter la douleur d'un départ, d'une absence. En général, ce sont des poèmes d'amour, l'auteur chante avant tout les charmes de la belle qu'il vient de quitter, puis au fur et à mésure qu'il progresse sur son chemin. Il note les péripéties de son voyage. Il les rapporte quand il peut à des souvenirs qui lui sont chers; en énumerant ainsi les noms de lieu sur son trajet il aura pour chacun d'eux une pensée affectueuse à l'adresse de sa bien-aimée." Paul Schweisguth, *Étude sur la littérature siamoise*, 90.

3. The *Chindamani* is a text on versification believed to have been composed during the reign of King Phra Narai (1656–1688), though the extant version is from the Rattanakosin period. The manual codifies the use of poetic vocabulary, spelling, pronunciation, and versification. See Phrachao Borommakot, *Chindamani*.

4. Two other *nirat* that are thought to predate *Chindamani* are *Khlong Thawathotsamat* and *Khlong Kamsuan Si Prat*.

5. Manas Chitakasem, "The Emergence," 143.

6. As Manas ("The Emergence," 146–47) observes, "Here the chronological process is converted into a time scale which is applied to a particular journey. The excursional process goes through a qualitative change which results in the conversion of the character of a literary figure to the poet writing about himself in his own poem. The fictional excursion described becomes the description of an actual journey taken at a prescribed moment or period and in a prescribed geographical setting."

7. Suchitra Chongstitvatana, "The Nature of Modern Thai Poetry," 18.

8. Manas Chitakasem, "The Emergence," 143.

9. Translated by Manas Chitakasem, "The Emergence," 144.

10. Manas Chitakasem ("The Emergence," 156–57) notes that "although the techniques of pun, transfers, and other ideas arising from the locale have been extensively employed, the conventional theme of love-longing and separation was partially broken. Emphasis has been placed on the poet's personal experiences of life in general. Place names and objects at each locale have been used to reflect ideas, observations, and attitudes toward human life and society in connection with the recollection of the poet's personal history. Other elements, for instance, etymology of the place names, history of the people and places, and humorous as well as philosophical passages, have frequently been included, perhaps to stimulate interest and to arouse questioning in the minds of the general readers."

11. As Manas Chitakasem ("The Emergence," 152) writes, "Sunthorn Phu brought to Nirat many elements, such as the concept of personal history as self-reflection, philosophical statements on life and people, social criticism, etc."

12. See Sunthon Phu, "Nirat Phukhao Thong," *Nirat Sunthon Phu*.

13. In this *nirat*, the poet expresses disdain for the countryside in verses 24 and 28 and states his preference for the city in verse 44.

14. Translated from the original text in Harald Hundius, *Das Nirat Müang Kläng von Sunthon Phu: Analyse und Übersetzung eines thailändischen Reisegedichtes*, 105. Hundius renders the passage as follows: "Thap Näng–Wehmut ergreift mich; man sieht nur Bauernhütten. Auch an den Bauernmädchen kann das Herz sich kaum erfreuen: mit einer dunklen, schorfigen Kruste ist ihre Haut bedeckt, als sei sie mit Indigo bestrichen. Die Mädchen in der Stadt, und seien es Sklavinnen, sind zwei-, dreimal hübscher als die Mädchen hier. Ach, hat man die Hauptstadt erst verlassen, findet Schönheit man nicht mehr! Je länger ich daran denke, desto bestürzter bin ich und sehne mich zurück nach Bangkok" (52).

15. Craig J. Reynolds, "Sedition in Thai History: A Nineteenth-Century Poem and Its Critics," 24.

16. Luang Phatthanaphongphakdi, *Nirat Nongkhai*.

17. See, for instance, Manas Chitakasem, "The Emergence," 139, as well as Hundius, *Das Nirat Müang Kläng*, 1.

18. Naowarat Pongpaiboon, *Krung Thep Thawarawadi: Jaruek Wai Nai Pi Thi 200 Haeng Krung Rattanakosin* (1986); Mala Khamjan, *Jao Jan Phom Hom: Nirat Phrathat In Khwaen* (1991).

19. These include Angkarn Kallayanapong, *Lamnam Phu Kradueng* (Kradueng Mountain Song) and *Bangkok Kaeo Kamsuan Rue Nirat Nakhon Si Thammarat* (Lament for Beloved Bangkok or Nirat Nakhon Si Thammarat).

20. Short poems with *nirat* character can be found in Angkarn Kallayanapong, *Kawiniphon Khong Angkarn Kallayanapong* (The Poetry of Angkarn Kallayanapong); *Bang Bot Jak Suan Kaeo* (Passages from the Crystal Garden); and *Panithan Kawi* (The Poet's Testament).

21. Thak Chaloemtiarana, *Thailand: The Politics of Despotic Paternalism*.

22. See, for example, "Ayuthaya," "Ayuthaya Wipayok," "Sinlapa Ayuthaya," "Sukhothai," and "Si Sachanalai" in *Kawiniphon* and "Ayuthaya" in *Lamnam Phu Kradueng*. The theme of Ayuthaya and the past is also echoed in several other poems, such as in "Laeng Wanakhadi" in *Kawiniphon*.

23. A *chedi* or *stupa* is a structure that houses relics.

24. A *bot* or *ubosot* is an ordination hall and a *vihan* is the building that houses the Buddha image or images.

25. A *kalpa* is a Buddhist term for a temporal span comparable to an eon.

26. *Khlong* and *kap* are the oldest meters used in Thai poetry.

27. See, for example, Naowarat Pongpaiboon and Sujit Wongthet.

28. What Chetana Nagavajara has called the "rugged austerity" of the Ayuthaya style that Angkarn seeks to emulate lends itself well to communicating the emotion of pain and the critical message of the poems on Ayuthaya and cultural loss. Chetana Nagavajara, "Art in Place of Nirvana," 213.

29. Trisilpa Boonkhachorn, "Intertextuality in Thai Literary and Social Contexts," 192. Regarding Angkarn's long *nirat*, *Lamnam Phu Kradueng*, Klaus Wenk remarks that, although the titles of many of the 102 poems mark new stations on the way to Phu Kradueng, the content of the poems exceeds the scope of the traditional *nirat*. According to Wenk, such formal criteria of *nirat* as the creation of links between the individual sections through certain formulas—the use of expressions like "having arrived in," for example—are also not used in Angkarn's *nirat*. Importantly, Wenk further remarks that Angkarn does not observe the traditionally strict metrical rules of *nirat*. Klaus Wenk, *Studien zur Literatur der Thai*, Band IV, 117–18.

30. Suchitra Chongstitvatana, "The Nature of Modern Thai Poetry," 20–21, 23.

31. See Liz Wilson, *Charming Cadavers*.

32. Suchitra Chongstitvatana, "The Nature of Modern Thai Poetry," 20. As she further notes, this stands in contrast to the invective with which he frequently describes women at other points in his poetry (21).

33. Suchitra Chongstitvatana, "The Nature of Modern Thai Poetry," 18–19.

34. Suchitra Chongstitvatana, "The Nature of Modern Thai Poetry," 24.

35. Temple names have been left in the original in the translation of this poem.

36. A *prang* is a spirelike part of temple architecture.

37. See "Jaruek Adid," *Kawiniphon*.

38. See "Krap Phra Boromakhru," *Panithan Kawi*.

39. See "Sanam Luang," *Bangkok Kaeo Kamsuan* and "Krung Thep Thailaen," *Lamnam Phu Kradueng*.

40. Thus, Naowarat Pongpaiboon reflects on the violent events of the 1970s in *Athit Thueng Jan* and *Tak Rung Rueang Payom*, as does Khomthuan Khanthanu in *Natakam Bon Lan Kwang*.

41. Thomas Hudak, "Thailand, Poetry of."

42. The year 2018 saw a Tang Chang exhibition at Chicago's Smart Museum titled *The Painting that is Painted with Poetry Is Profoundly Beautiful*. Nora Taylor reviews the exhibition that integrates Tang's conceptual poetry with painting in Nora A. Taylor, "Tang Chang," 113.

43. This term denotes a hierarchized system of social ranking introduced in the Ayuthaya period that was originally based on control over land. *Sakdina* is sometimes translated as "feudal," and has in the present come to mean "elite."

44. See Chit Phumisak's 1957 *Sinlapa Phuea Chiwit Sinlapa Phuea Prachachon* (Art for Life, Art for the People) and Atsani Phonlachan's 1972 *Sinlapa Haeng Kap Klon* (The Art of Poetry), as well as a 1979 volume that assembles his essays, *Kho Khit Jak Wanakhadi* (Thoughts from Literature).

45. See Kasian Tejapira, *Commodifying Marxism: The Formation of Modern Thai Radical Culture, 1927–1958*. See also Yuangrat and Paul Wedel, *Radical Thought, Thai Mind: The Development of Revolutionary Ideas in Thailand*, 77–87.

46. These poets include Naowarat Pongpaiboon and Sujit Wongthet, as well as Khomthuan Khanthanu.

47. It is important to note that Anderson's and other researchers' contextualization of Thai history within US politics and global influence must be understood also within the context of these researchers' language competencies and access to archives. Had there been significant attention to and review of Chinese- or Japanese-language archives at the time, our understanding of the Thai history and politics of the Cold War would differ significantly.

See Benedict Anderson, *In the Mirror: Literature and Politics in Siam in the American Era*, 12ff.

48. The idea that the period from 1973 through 1976 represented an ideal of democratic rule also has to be qualified. This period included particularly violent phases and events as reactionary forces retaliated against democratic gains. See, for instance, Tyrell Haberkorn, *Revolution Interrupted*.

49. Naowarat Pongpaiboon, *Phiang Khwam Khluean Wai* (Mere Movement).

50. The poem "Krathum Baen" takes its title from the name of a working-class neighborhood in Bangkok.

51. See "Kawi" ("Poet/ry") in Naowarat Pongpaiboon, *Phleng Khlui Phiu*. See also Angkarn's "Panithan Khong Kawi" ("The Pledge of the Poet") in *Kawiniphon* and "Panithan Kawi ("The Poet's Testament") in *Panithan Kawi*.

52. See the important piece by Suchitra Chongstitvatana, "Kawiniphon Khong Angkarn Kallayanapong" (The Poetry of Angkarn Kallayanapong).

53. Thak Chaloemtiarana, *Thailand*, 147.

54. David K. Wyatt, *Thailand: A Short History*, 281.

55. Thak Chaloemtiarana, *Thailand*, 99.

56. David Wyatt, *Thailand*.

57. Wyatt notes that there was "little social and political differentiation" in Sukhothai. David Wyatt, *Thailand*, 58.

58. Sheldon I. Pollock, *Language of the Gods in the World of Men: Sanskrit, Culture, and Power in Premodern India*, 1.

59. Pollock details how Sanskrit was tied to notions of imperial order and kingship: "If the order of Sanskrit poetry was tied to the order of Sanskrit grammar, that order was itself a model or prototype of the moral, social, and political order. A just (*sādhu*) king was one who himself used and promoted the use of correct language (*sādhuśabda*). Not only was Sanskrit therefore the appropriate vehicle for the expression of royal will, but Sanskrit learning became a component of kingliness." Sheldon Pollock, "The Cosmopolitan Vernacular," 14.

60. See Barend Jan Terwiel, "The Introduction of Indian Prosody among the Thais," and Klaus Rosenberg, *Die epischen Chan-Dichtungen in der Literatur Thailands*.

61. Angkarn Kallayanapong, *Kawiniphon*, 57–59.

62. See Bhawan Ruangsilp, *Dutch East India Company Merchants at the Court of Ayutthaya: Dutch Perceptions of the Thai Kingdom, ca. 1604–1765*, and Dhiravat na Pombejra, *Court, Company, and Campong: Essays on the VOC Presence in Ayutthaya*. See also Chris Baker and Pasuk Pongphaichit, *A History of Ayutthaya: Siam in the Early Modern World*, and Charnvit Kasetsiri, *Ayutthaya: Prawatisat lae Kan Mueang* (Ayutthaya: History and Politics).

63. Dhiravat na Pombejra, *Court, Company, and Campong*, 25.

64. Krom Wichakan, *Wicha Prawattisat Chan Mathayomsueksa Pi Thi 2* (Social Studies Textbook: History, Eighth Grade), 60–61.

65. Krom Wichakan, *Wicha Prawattisat*, 1963, 57.

66. Krom Wichakan, *Wicha Prawattisat*, 1963, 40–41.

67. Krom Wichakan, *Wicha Prawattisat*, 1964, 38.

68. Krom Wichakan, *Wicha Prawattisat*, 1964, 45.

69. As Trisilpa remarks, "It can be concluded that the first priority of poetic values or literariness is the musicality of words." Trisilpa Boonkhachorn, "Intertextuality," 77. See also Manas Chitakasem, "Poetic Conventions and Modern Thai Poetry," 39, and Klaus Rosenberg, *Die epischen Chan-Dichtungen in der Literatur Thailands*, 22.

70. Trisilpa Boonkhachorn, "Intertextuality," 192.

71. B. J. Terwiel, "The Introduction of Indian Prosody among the Thais." For an analysis of the poetics of politics and the role of Sanskrit in relation to vernacular languages in South and Southeast Asia, see Sheldon Pollock, *Language of the Gods in the World of Men* and "The Cosmopolitan Vernacular."

72. *Kaphayasarawilasini* and *Kaphayakantha* likely predate *Cindamani*. These treatises on the *khlong* and *kap* meters are written in both Pali and Thai; it is not certain in which language they were originally composed. *Tamra Chan Wanaphruet lae Matraphruet* is a textbook on *chan* meters translated from the Pali *Vutthodaya* by Phraparamanuchit during the reign of Rama III (1824–1851) that explains and indigenizes 50 *chan wanaphruet*, *chan* governed by numbers of syllables, and 8 *chan matraphruet*, *chan* governed by syllabic instants. See Klaus Rosenberg, *Die epischen Chan-Dichtungen in der Literatur Thailands*.

73. See, for example, Klaus Rosenberg, *Die epischen Chan-Dichtungen in der Literatur Thailands*, and Thomas Hudak, *The Indigenization of Pali Meters in Thai Poetry*.

74. Trisilpa Boonkhachorn, "Intertextuality," 156.

75. Trisilpa Boonkhachorn, "Intertextuality," 202–3. *Klon*, for instance, is a meter thought to have folk origins. It was appropriated by the Ayuthaya court in the eighteenth century and later made use of for purposes of resistance to the dictatorships of the 1970s. Thus, it becomes more difficult to assign definite connotations of resistance or consent to genres and forms.

76. Suchitra Chongstitvatana, "Thai Concepts of Poets and Poetry," in "The Nature of Modern Thai Poetry," 281–96.

77. The verb *boriphat* means to reproach, censure, accuse, criticize, or revile. Suchitra Chongstitvatana, class lecture, 1990.

78. "Benjasin" ("Five Precepts"), *Bangkok Kaeo Kamsuan*, 125.

79. Untitled, *Panithan Kawi*, 39.

80. The language of the Bangkok poems also evokes the Vietnam War years, a period in which the influx of American GIs seeking "Rest and Recreation" contributed toward shaping Thai cultural forms (Personal communication, Thak Chaloemtiarana, June 25, 2009).

81. Michael Wright, *Ongkan Chaeng Nam* (Thai with English translation).

82. Klaus Wenk, *Phali lehrt die Jüngeren* (*Phali Son Nong*).

83. Not all forms of *khlong* are complex, but forms such as *khlong si suphap* can be considered complex.

84. Trisilpa Boonkhachorn, "Intertextuality," 187.

85. Trisilpa Boonkhachorn, "Intertextuality," 190. *Kap* probably originated from the Pali meters *kap sarawilasini* and *kap kantha*.

Chapter 4

1. Martin Puchner, *Poetry of the Revolution: Marx, Manifestos, and the Avant-gardes*, 1.

2. See in Angkarn Kallayanapong, *Kawiniphon*: "Laeng Wanakadi" (36), "Phi Phung Tai" (61), "Om" (91), "Ku Duang Jai" (130), "Lak Chai" (131), "Wang Sawaeng Arai Nai Chiwa" (170), "Koed Ma Thammai Nai Chat Ni" (183), "Duek Ni Chiwi Ko San Long" (194), and "Phutnaisawan" (248); in *Lamnam Phu Kradueng*: "Om" (32), "Om Nom Wai Phra Saratsawadi" (39), "Khon Kaen Kho Thaen Kha Chiwit" (75), "Khon Kaen Phaen Din Sin Nang Kaeo" (87), "Kha Noi Mi Khru Yu Thua Fa" (240); in *Bangkok Kaeo Kamsuan*: "Kroen" (189) and "Pakka Thip" (338); and in *Panithan Kawi*: "Din Sai Chiwit Lae Amatasin" (27), "Krap Phra Boromakhru" (45), "Raluek Thueng Phra Saphanyu" (54), and "Jiaranai Kaeo Mani Haeng Chiwit" (73).

3. Mary Ann Caws, *Manifesto: A Century of Isms*, xxi.

4. Mary Ann Caws, *Manifesto*, xxi.

5. It is Suchitra Chongstitvatana's 1987 essay, "Kawiniphon Khong Angkarn Kallayanapong (The Poetry of Angkarn Kallayanapong), that establishes *panithan* also as a critical term.

Sulak Sivaraksa and Hiram Woodward translate *panithan* as "testament." Further possible translations include "vow, dedication, resolution, determination." The *Potjananukrom Chabab Ratchabandithayasathan* (Royal Institute Dictionary) definition of the Sanskrit-derived *pranithan* is "the establishing of a desire." Rachabandithayasathan, *Pojananukrom Chabab Rachabandithayasathan* (Royal Institute Dictionary), s.v. *pranithan*. The corresponding Sanskrit term is *praṇidhāna*, defined as "attention paid to, vehement desire, vow," from *pra-ni-dhā*, "to resolve upon, give the whole attention to." Monier-Williams, Cappeller, and Leumann's *Sanskrit-English Dictionary* also lists "Exertion, endeavor." Monier Monier-Williams, Carl Cappeller, and Ernst Leumann. *Sanskrit-English Dictionary: Etymologically and Philologically Arranged With Special Reference to Cognate Indo-European Languages*, s.v. *praṇidhāna, pra-ni-dhā*.

Rhys Davids and Stede's *Pali-English Dictionary* explains *paṇidhāna* as "aspiration, longing, prayer." Thomas Williams Rhys Davids and William Stede, comps., *Pali English Dictionary*, s.v. *paṇidhāna*.

6. Mary Ann Caws, *Manifesto*, xix.

7. Suchitra Chongstitvatana, "The Nature of Modern Thai Poetry," 281–85.

8. I have chosen the translation "testament" for easier distinction between the two *panithan*. In addition, testament might also signify the augmentation of dedication that occurs between the two poems. See Chamnongsri L. Rutnin, trans., in *The S.E.A. Write Anthology of Thai Short Stories and Poems*, 107–9. See Rutnin in Michael Wright, *Angkarn Kalyanapong: A Contemporary Siamese Poet*, 31.

9. *Kap* is a type of meter.

10. Types of meters.

11. Suchitra Chongstitvatana, "Kawiniphon Khong Angkarn Kallayanapong," 36–37.

12. Suchitra quotes the pieces "Tha Ta Bod Rai Nai Din Daen" and "Hom Wan Sukhanthaman Ming Mai" that support this unique perspective.

13. Other poems such as "Wiman Nam Khang" ("Celestial Mansion of Dew," *Panithan Kawi*) end with the demand "What work have you to present this world with?"

14. Suchitra Chongstitvatana, "Kawiniphon Khong Angkarn Kallayanapong," 38.

15. Suchitra Chongstitvatana, "Kawiniphon Khong Angkarn Kallayanapong," 40.

16. Suchitra Chongstitvatana, "Kawiniphon Khong Angkarn Kallayanapong."

17. Suchitra Chongstitvatana, "Kawiniphon Khong Angkarn Kallayanapong," 42.

18. Suchitra Chongstitvatana, "Kawiniphon Khong Angkarn Kallayanapong," 42.

19. Suchitra Chongstitvatana, "Kawiniphon Khong Angkarn Kallayanapong," 45.

20. Suchitra Chongstitvatana, "Kawiniphon Khong Angkarn Kallayanapong," 46–48: "Perhaps it can be said that from the two versions of *Lamnam Phu Kraduang* we can see the development in his teachings, which become much clearer. From 'dhamma' from nature he goes on to 'buddhadhamma,' which is derived from both nature and things of beauty. His revising and adding elements of the teachings

of the Buddha to make them [the teachings] become more concentrated helps to reflect the poet's intention of stressing the substance of the Buddhist teachings more distinctly than in the first issue." Suchitra Chongstitvatana, "Kawiniphon Khong Angkarn Kallayanapong," 48.

21. See Suchitra Chongstitvatana, "The Nature of Modern Thai Poetry."

22. *Chom nang chom mueang* passages are passages of admiration for a woman or for a city-kingdom.

23. Chetana Nagavajara, "Art in Place of Nirvana" 44.

24. Chetana Nagavajara, "Art in Place of Nirvana," 45.

25. Chetana Nagavajara, "Art in Place of Nirvana," 45. Chetana describes Angkarn's basic attitude as contrary to Buddhist doctrine, because he views him as professing and advocating attachment rather than detachment. In the course of his essay, Chetana traces Angkarn's aesthetic concept back to the influence of Western thinking on aesthetics, namely, that of Angkarn's Italian teacher, Silpa Bhirasri.

26. Suchitra Chongstitvatana, "The Nature of Modern Thai Poetry," 50, 53.

27. Chetana Nagavajara, "Art in Place of Nirvana," 45.

28. The definition for *akāliko* is "not subject to time, non-temporal," one of the *dhammaguna*, the virtues or attributes of the *dhamma*.

29. Chusak Pattarakulvanit and Nopporn Prachakul, "Thruesadi Wannakam Naeo Deconstruction" (Deconstructionist Literary Theory), 261.

30. A Buddhist eon.

31. *Klɔn* is a type of meter.

32. *Ahangkan* denotes haughty pride, self-assurance, self-confidence (Sanskrit, *ahaṃkāra*, or *ahaṅkāra*, conceit or conception of individuality). For the concept's use in Buddhist thought, see Steven Collins, *Selfless Persons*, 102.

Throughout Angkarn's oeuvre, other poems make similar claims. Thus "Om" (*Lamnam Phu Kradueng*) invokes Gaṇeśa and asks for inspiration, further supporting the idea of literature's connection with the divine—even with the entire pantheon of Hindu deities (stanza 4/page 32). The poem's fifth stanza pairs beauty with the earth, water, sky, and heavens, and the sixth makes apparent the close link between literature and knowledge in Angkarn's framework of thought. The first stanza of "Khɔn Kaen Kho Thaen Kha Chiwit" also depicts literary art as the partner of eternity and in the ninth stanza of "Krap Phra Boromakhru" (*Panithan Kawi*), the earth is again elevated to a status above heaven.

33. Angkarn Kallayanapong, "Yat Nam Khang Khue Namta Khong Wela."

34. See especially Steven Collins, *Selfless Persons*.

35. For a political history of this period, see Thak Chaloemtiarana, *Thailand*.

36. See, for instance, Mark G. Rolls, "Thailand's Post-Cold War Security Policy and Defence Programme."

37. Suchitra writes about Naowarat's *Kham Yad*: "This first book reflects his deep concern about the verse form and the melodious effect of poetry with the evident influence of Sunthon Phu." Suchitra Chongstitvatana, "The Nature of Modern Thai Poetry," 119.

38. My translation from the German. Christian Bauer, "Naowarat Pongpaiboon: beīyaṅ gwām gleīån¹ hway." *Kindlers Literatur Lexikon*, Stuttgart: J. B. Metzler, entry from September 2012, http://www.kll-online.de.

39. Naowarat Pongpaiboon, *Phiang Khwam Khluean Wai* (Mere Movement), 46–48.

40. I translate *kawi* here as "poet/ry," since the first part of the poem describes the qualities of poetry, the second those of the poet. "Kawi" appears as poem no. 25 in Naowarat Pongpaiboon's 1980 volume *Phleng Khlui Phiu*.

41. Suchitra Chongstitvatana, *Wang Sang Sin Naruemit Phroet Phraeo: Kan Sueb Thod Khanob Kap Kan Sang San Wannasin Nai Kawiniphon Thai Samai Mai* (Hoping to Create Sublime Art: The Continuities of Convention and the Creation of the Literary in Modern Thai Poetry), 36–39.

42. Suchitra Chongstitvatana, "The Nature of Modern Thai Poetry," 154.

43. From Sanskrit, *anubhāva*, "dignity, authority, consequence." Monier Monier-Williams, Carl Cappeller, and Ernst Leumann. *Sanskrit-English Dictionary*, s.v. *anubhāva*.

44. McFarland lists the definitions "influence, majesty." George Bradley McFarland, *English-Thai Dictionary*, s.v. *anuphap*.

45. Khomthuan Khanthanu, *Natakam Bon Lan Kwang*, 51.

46. Cynthia Marshall, *The Shattering of the Self: Violence, Subjectivity, and Early Modern Texts*, 2, 3–4.

47. Marc Weeks and Frederic Maurel, "Voyages across the Web of Time," 327.

48. A *salok* is a meter derived from Sanskrit.

49. The authors write, "And this too is implied by eternal recurrence, the will to make of one's life something more enduring than the ephemeral physical being. It is an aestheticist philosophy, regarding life and 'reality' as artworks." Marc Weeks and Frederic Maurel, "Voyages across the Web of Time," 331.

50. Thai unit of measurement.

51. See Michael K. Connors, "Goodbye to the Security State: Thailand and Ideological Change"; "Ministering Culture: Hegemony and the Politics of Culture and Identity in Thailand"; and *Democracy and National Identity in Thailand*.

52. Buddhist eons.

53. Cynthia Marshall, *The Shattering of the Self*, 2, 3–4.

54. Marc Weeks and Frederic Maurel, "Voyages across the Web of Time," 334–35.

55. Chetana likewise stresses the individualist bent of Angkarn's Buddhist framework of thinking and large emphasis on self-fashioning: "He believes that humans can 'build' themselves," in Ruenruethai Sajjaphan, ed., *80 Pi Angkarn Kallayanapong*, 76.

56. Mikhail Bakhtin, *The Dialogic Imagination: Four Essays*, 293. The glossary provides the following definition for heteroglossia:

The base condition governing the operation of meaning in any utterance. It is that which insures the primacy of context over text. At any given time, in any given place, there will be a set of conditions—social, historical, meteorological, physiological—that will insure that a word uttered in that place and at that time will have a meaning different than it would have under any other conditions; all utterances are heteroglot in that they are functions of a matrix of forces practically impossible to recoup, and therefore impossible to resolve. Heteroglossia is as close a conceptualization as is possible of that locus where centripetal and centrifugal forces collide; as such, it is that which a systematic linguistics must always suppress. (428)

57. Mikhail Bakhtin, *The Dialogic Imagination*, 293.

58. A good example of Angkarn's early use of a heteroglot vocabulary is provided by two poems from 1964 and 1965 in *Kawiniphon*, which use terms such as "Chivas," "virus," "parade," "cheer," "malaria," "bar," and "corruption" to critique the presence of foreign persons and influence in Thailand (140–44).

Chapter 5

1. Ruenruethai Sajjaphan, ed., *80 Pi Angkarn Kallayanapong*, 78.

2. Shane Weller, "From 'Gedicht' to 'Genicht': Paul Celan and Language Scepticism," 70, 73.

3. Shane Weller, "From 'Gedicht' to 'Genicht,'" 72, 73. For the full text of the Meridian, see the critical edition, Paul Celan, *Der Meridian: Endfassung—Entwürfe—Materialien*. For an English translation, see Rosemarie Waldrop, trans., "The Meridian: Speech on the Occasion of Receiving the Georg Büchner Prize, Darmstadt, 22 October 1960," 37–55.

4. Shane Weller, "From 'Gedicht' to 'Genicht,'" 73.

5. Shane Weller, "From 'Gedicht' to 'Genicht,'" 74.

6. Shane Weller, "From 'Gedicht' to 'Genicht,'" 74, 77.

7. The authors describe how in the "American Era" Thailand shifted into closer alliance with the United States and its Cold War, anticommunist policies and economic strategies (287–88). Thus, under Sarit Thanarat's government with its developmentalist policy, greater US involvement in state affairs came about: "US advisers helped to install a stronger institutional base for managing this larger budget and more complex task." Chris Baker and Pasuk Pongphaichit, "A Short Account of the Rise and Fall of the Thai Technocracy," 287.

8. Chris Baker and Pasuk Pongphaichit, "A Short Account of the Rise and Fall of the Thai Technocracy," 289.

9. Steven Collins introduced the formulation of a "Pali imaginaire," a term that figures also in the title of his 1998 volume *Nirvana and other Buddhist Felicities: Utopias of the Pali Imaginaire*.

10. Mikhail Bakhtin, *The Dialogic Imagination*, 287. Donald Wesling summarizes Bakhtin's critique of poetic language as follows:

> For Bakhtin, in his polemical response to this prejudice [the superiority of poetry over prose], the basic position was that poetry was asocial because it was monologic, single-voiced, suppressing half of a dialogue; that in particular, lyric poetry was non-narrative, less able therefore to bring in a thick reference to social fact, the conflict of languages and perspectives in historical social life; and finally, as one result of traditional rules, as well as of single-voicing, poetic rhythm regularized sound and sense in the utterance, so that what was self-centered was also paradoxically turned into a strict procrustean bed of convention.

Donald Wesling, *Bakhtin and the Social Moorings of Poetry*, 21–22.

11. Mikhail Bakhtin, *The Dialogic Imagination*, 287n12.
12. Michael Eskin, "Bakhtin on Poetry," 279.
13. Michael Eskin, "Bakhtin on Poetry," 380.
14. Michael Eskin, "Bakhtin on Poetry," 387.
15. Michael Eskin, "Bakhtin on Poetry," 388.
16. Michael Eskin, "Bakhtin on Poetry," 390.
17. Michael Eskin, "Bakhtin on Poetry," 380; Bakhtin, *The Dialogic Imagination*, 287.
18. Mikhail Bakhtin, *The Dialogic Imagination*, 287.
19. Mikhail Bakhtin, *The Dialogic Imagination*, 287n12.
20. See Michael Warner's *Publics and Counterpublics* for what constitutes such an aspirational community or "public."
21. Suchitra Chongstitvatana, "The Nature of Modern Thai Poetry," 74.
22. Mikhail Bakhtin, *The Dialogic Imagination*, 293.
23. Shane Weller, "From 'Gedicht' to 'Genicht,'" 90–91.
24. Shane Weller, "From 'Gedicht' to 'Genicht,'" 91.
25. Untitled poem, *Panithan Kawi*, 75.
26. Amir Eshel, "Paul Celan's Other: History, Poetics, and Ethics," 64.
27. Thus, Eshel writes, "When Heidegger's work is read with Celan's, the philosopher's appears to be an abstract, postmetaphysical critique of what, for Celan, is marked by the concrete, unsubsumable names of places where the terror of monolingualism and racism led to the extermination of human beings." Amir Eshel, "Paul Celan's Other," 71.

28. Amir Eshel, "Paul Celan's Other," 72.

29. Walter Benjamin, "Zum Begriff der Geschichte," 255.

30. See Daniel Weidner, "Thinking Beyond Secularization: Walter Benjamin, the 'Religious Turn,' and the Poetics of Theory."

31. See for instance, "Mandorla," *Die Niemandsrose*, in Paul Celan, *Die Gedichte: Kommentierte Gesamtausgabe*, 142.

32. "Le Contrescarpe," *Die Niemandsrose*, in Paul Celan, *Die Gedichte: Kommentierte Gesamtausgabe*, 160–63.

33. Paul Celan, "Die Schleuse," *Die Niemandsrose*, in Paul Celan, *Die Gedichte: Kommentierte Gesamtausgabe*, 131.

34. See especially Weller's discussion of negation on pages 78–79 of "From 'Gedicht' to 'Genicht.'"

35. Paul Celan, "Psalm," *Die Niemandsrose*, in Paul Celan, *Die Gedichte: Kommentierte Gesamtausgabe*, 132.

36. Shane Weller, "From 'Gedicht' to 'Genicht,'" 70.

37. Pheng Cheah, *What Is a World?*, 204.

38. In addition to Pheng Cheah, see Dipesh Chakrabarty, *Provincializing Europe: Postcolonial Thought and Historical Difference* and "The Time of History and the Time of Gods"; and Bliss Cua Lim, *Translating Time*.

39. See Suchitra Chongstitvatana "Buddhist Environmentalism in Modern Thai Poetry," 184–94, and "The Harmony between Nature and Man in Thai Poetry."

40. Suchitra Chongstitvatana, "The Nature of Modern Thai Poetry," 32. She discusses Angkarn's deployment of nature as beauty and inspiration, as teacher, as *dhamma*, and as literary medium also in *Wang Sang Sin*, 49–71.

41. Suchitra Chongstitvatana, "The Nature of Modern Thai Poetry," 216.

42. See Suchitra Chongstitvatana, "The Nature of Modern Thai Poetry," 33–38; and Chetana Nagavajara, "The Sense of the Past in the Poetry of Angkarn Kalayanaphong," 204.

43. Compare to Chetana Nagavajara's rendition of the poem in his essay "The Sense of the Past," 202–3.

44. Compare also to Michael Wright's translation of the poem in *Angkarn Kalyanapong*, 13–14.

45. Suchitra explains that the theme of time in Angkarn's poetry is closely related to the image of water. Suchitra Chongstitvatana, "The Nature of Modern Thai Poetry," 55–60.

46. Nick Admussen, "Genre Occludes the Creation of Genre Bing Xin, Tagore, and Prose Poetry," 578.

47. Nick Admussen, "Genre Occludes the Creation of Genre," 580.

48. Nick Admussen, "Genre Occludes the Creation of Genre," note 24.

49. Nick Admussen, "Genre Occludes the Creation of Genre," 582.

50. Nick Admussen, "Genre Occludes the Creation of Genre," 586.
51. See Chetana Nagavajara, "Art in Place of Nirvana."

Chapter 6

1. See Tony Day, 2010; Rebecca Hong, 2005; Roland Burke, 2016; Greg Barnhisel, 2015. See also *Parapolitics: Cultural Freedom and the Cold War*, exhibition, Haus der Kulturen der Welt, Berlin, November 3, 2017–January 8, 2018, https://www.hkw.de/en/programm/projekte/2017/parapolitics/parapolitics_start.php.

2. See e.g., Eugene Ford, *Cold War Monks: Buddhism and America's Secret Strategy in Southeast Asia*.

3. Angkarn Kalyanapongs, "I Lost You," trans. Allen Ginsberg, *International Portland Review* 26 (1980), 400.

4. Ginsberg's translation of "The Poet's Testament" can be found in Sathirakoses-Nagapradipa Foundation, *Three Thai Poets: Angkarn Kalyanapongs, Naowarat Pongpaiboon, Witayakorn Chiengkul*, 12. Ginsberg's rendition of "Scoop Up the Sea" is contained in Chand Chirayu Rajani, "Notes: Thai Poetry Translation and Some New Examples," 135.

5. Ormkaew Kallayanapong, *Pho Angkarn: Phu Ma Jak Dao Lok* (Father Angkarn: He Who Came from Planet Earth), 80–81. Sulak Sivaraksa further confirms that he took Ginsberg to see Angkarn in 1963. Interview by the author with Sulak Sivaraksa, Bangkok, July 27, 2017.

6. Personal communication with Peter Hale, August 7, 2016.

7. The first of the next two scans that Tim Noakes sends contains the continuation of Ginsberg's poem "Angkor Wat," more dreams recorded on his brief return to Saigon, and then chronicles his onward journey to and in Japan. Allen Ginsberg Papers, M0733, Box 15, folder 8, Department of Special Collections, Stanford University Libraries. The third scan is of a box from 1971. It contains a mention of Bangkok, but seems merely to be a recollection and does not provide documentation of further travel to the country. Allen Ginsberg Papers, M0733, Box 24, folder 11, Department of Special Collections, Stanford University Libraries.

8. It is with a gesture toward this entry that Ginsberg's *published* account of his sojourn in India leaves off:

Bankok—May 28, '63
Chinese meats hanging in shops—

Allen Ginsberg, *Indian Journals, March 1962–May 1963: Notebooks, Diary, Blank Pages, Writings*, 210.

9. Allen Ginsberg, *Collected Poems, 1947-1997*, 311-13.

10. Allen Ginsberg Papers, M0733, Box 15, folder 7: 148-49. Excerpts from the Allen Ginsberg Papers at Stanford by Allen Ginsberg. Copyright © 1963 by Allen Ginsberg, used by permission of The Wylie Agency LLC.

11. "CIA Dope Calypso—Allen Ginsberg," Ecohustler, March 18, 2014, available from https://ecohustler.com/culture/cia-dope-calypso-allen-ginsberg/.

12. See also Alfred W. McCoy, *The Politics of Heroin: CIA Complicity in the Global Drug Trade, Afghanistan, Southeast Asia, Central America, Colombia*, a research project to which Ginsberg contributed information (x-xi).

13. "Benjasin" ("Five Precepts"), *Bangkok Kaeo Kamsuan*, 125.

14. See Saiwaroun Noinimit, "Laksana Soerialit Nai Kawiniphon Khong Angkarn Kallayanapong" (Surrealism in the Poetry of Angkarn Kallayanapong) and Sodchuen Chaiprasat, *Chittrakam lae Wannakam Naeo Soerialit nai Prathet Thai, Pho. So. 2507-2527* (Surrealist Trends in Painting and Literature in Thailand, 1964-1984).

15. Prabhu attaches the following explanation in note 13: "Robert Bennett, 'Teaching the Beat Generation to Generation X,' in *The Beat Generation: Critical Essays*, edited by Myrsiades Kostas (New York: Peter Lang, 2002), 2." In Gayathri Prabhu, "Figurations of the Spiritual Squalid in Allen Ginsberg's Indian Journals: Transformation of India in Post-War Beat and American Imagination," https://tracecreativity.com/community/projects-and-channels/the-transnational-journal/.

16. Gayathri Prabhu, "Figurations of the Spiritual Squalid in Allen Ginsberg's Indian Journals."

17. Interview by author with Sulak Sivaraksa, Bangkok, July 27, 2017.

18. Angkarn Kalyanapong, "Scoop Up the Sea," trans. Allen Ginsberg, in Chand Chirayu Rajani M.C., "Thai Poetry Translation: A Review and Some New Examples," 135.

19. Jane Augustine, "The American Poetic Diamond Vehicle: Allen Ginsberg and Anne Waldman Re-work Vajrayana Buddhism," 159.

20. Jane Augustine, "The American Poetic Diamond Vehicle," 158, 159.

21. Jane Augustine, "The American Poetic Diamond Vehicle," 160.

22. Angkarn Kalyanapong, "Scoop Up the Sea," trans. Sulak Sivaraksa and Hiram Woodward, in *Angkarn Kalyanapong: A Contemporary Siamese Poet*, ed. Michael Wright, 41-42.

23. I translate this poem as "The Pledge of the Poet" to distinguish it from Angkarn's similarly named 1986 poem.

24. Sathirakoses-Nagapradipa Foundation, *Three Thai Poets*, 12.

25. Angkarn Kalyanapongs, "I Lost You."

26. Allen Ginsberg Papers, M0733, Box 15, folder 7: 159. Excerpts from the Allen Ginsberg Papers at Stanford by Allen Ginsberg. Copyright © 1963 by Allen Ginsberg, used by permission of The Wylie Agency LLC.

27. Allen Ginsberg Papers, M0733, Box 15, folder 7: 160–61. Excerpts from the Allen Ginsberg Papers at Stanford by Allen Ginsberg. Copyright © 1963 by Allen Ginsberg, used by permission of The Wylie Agency LLC.

28. Allen Ginsberg, *Collected Poems, 1947–1997*, 314–31.

29. Tony Trigilio, *Allen Ginsberg's Buddhist Poetics*, 37.

30. Tony Trigilio, *Allen Ginsberg's Buddhist Poetics*, 37.

31. Tony Trigilio, *Allen Ginsberg's Buddhist Poetics*, 40.

32. Allen Ginsberg, *Collected Poems, 1947–1997*, 319.

33. Tony Trigilio, *Allen Ginsberg's Buddhist Poetics*, 39.

34. Tony Trigilio, *Allen Ginsberg's Buddhist Poetics*, 102.

35. Tony Trigilio, *Allen Ginsberg's Buddhist Poetics*, 41.

36. Tony Trigilio, *Allen Ginsberg's Buddhist Poetics*, 40.

37. Allen Ginsberg, *Collected Poems, 1947–1997*, 325.

38. Angkarn Kallayanapong, *Kawi Sri Ayuthaya* (Poet of Ayuthaya), 119–20.

39. Interview by the author with Ormkaew Kallayanapong, Bangkok, December 9, 2016.

40. Interview by the author with Sulak Sivaraksa, Bangkok, July 27, 2017.

41. Sudarat Musikawong, "Art for October: Thai Cold War State Violence in Trauma Art," 44.

42. Angkarn Kallayanapong, *Alangkan Jak Angkarn Kallayanapong* (Magnificence by Angkarn Kallayanapong).

43. Sathirakoses-Nagapradipa Foundation and Power of Thai Foundation, *Rachasadudi Ming Khwan Prachathipatai* (Panegyric for Treasured Democracy).

44. Erik Mortensen, "Keeping Vision Alive: The Buddhist Stillpoint in the Work of Jack Kerouac and Allen Ginsberg," 127.

45. Erik Mortensen, "Keeping Vision Alive," 128.

46. Pheng Cheah, *What Is a World?*, 204.

47. Erik Mortensen, "Keeping Vision Alive," 129.

48. Jane Augustine, "The American Poetic Diamond Vehicle," 156.

49. Jane Augustine, "The American Poetic Diamond Vehicle," 163.

50. Jane Augustine, "The American Poetic Diamond Vehicle," 163.

51. Suchitra Chongstitvatana, *Phuthatham Nai Kawiniphon Samai Mai* (Buddha Dharma in Modern Thai Poetry), 178.

52. See Donald K. Swearer, ed., *Me and Mine: Selected Essays by Bhikkhu Buddhadasa*.

53. Interview by the author with Ormkaew Kallayanapong, December 9, 2016.

54. Pheng Cheah, *What Is a World?*, 212.

Appendix

1. Khled Thai's fifth edition of *Kawiniphon* from 1986 includes some poems that Angkarn wrote after 1964.

2. *Kap* is a type of meter.
3. A *chedi* or *stupa* is a structure that houses relics.
4. Temple names have been left in the original in the translation of this poem.
5. A *bot* or *ubosot* is an ordination hall and the *vihan* is the building that houses the Buddha image or images.
6. A *kalpa* is a Buddhist term for a temporal span comparable to an eon.
7. Decorative pattern.
8. Temple names have been left in the original in the translation of this poem.
9. A *prang* is a spirelike part of temple architecture.
10. A kind of lute.
11. *Thap saming khla* is a blue krait snake.
12. A *salok* is a meter derived from Sanskrit.
13. *Dāna* are offerings.
14. A Buddhist eon.
15. *Klon* is a type of meter.
16. Types of meters.
17. The "no-self executes the self."
18. Phra Si An is a messianic, future Buddha, known in other traditions as Ariya Maitreya.
19. Buddhist eons.
20. Thai unit of measurement.
21. A species of climber.
22. A detail of the roof in temple architecture.
23. Angkarn Kallayanapong, *Kawi Sri Ayuthaya* (Poet of Ayuthaya), 119–20.

Bibliography

Admussen, Nick. "Genre Occludes the Creation of Genre: Bing Xin, Tagore, and Prose Poetry." In *The Oxford Handbook of Modern Chinese Literatures*, 578–96, ed. Andrea Bachner and Carlos Rojas. Oxford University Press, 2016.

Allen Ginsberg Papers, M0733, Box 15, folder 7, 1963. Excerpts from the Allen Ginsberg Papers at Stanford by Allen Ginsberg. Copyright © 1963 by Allen Ginsberg, used by permission of The Wylie Agency LLC.

Allen Ginsberg Papers, M0733, Box 15, folder 8, 1963. Excerpts from the Allen Ginsberg Papers at Stanford by Allen Ginsberg. Copyright © 1963 by Allen Ginsberg, used by permission of The Wylie Agency LLC.

Allen Ginsberg Papers, M0733, Box 24, folder 11, 1971. Excerpts from the Allen Ginsberg Papers at Stanford by Allen Ginsberg. Copyright © 1963 by Allen Ginsberg, used by permission of The Wylie Agency LLC.

Anderson, Benedict. *Imagined Communities: Reflections on the Origin and Spread of Nationalism*. London: Verso, 1983.

———. *In the Mirror: Literature and Politics in Siam in the American Era*. Ithaca, NY: Cornell University Southeast Asia Program Publications, 1985.

Angkarn Kalyanapong. "I Lost You." Trans. Allen Ginsberg. *International Portland Review* 26 (1980): 400.

Angkarn Kallayanapong. *Alangkan Jak Angkarn Kallayanapong* (Magnificence by Angkarn Kallayanapong), ed. Usa Thewi. Bangkok: Sathirakoses-Nagapradipa Foundation, 2008.

———. *Bang Bot Jak Suan Kaeo* (Passages from the Crystal Garden). Bangkok: Sueksit Sayam, 1972.

———. *Bangkok Kaeo Kamsuan Rue Nirat Nakhon Si Thammarat* (Lament for Beloved Bangkok or Nirat Nakhon Si Thammarat). Bangkok: Sayam, 1991 [1978].

———. *Kawiniphon Khong Angkarn Kallayanapong* (The Poetry of Angkarn Kallayanapong). Bangkok: Khled Thai, 5th ed. 1986 [1964].

———. *Kawi Sri Ayuthaya* (Poet of Ayuthaya). Bangkok: Khled Thai, 1999.

———. *Klap Ban Koed* (Returning Home). 2013.

———. *Lamnam Phu Kradueng* (Kradueng Mountain Song). Bangkok: Sayam, 1991 [1969].
———. *Makhawan Rangsan* (Makhawan Creation). Bangkok: Ban Phra Athit, 2008.
———. *Panithan Kawi* (The Poet's Testament). Bangkok: Karat, 1986.
———. *Rachasadudi Ming Khwan Prachathipatai* (Panegyric for Treasured Democracy), Bangkok: Sathirakoses-Nagapradipa Foundation and Power of Thai Foundation, 1992.
———. *Sukhothai* (Sukhothai: Dawn of Happiness). Bangkok: Department of Fine Arts, 1978.
———. *Sumalai Poralok* (Flowers of a Future World). Bangkok: Sathirakoses-Nagapradipa Foundation, 1994.
———. *Yad Nam Khang Khue Namta Khong Wela* (Dew Drops Are the Tears of Time). Bangkok: Thienwan, 1987.
Atsani Phonlachan. *Kho Khit Jak Wanakhadi* (Thoughts from Literature). 4th ed. Bangkok: Chomrom Nangsue Namkhaeng, 1979.
———. *Sinlapa Haeng Kap Klon* (The Art of Poetry). Bangkok: Charoenwit Kanphim, 1972.
Augustine, Jane. "The American Poetic Diamond Vehicle: Allen Ginsberg and Anne Waldman Re-work Vajrayana Buddhism." In *The Emergence of Buddhist American Literature*, ed. John Whalen-Bridge and Gary Storhoff, 155–74. Albany: SUNY Press, 2009.
Baker, Chris, and Pasuk Pongphaichit. *A History of Ayutthaya: Siam in the Early Modern World*. Cambridge and New York: Cambridge University Press, 2017.
———. *A History of Thailand*. Cambridge: Cambridge University Press, 2014 [2005].
———. "A Short Account of the Rise and Fall of the Thai Technocracy." *Southeast Asian Studies* 3, no. 2 (August 2014): 283–98.
Bakhtin, Mikhail. *The Dialogic Imagination: Four Essays*. Austin and London: University of Texas Press, 1981.
Balslev, Anindita Niyogi. *A Study of Time in Indian Philosophy*. Wiesbaden: Harrassowitz, 1983.
Barlow, Tani E. "Advertising Ephemera and the Angel of History." *positions: asia critique* 20, no. 1 (2012, Winter): 111–58.
———. "Debates over Colonial Modernity in East Asia and Another Alternative." *Cultural Studies* 26, no. 5 (2012): 617–44.
Bauer, Christian. "Angkarn Kalyanapong: Das lyrische Werk" (Angkarn Kalyanapong: The Poetic Oeuvre), entry, *Kindlers Literatur Lexikon*. Stuttgart: J. B. Metzler. http://www.kll-online.de.
———. "Naowarat Pongpaiboon: beīyaṅ gwām gleṙån[1] hway" (Naowarat Pongpaiboon: Mere Movement), entry, *Kindlers Literatur Lexikon*. Stuttgart: J. B. Metzler, 2012. http://www.kll-online.de.

Belletto, Steven. "The Beat Generation Meets the Hungry Generation: U.S.–Calcutta Networks and the 1960s 'Revolt of the Personal.'" *Humanities* 8, no. 3 (2019). https://www.mdpi.com/2076-0787/8/1/3/htm.

Benjamin, Walter. "Über den Begriff der Geschichte." In *Illuminationen: Ausgewählte Schriften 1*, ed. Siegfried Unseld, 251–61. Frankfurt am Main: Suhrkamp, 1955.

Bhawan Ruangsilp. *Dutch East India Company Merchants at the Court of Ayutthaya: Dutch Perceptions of the Thai Kingdom, ca. 1604–1765*. Leiden and Boston: Brill, 2007.

Borommakot, Phrachao. *Chindamani*. Bangkok: Fine Arts Department, 2015.

Cassaniti, Julia L. *Living Buddhism: Mind, Self, and Emotion in a Thai Community*. Ithaca, NY: Cornell University Press, 2015.

———. *Remembering the Present: Mindfulness in Buddhist Asia*. Ithaca, NY: Cornell University Press, 2018.

Caws, Mary Ann. *Manifesto: A Century of Isms*. Lincoln: University of Nebraska Press, 2001.

Celan, Paul. *Der Meridian: Endfassung—Entwürfe—Materialien*, ed. Bernhard Böschenstein and Heino Schmull. Frankfurt: Suhrkamp, 1999.

———. *Die Gedichte· Kommentierte Gesamtausgabe*. Frankfurt: Suhrkamp, 2003.

Chakrabarty, Dipesh. *Provincializing Europe: Postcolonial Thought and Historical Difference*. Princeton, NJ: Princeton University Press, 2000.

———. "The Time of History and the Times of Gods." In *The Politics of Culture in the Shadow of Capital*, ed. Lisa Lowe and David Lloyd, 35–59. Durham, NC: Duke University Press, 1997.

Chamnongsri L. Rutnin, trans. In *The S.E.A. Write Anthology of Thai Short Stories and Poems*, ed. Nitaya Masavisut and Matthew Grose, 107–9. Chiang Mai: Silkworm Books, 1998.

Chand Chirayu Rajani, M.C. "Thai Poetry Translation: A Review and Some New Examples." *Journal of the Siam Society* 67, no. 1 (1979): 132–39.

Chang Sae Tang. *Yam Chao: Bang Bot Khong "Bot Kawi Pho Kap Mae," Pho. So. 2509-2514* (Morning: Passages from the Poems "Father and Mother," B.E. 2509-2514). Bangkok: Poet Tang Chang's Institute of Modern Art, 1985.

Charnvit Kasetsiri. *Ayutthaya: Prawatisat lae Kan Mueang* (Ayutthaya: History and Politics). Bangkok: Toyota Foundation Thailand, 1999.

Cheah, Pheng. *What Is a World? On Postcolonial Literature as World Literature*. Durham, NC and London: Duke University Press, 2016.

Chetana Nagavajara, "Art in Place of Nirvana: Western Aesthetics and the Poetry of Angkarn Kalayanaphong." *Solidarity* 130 (1991): 44–52.

———. "Art in Place of Nirvana: Western Aesthetics and the Poetry of Angkarn Kalayanaphong." In *Comparative Literature from a Thai Perspective: Collected Articles, 1978–1992*, 213–28. Bangkok: Chulalongkorn University, 1996.

Chiranan Pitpreecha. *Bai Mai Thi Hai Pai: Kawiniphon Haeng Chiwit*. Bangkok: Samnak Phim An Thai, 1989.

Chit Phumisak. *Sinlapa Phuea Chiwit Sinlapa Phuea Prachachon* (Art for Life, Art for the People). Bangkok: Nitisart, 1957.

Cho, Francisca. *Seeing Like the Buddha: Enlightenment through Film*. Albany: SUNY Press, 2017.

Chusak Pattarakulvanit and Nopporn Prachakul. "Thruesadi Wannakam Naeo Deconstruction" (Deconstructionist Literary Theory). In *80 Pi Angkarn Kallayanapong* (80 Years of Angkarn Kallayanapong), CD appendix, ed. Ruenruethai Sajjaphan, 259–61. Bangkok: Thailand Research Fund, 2011 [1996].

Collins, Steven. *Nirvana and other Buddhist Felicities: Utopias of the Pali Imaginaire*. Cambridge: Cambridge University Press, 1998.

———. *Selfless Persons: Imagery and Thought in Theravada Buddhism*. Cambridge: Cambridge University Press, 1982.

Connors, Michael K. *Democracy and National Identity in Thailand*. New York: Routledge Curzon, 2003.

———. "Goodbye to the Security State: Thailand and Ideological Change." *Journal of Contemporary Asia* 33, no. 4 (2003): 431–48.

———. "Ministering Culture: Hegemony and the Politics of Culture and Identity in Thailand." *Critical Asian Studies* 37, no. 4 (2005): 532–51.

Davis, Erik. *Deathpower: Buddhism's Ritual Imagination in Cambodia*. New York: Columbia University Press, 2016.

Dhanate Vespada. "Lila Nai Ngan Roi Kaeo Khong Angkhan Kalayanapong" (Style in Angkhan Kalayanapong's Poetical Prose). Master's thesis, Chulalongkorn University, 1990.

Dhiravat na Pombejra. *Court, Company, and Campong: Essays on the VOC Presence in Ayutthaya*. Ayuthaya, Thailand: Ayutthaya Historical Study Centre, Occasional Paper No. 1, 1992: 25–42.

Eshel, Amir. "Paul Celan's Other: History, Poetics, and Ethics." *New German Critique*, no. 91, Special Issue on Paul Celan (Winter 2004): 57–77.

Eskin, Michael. "Bakhtin on Poetry." *Poetics Today* 21, no. 2 (Summer 2000): 379–91.

Ford, Eugene. *Cold War Monks: Buddhism and America's Secret Strategy in Southeast Asia*. New Haven, CT: Yale University Press, 2017.

Fuhrmann, Arnika. *Ghostly Desires: Queer Sexuality and Vernacular Buddhism in Contemporary Thai Cinema*. Durham, NC: Duke University Press, 2016.

Ginsberg, Allen. *Collected Poems, 1947–1997*. New York: HarperCollins, 2006.

———. *Indian Journals, March 1962–May 1963: Notebooks, Diary, Blank Pages, Writings*. San Francisco: Dave Haselwood Books and City Light Books, 1970.

Gombrich, Richard. *Theravada Buddhism: A Social History from Ancient Benares to Modern Colombo*. London: Routledge, 1988.

Gray, Christine. "Thailand: The Soteriological State in the 1970s." PhD diss., University of Chicago, 1986.

Haberkorn, Tyrell. *Revolution Interrupted: Farmers, Students, Law, and Violence in Northern Thailand*. Madison: University of Wisconsin Press, 2011.

Hall, Stuart. "Notes on Deconstructing 'the Popular.'" In *Cultural Theory and Popular Culture: A Reader*, ed. John Storey, 442–53. London: Prentice Hall, 1998.

Harootunian, Harry. "Remembering the Historical Present." *Critical Inquiry* 33, no. 3 (Spring 2007): 471–94.

Harrison, Rachel, ed. *Disturbing Conventions: Decentering Thai Literary Cultures*. London: Rowman & Littlefield International, 2014.

Hong Lysa. "Invisible Semicolony: The Postcolonial Condition and Royal National History in Thailand." *Postcolonial Studies* 11, no. 3 (2008): 315–27.

Hudak, Thomas J. *The Indigenization of Pali Meters in Thai Poetry*. Athens: Ohio University Center for International Studies, 1990.

———. "Thailand, Poetry of." In *The Princeton Encyclopedia of Poetry and Poetics*, ed. Roland Greene. Online ed. Princeton, NJ: Princeton University Press, 2017. https://www-oxfordreference-com.proxy.library.cornell.edu/view/10.1093/acref/9780190681173.001.0001/acref-9780190681173.

Hundius, Harald. *Das Nirat Müang Kläng von Sunthon Phu: Analyse und Übersetzung eines thailändischen Reisegedichtes*. Wiesbaden: Harrassowitz, 1976.

Jackson, Peter A. "Buddhadāsa on Rebirth and Paṭiccasamuppāda." In *Buddhadāsa: Theravada Buddhism and Modernist Reform in Thailand*, 101–27. Bangkok: Silkworm Books, 2003 [1987].

Kasian Tejapira. *Commodifying Marxism: The Formation of Modern Thai Radical Culture, 1927–1958*. Kyoto: Kyoto University Press, 2001.

Kepner, Susan. *A Civilized Woman: M. L. Boonlua Debhayasuwan and the Thai Twentieth Century*. Chiang Mai, Thailand: Silkworm Books, 2013.

———. *The Lioness in Bloom: Modern Thai Fiction about Women*. Berkeley: University of California Press, 1996

Keyes, Charles. *Thailand: Buddhist Kingdom as Modern Nation-State*. Boulder, CO: Westview, 1987.

Khomthuan Khanthanu. *Natakam Bon Lan Kwang* (Theatre in the Public Square). Bangkok: Ming Khwan, 1993 [1983].

Kirsch, A. Thomas. "Complexity in the Thai Religious System: An Interpretation." *The Journal of Asian Studies* 36, no. 2 (February 1977): 241–66.

Krom Wichakan. *Wicha Prawattisat Chan Mathayomsueksa Pi Thi 1*. Phranakhon: Ro. Pho. Khurusapha, 5th ed. 2507 (1964).

Krom Wichakan. *Wicha Prawattisat Chan Mathayomsueksa Pi Thi 2*. Phranakhon: Ro. Pho. Khurusapha, 3rd ed. 2506 (1963).

Lim, Bliss Cua. *Translating Time: Cinema, the Fantastic, and Temporal Critique*. John Hope Franklin Center Book Series. Durham, NC: Duke University Press, 2009.

Loos, Tamara. *Subject Siam: Family, Law, and Colonial Modernity in Thailand*. Ithaca, NY: Cornell University Press, 2006.

Mala Khamjan. *Jao Jan Phom Hom: Nirat Phrathat In Khwaen*. Bangkok: Khanathorn Book Review, 1991.

Manas Chitakasem. "The Emergence and Development of the Nirat Genre in Thai Poetry." *Journal of the Siam Society* 60, no. 2 (1972): 135–68.

———. "Poetic Conventions and Modern Thai Poetry." In *Thai Constructions of Knowledge*, ed. Manas Chitakasem and Andrew Turton, 37–62. London: University of London, School of Oriental and African Studies, 1991.

Marshall, Cynthia. *The Shattering of the Self: Violence, Subjectivity, and Early Modern Texts*. Baltimore: Johns Hopkins University Press, 2003.

Mattioli, John. "Past Inscription: The Mythopoetics of Angkarn Kalyanapong." *Explorations in Southeast Asian Studies* 5, no. 1 (Spring 2004). https://www.cseashawaii.org/wp-content/uploads/2016/10/Explorations_5-1.pdf.

McCoy, Alfred W. *The Politics of Heroin: CIA Complicity in the Global Drug Trade, Afghanistan, Southeast Asia, Central America, Colombia*. New York: HarperCollins, 2003 [1972].

McDaniel, Justin. *Architects of Buddhist Leisure: Socially Disengaged Buddhism in Asia's Museums, Monuments and Amusement Parks*. Honolulu: University of Hawai'i Press, 2016.

———. *The Lovelorn Ghost and the Magical Monk: Practicing Buddhism in Modern Thailand*. New York: Columbia University Press, 2011.

McFarland, George Bradley. *English-Thai Dictionary*. Stanford, CA: Stanford University Press, 1956.

Monier-Williams, Monier, Carl Cappeller, and Ernst Leumann. *Sanskrit-English Dictionary: Etymologically and Philologically Arranged with Special Reference to Cognate Indo-European Languages*. New Delhi: Munshiram Manoharlal Publishers, 1976.

Mortensen, Erik. "Keeping Vision Alive: The Buddhist Stillpoint in the Work of Jack Kerouac and Allen Ginsberg." In *The Emergence of Buddhist American Literature*, ed. John Whalen-Bridge and Gary Storhoff, 123–137. Albany: SUNY Press, 2009.

Naowarat Pongpaiboon. *Kham Yad* (Word Drops). Bangkok: Krung Sayam Kan Phim, 1969.

———. *Krung Thep Thawarawadi: Jaruek Wai Nai Pi Thi 200 Haeng Krung Rattanakosin* (Krung Thep Thawarawadi: Recorded in the 200th Year of the Rattanakosin Era). Bangkok: Sinlapawatthanatham, 1986.

———. *Phiang Khwam Khluean Wai* (Mere Movement). Bangkok: Chaophraya, 1980.

———. *Phiang Khwam Khluean Wai (Mere Movement)*. Trans. Juangjan Bunnag, Robert Cumming, and Michael Wright. Bangkok: Kled Thai, 1988.

———. *Phleng Khlui Phiu* (Flute Song). 3rd ed. Bangkok: Pla Taphian, 1986 [1983].

Nerlekar, Anjali. *Bombay Modern: Arun Kolatkar and Bilingual Literary Culture*. Evanston, IL: Northwestern University Press, 2016.

Ormkaew Kallayanapong. *Pho Angkarn: Phu Ma Jak Dao Lok* (Father Angkarn: He Who Came from Planet Earth). Bangkok: Ormkaew Kallayanapong, 2014.

Pattana Kitiarsa. "Beyond Syncretism: Hybridization of Popular Religion in Contemporary Thailand." *Journal of Southeast Asian Studies* 36, no. 3 (October 2005): 461–87.

Phatthanaphongphakdi (Thim), Luang, *Nirat Nongkhai*. Bangkok: Fine Arts Department, 2016.

Platt, Martin B. *Isan Writers, Thai Literature: Writing and Regionalism in Modern Thailand*. Honolulu: University of Hawai'i Press, 2013

Phillips, Herbert. *Modern Thai Literature: With an Ethnographic Interpretation*. Honolulu: University of Hawai'i Press, 1987.

Pollock, Sheldon I. "The Cosmopolitan Vernacular." *Journal of Asian Studies* 57, no. 1 (1998): 6–37.

———. *Language of the Gods in the World of Men: Sanskrit, Culture, and Power in Premodern India*. Berkeley: University of California Press, 2006.

Prabhu, Gayathri. "Figurations of the Spiritual Squalid in Allen Ginsberg's Indian Journals: Transformation of India in Post-War Beat and American Imagination." *Transnational Literature* 6, no. 1, 2013. http://fhrc.flinders.edu.au/transnational/home.html.

Prasad, Hari Shankar. "The Concept of Time in Pali Buddhism." *East and West* 38, no. 1 (December 1998): 107–36.

Puchner, Martin. *Poetry of the Revolution: Marx, Manifestos, and the Avant-gardes*. Princeton: Princeton University Press, 2006.

Rachabandithayasathan. *Pojananukrom Chabab Rachabandithayasathan* (Royal Institute Dictionary). Bangkok: Nanmi Buk, 2003 [2546].

Reynolds, Craig J. "Sedition in Thai History: A Nineteenth-Century Poem and Its Critics." In *Thai Constructions of Knowledge*, ed. Manas Chitakasem and Andrew Turton, 15–36. London: University of London, School of Oriental and African Studies, 1991.

Rhys Davids, T. W., and William Stede. *Pali-English Dictionary*. Delhi: Munshiram Manoharlal, 1989.

Rolls, Mark G. "Thailand's Post-Cold War Security Policy and Defence Programme." *Post-Cold War Security Issues in the Asia-Pacific Region*, ed. Colin McInnes and Mark G. Rolls, 94–111. Ilford, Essex: Frank Cass, 1994.

Rosenberg, Klaus. *Die epischen Chan-Dichtungen in der Literatur Thailands. Mit einer vollständigen Übersetzung des Anirut Kham Chan*. Hamburg: Gesellschaft für Natur- und Völkerkunde Ostasiens, 1976.

Rotman, Andy. *Thus I Have Seen: Faith in Early Indian Buddhism*. New York: Oxford University Press, 2009.

Ruenruethai Sajjaphan, ed. *80 Pi Angkarn Kallayanapong* (80 Years of Angkarn Kallayanapong). Bangkok: Thailand Research Fund, 2011.

Saiwaroun Noinimit. "Laksana Soerialit Nai Kawiniphon Khong Angkarn Kallayanapong" (Surrealism in the Poetry of Angkarn Kallayanapong). Master's thesis, Chulalongkorn University, 1990.

Sathirakoses-Nagapradipa Foundation. *Three Thai Poets: Angkarn Kalyanapongs, Naowarat Pongpaiboon, Witayakorn Chiengkul.* Bangkok: Sathirakoses-Nagapradipa Foundation, 1978.

Schweisguth, Paul. *Étude sur la littérature siamoise.* Paris: Imprimerie Nationale, 1951.

Sodchuen Chaiprasat. *Chittrakam lae Wannakam Naeo Soerialit nai Prathet Thai, Pho. So. 2507–2527* (Surrealist Trends in Painting and Literature in Thailand, 1964–1984). Bangkok: Sayamsamakhom, 1996.

Spiro, Melford E. *Buddhism and Society: A Great Tradition and Its Burmese Vicissitudes.* New York: Harper and Row, 1970.

Suchitra Chongstitvatana. "Buddhist Environmentalism in Modern Thai Poetry." In *Buddhism without Borders: Proceedings of the International Conference on Globalized Buddhism*, Bumthang, Bhutan May 21–23, 2012, ed. Dasho Karma Ura and Dendup Chophel, 184–94. Thimphu, Bhutan: The Centre for Bhutan Studies, 2012.

———. "The Green World of Angkhan Kalayanaphong: A Vision on Nature and Environment." In *Thai Literary Traditions*, ed. Manas Chitakasem, 148–157. Bangkok: Chulalongkorn University Press, 1995.

———. "The Harmony between Nature and Man in Thai Poetry." Paper presented at the 3rd Euroseas Conference, London, September 6–8, 2001.

———. "Kawiniphon Khong Angkarn Kallayanapong: Sasana Haeng Sunthari" (The Poetry of Angkarn Kallayanapong: The Religion of Aesthetics). *Pajarayasan* 14, no. 1 (1987): 35–51.

———. "The Nature of Modern Thai Poetry Considered with Reference to the Works of Angkhan Kalayanaphong, Naowarat Phongphaibun and Suchit Wongthet." PhD diss., School of Oriental and African Studies, University of London, 1984.

———. *Phuthatham Nai Kawiniphon Samai Mai* (Buddha Dharma in Modern Thai Poetry). Bangkok: Khrongkan Phoei Phrae Phonngan Wichakan, Faculty of Arts, Chulalongkorn University, 2001.

———. *Wang Sang Sin Naruemit Phroet Phraeo: Kan Sueb Thod Khanob Kap Kan Sang San Wannasin Nai Kawiniphon Thai Samai Mai* (Hoping to Create Sublime Art: The Continuities of Convention and the Creation of the Literary in Modern Thai Poetry). Bangkok: Scholarly Publication Dissemination Program, Faculty of Arts, Chulalongkorn University, 2013.

Sudarat Musikawong. "Art for October: Thai Cold War State Violence in Trauma Art." *positions: east asia cultures critique* 18, no. 1 (Spring 2010): 19–50.

Sunthon Phu. "Nirat Phukhao Thong." In *Nirat Sunthon Phu*. Bangkok: Thanpanya, 2000.
Swearer, Donald K., ed. *The Buddhist World of Southeast Asia*. Albany: SUNY Press, 1995.
———. *Me and Mine. Selected Essays by Bhikkhu Buddhadasa*. Albany: SUNY Press, 1989.
Tambiah, Stanley. *World Conqueror and World Renouncer: A Study of Buddhism and Polity in Thailand against a Historical Background*. Cambridge Studies in Social and Cultural Anthropology Series. Cambridge: Cambridge University Press, 1976.
Taylor, Nora A., "Tang Chang: The Painting that Is Painted with Poetry Is Profoundly Beautiful." *Art Asia Pacific*, July–August 2018. http://artasiapacific.com/Magazine/109/ThePaintingThatIsPaintedWithPoetryIsProfoundlyBeautiful.
Terwiel, B. J. "The Introduction of Indian Prosody among the Thais." In *Ideology & Status of Sanskrit: Contributions to the History of the Sanskrit Language*, ed. Jan E. M. Houben, 307–23. Leiden: E. J. Brill, 1996.
———. *Monks and Magic: Revisiting a Classic Study of Religious Ceremonies in Thailand*. Copenhagen: NIAS Press, 2012 [1975].
Thak Chaloemtiarana. *Read Till It Shatters: Nationalism and Identity in Modern Thai Literature*. Acton: Australian National University Press, 2018.
———. *The Sarit Regime, 1957–1963: The Formative Years of Modern Thai Politics*. PhD diss., Cornell University, 1974.
———. *Thailand: The Politics of Despotic Paternalism*. Ithaca, NY: Southeast Asia Program, Cornell University, 2007.
Trigilio, Tony. *Allen Ginsberg's Buddhist Poetics*. Carbondale: Southern Illinois University Press 2007.
Trisilpa Boonkhachorn. "Intertextuality in Thai Literary and Social Contexts: A Study of Contemporary Poets." PhD diss., University of Michigan, Ann Arbor, 1992.
Waldrop, Rosemarie, trans. "The Meridian: Speech on the Occasion of Receiving the Georg Büchner Prize, Darmstadt, 22 October 1960." In *Paul Celan Collected Prose*, 37–55. New York: Routledge, 2003.
Warner, Michael. *Publics and Counterpublics*. New York: Zone Books, 2002.
Wedel, Yuangrat and Paul. *Radical Thought, Thai Mind: The Development of Revolutionary Ideas in Thailand*. Bangkok: ABAC, 1987.
Weeks, Marc, and Frederic Maurel. "Voyages across the Web of Time: Angkarn, Nietzsche and Temporal Colonization." *Journal of Southeast Asian Studies* 30, no. 2 (September 1999): 325–37.
Weidner, Daniel. "Thinking beyond Secularization: Walter Benjamin, the 'Religious Turn,' and the Poetics of Theory." *New German Critique* 111, 37, no. 3 (2010): 131–48.
Weller, Shane. "From 'Gedicht' to 'Genicht': Paul Celan and Language Scepticism." *German Life and Letters* 69, no. 1 (2016): 69–91.

Wenk, Klaus. *Phali lehrt die Jüngeren (Phali Son Nong): Ein Beitrag zur Literatur und Soziologie Thailands*. Hamburg: Gesellschaft für Natur- und Völkerkunde Ostasiens, 1977.

———. *Studien zur Literatur der Thai*, Band IV. Hamburg: Gesellschaft für Natur- und Völkerkunde Ostasiens, 1989.

Wesling, Donald. *Bakhtin and the Social Moorings of Poetry*. Lewisburg, PA: Bucknell University Press, 2003.

Wilson, Liz. *Charming Cadavers: Horrific Figurations of the Feminine in Indian Buddhist Hagiographic Literature*. Chicago: University of Chicago Press, 1996.

Wright, Michael. *Angkarn Kalyanapong: A Contemporary Siamese Poet*. Bangkok: Sathirakoses-Nagapradipa Foundation, 1986.

———. *Ongkan Chaeng Nam*. Bangkok: Matichon, 2000 (Thai with English translation).

Wyatt, David K. *Thailand: A Short History*. New Haven, CT: Yale University Press, 1984.

Index

Admussen, Nick: "Genre Occludes the Creation of Genre: Bing Xin, Tagore, and Prose Poetry," 140–41
aesthetics, 2; Buddhism and, 4, 20; Thai Marxist, 71. *See also under* Angkarn Kallayanapong
affect, 21, 57, 104, 105, 126, 166–67
Alangkan Jak Angkarn Kallayanapong (Magnificence by Angkarn Kallayanapong) (Angkarn), 32
"Amnat Rai Khong Cholesterol" ("Evil Power of Cholesterol") (Angkarn), 32
Anderson, Benedict, 53, 72
Angkarn Kallayanapong:
 addressee, of work, 133–34
 anti-institutionalist outlook of, 84, 149
 Art for Life movement and, 15, 17, 19, 26, 69, 71, 125
 artistic/aesthetic concerns, in work of, 2, 12, 35, 49, 65, 94, 167: art as eternal, 92, 96–97; art and ethics, 97; art/literature as redemptive, 93, 100, 105; beauty and *dhamma*, 94; beauty and impermanence, 48, 50; dedication to art, 90

awards, 18, 30, 32–33
Ayuthaya period, in work of, 3, 12, 52, 55, 61–69, 74–77: cultural purity of, 84; use of forms of, 83, 166–67
Bangkok, in work of, 67–68, 77, 80–82, 84, 148
belatedness (*Nachträglichkeit*), in work of, 50
biographical details, 159
boriphat, in work of, 80
Buddhist concerns in work of: 1–3, 5–9, 12, 27, 35–36, 112, 135: attachment/detachment, 37–38, 50–51; Bodhisattvahood, 94, 161–62; in contemporary life, 144, 145, 163; cosmology, 113, 163; counter-doctrinality, 96, 101; *dhamma* and art/literature, 93–94, 97, 113; impermanence, 13, 38, 40–41, 46–51, 113, 116, 167; *karma*, 53–54; meritorious actions, 9, 43, 93, 101, 102; *mokṣa*, 53–54; the nibbanic, 50–51, 101–2; nirvana, 92, 139; *saṃsāra*, 53–54, 119, 136–37; soteriology, 23, 113; temporality, 11, 28, 164–66
Celan's work and, 25, 122–25, 128, 133, 135

Angkarn Kallayanapong *(continued)*
  cosmological concerns, in work of, 6, 7, 42, 68, 110–11
  cosmopolitanism, in work of, 12, 84, 164, 169
  critique, work as: Buddhism, as basis of, 163; of capitalism, 127; of class, 134; of culture, 1–3, 19, 35, 52, 55–56, 64, 69–70, 144; of elites, 83–84; forms for, 85; in general, 145; of materialism, 108–9; of modernity, 164
  deconstructive reading, of Angkarn's work, 97–98
  dialogism, of Angkarn's work, 130–31: contradiction, in work of, 10, 54, 117
  didacticism, in work of, 45, 83, 95, 118
  ethical concerns, in work of, 3, 7, 9, 46, 48–50, 52, 73–74: and aesthetic endeavors, 97, 109
  emotions, use of, 42, 43, 48, 165
  gender/sexuality concerns, in work of, 27–28, 159, 230n32
  Ginsberg, Allen, and, 25: meeting with, 145; work of both compared, 143, 148, 156, 159–63
  globalization concerns, in work of, 12, 55, 142
  Hinduism, in work of, 6, 111, 135, 148, 235n32
  hybridity, in work of, 4, 55, 80, 82
  individualism, in work of, 9–10, 38–43
  longing/loss, in work of, 24, 65, 69, 122: cultural, 7, 38, 83, 121
  the nation/nationalism, 32: in work of, 12, 68, 72–73, 77–78, 122, 159
  nature concerns, in work of, 22, 45, 49, 93, 94, 239n40: eco-poetics, 49, 136–40

nirat and, 18, 22, 55–56, 60–69, 80: transformation of, 84
ontological concerns, 8, 139: cultural strata, in work of, 63, 77, 85, 134, 137; egalitarian nature of, 94, 128, 134, 137, 139, 150–51
panithan (manifestos), 24, 61, 73, 87, 96: v. Naowarat's, 105–6; temporality and, 88
performative aspects, in work of, 165–67
poetology, 2, 12, 122
poetic prose of, 5, 15, 23, 35, 39, 45, 46, 47, 122, 166: prose poetry, 7, 30
poetics 3, 23, 56, 64, 79–80: eco-poetics, 49, 136–40; grammar, 130–33; heteroglossia, 117–18, 128–31, 237n58; linguistic innovations, 4, 17, 122–27, 167–68; meter, 4, 70, 83, 118, 130; Sanskritic idiom, 82
poetry: as divine, 105; as indispensable; 98; as religion, 93
political concerns, in work of, 26–27, 31–32, 72–73, 143, 148, 157–59
postcoloniality, in work of, 5, 11, 124, 136
publication and circulation history, 30–32
redemptive/reparative concerns, 1, 5, 19, 165: and art, 73, 87
Sarit regime and, 17, 61, 77–78
subjectivity, in work of, 13–14, 88–89: *ahangkan* and, 45, 100, 226n13, 235n32; artistic, 98–102, 167; conflicted, 107–18; within cosmological framework, 113–14; humility, 40, 45, 94, 101; redemptive, 92–93

surrealism, in work of, 148–49
temporality, in work of, 2–4, 5–12,
  45, 92, 142: dimensionality
  of time, 38, 43, 47, 54, 68;
  linearity of time, 52; ontology
  of time, 35–38, 46–47, 165;
  personifications of time, 37,
  39, 47–48, 52; poetic language
  and, 132–33; pressure of time,
  38–39, 51, 114; resacrilization of
  time, 52, 135–36, 168; Sukhothai
  period, 75–77, 84; "time as
  conflict," 36, 38, 51–52; time as
  productive/destructive, 39–40
Thai modernity and, 3, 4, 5, 35–36,
  53, 55–87, 142, 154, 168
translations of, 22–25
transnationality, in work of, 25–26,
  121–22, 141–42, 153, 167, 168
visual art by, 26, 32
vocabulary, 167–68, 237n58:
  Buddhist, 23, 119, 125–28;
  Greek/Latinate, 23, 119, 125–27;
  Khmer, 127
vulgarity, in work of, 56, 79, 82, 149
as xenophobic, 12, 78, 84. See
  also specific works of art and
  literature
Angkarn Kallayanapong, works
  of: *Alangkan Jak Angkarn
  Kallayanapong* (Magnificence by
  Angkarn Kallayanapong), 32;
  "Amnat Rai Khong Cholesterol"
  ("Evil Power of Cholesterol"),
  32; "Ayuthaya," 24 61–65, 80,
  173–75: meters in 63; "Ayuthaya
  Wipayok" ("The Perishing of
  Ayuthaya"), 65–67, 69, 80,
  178–80; *Bang Bot Jak Suan
  Kaeo* (Passages from the Crystal
  Garden), 30, 61; *Bangkok Kaeo
  Kamsuan Rue Nirat Nakhon Si

Thammarat (Lament for Beloved
  Bangkok or Nirat Nakhon Si
  Thammarat), 6, 30, 35, 60–61,
  73, 81, 87, 110, 194–96; "Beng
  Ngan Bat Sop Jop Phop Trai"
  ("Excreting Work Eternally Vile"),
  81; "Benjasin" ("Five Precepts"),
  81–82, 148; "Jaruek Adid"
  ("Inscription from the Past"), 24,
  137–39, 188–89; "Jiaranai Kaeo
  Mani Haeng Chiwit" ("Cutting
  the Crystal Gems of Life"),
  115–16, 201–2; "Kalajak" ("The
  Wheel of Time"), 38–39, 183–84;
  "Kala Khue Arai" ("What Is
  Time?"), 6, 191–92; "Kamakon
  Khom Khuen Sak Sop Sau Tang
  Prathet" ("Workers Rape the
  Corpse of a Foreign Woman"),
  32; *Kawiniphon Khong Angkarn
  Kallayanapong* (The Poetry of
  Angkarn Kallayanapong), 6,
  7, 30, 35, 38, 40, 61, 75–76,
  87, 89, 117, 171–89; *Kawi Sri
  Ayuthaya* (Poet of Ayuthaya), 30,
  31–32, 220–21; "Kha Mi Khru
  Yu Thua Fa" ("I Have Teachers
  All over the Heavens"), 95;
  "Khwam Fan Khong Thueak Pha
  Luang" ("Dream of the Rocks"),
  38; "Kroen" ("Foreword"),
  110–11, 194–95; "Ku Duang Jai"
  ("Redeeming the Heart"), 108–9,
  186–87; "Laeng Wanakhadi"
  ("Devoid of Literature"), 7,
  98, 109–10, 137, 172–73;
  "Lak Chai" ("The Grounds
  of Accomplishment"), 93,
  187–88; *Lamnam Phu Kradueng*
  (Kradueng Mountain Song), 5,
  6, 30, 35, 60, 87, 95, 190–93,
  230n29; "Lok" ("The World"),

Angkarn Kallayanapong, works of (*continued*)
137; *Melting Men* (drawings), 159; "Nimit Nai Sai Rung" ("*Nimitta* in the Rainbow"), 7, 35, 51, 205–7: ontology of time in, 36–38; "Oh Hok Tula Maha-amahit" ("Oh Brutal Sixth of October"), 159; "Om" (*Kawiniphon*), 40–41, 186; "Pakka Thip" ("The Divine Pen"), 99–100, 195–96; *Panithan Kawi* (The Poet's Testament), 6, 8, 18, 30–31, 35, 40, 61, 80–81, 87, 112, 113, 133, 196–205: globalization and, 125; hybridized vocabulary of, 117–18, 127; "Panithan Kawi" ("The Poet's Testament"), 88, 90–93, 95, 104, 197–99: deconstructive reading of, 97–98; eco-poetics and, 136, 139–40; *klon* 8 meter of, 118; vocabulary of, 119, 126–28; "Panithan Khong Kawi" ("Pledge of the Poet" or "The Poet's Pledge"), 24–25, 87–90, 96–97, 105, 117, 171–72: Ginsberg's version ("The Poet's Testament"), 144, 153; *khlong* meter of, 118; v. "The Poet's Testament," 136; "Phiang Khru Nueng Ko Muai Samoe Fan" ("In One Instant Dead, like in a Dream"), 113, 114, 204–5; "Phi Phung Tai" ("Shooting Star"), 41–42, 182–83; "Phlapphlueng" ("Lily,"), 39, 185; "Phutharom" ("Buddhist Spirit"), 8–10, 101, 196–97; *Rachasadudi Ming Khwan Prachathipatai*, 31; "Raluek Thueng Phra Saphanyu" ("Remembering Phra Saphanyu"), 40; "Sanam Luang," 73; "Sia Jao" ("I Lost You"), 24–25, 42–43, 185–86: translation by Ginsberg, 145, 153–55; "Sinlapa Ayuthaya" ("The Art of Ayuthaya"), 68–69, 80, 175–78; "Si Sachanalai," 76, 180–82; "Sith Isara Seri Khong Puang Pracharat—Prakat Jetanarom 14 Tula Udomsith Isara" ("The People's Right to Freedom—Statement of Intention 14 October Rights and Freedom"), 32, 158–59, 163, 220–21; "Sukhothai," 76; "Su Krasae Chara" ("Against the Stream of Aging"), 5, 39–40, 192–93; *Sumalai Poralok*, 31; "Tuen Thoet Lok Manut" ("Awake, Humanity!"), 80–81, 101, 199–200: vocabulary, 126; "Unnamed" (p. 39), 82, 126, 200–201; "Unnamed" (p. 75), 112, 133, 202; "Waeo Ta Khong Wela" ("The Eye of Time"), 39; "Wak Thale" ("Scoop Up the Sea"), 25: translation by Ginsberg, 144, 150–51, 152–53; translation by Sulak/Woodward, 151–53; "Wela Khue Chiwa" ("Time Is Life"), 1–3, 6, 40, 190–91; "Wiman Nam Khang" ("Celestial Mansion of Dew"), 114–15, 203–4; *Yad Nam Khang Khue Namta Khong Wela* (Dew Drops Are the Tears of Time), 6, 30, 31, 35, 205–20; "Yad Nam Khang Khue Namta Khong Wela" ("Dew Drops Are the Tears of Time"), 45–50, 101, 207–20

Angkor Wat, 155–56

"Angkor Wat" (Ginsberg), 146, 155–57

Anuk Pitukthanin, 31

Architects of Buddhist Leisure: Socially Disengaged Buddhism in Asia's Museums, Monuments, and

Amusement Parks (McDaniel), 21
art: and Buddhism, 7, 9; and humanity, 7; as supratemporal, 29
Art for Life, Art for the People (Chit), 71
Art for Life movement, 15, 17, 26, 61, 69–72, 106, 125, 158: folk elements in work of, 71
Atsani Phonlachan, 71
Augustine, Jane, 151, 161–62
"Ayuthaya" (Angkarn), 24, 61–65, 80, 173–75: meters in, 63
Ayuthaya: city, 65, 67; cosmopolitan nature of, 75–77, 84
Ayuthaya period, 3, 12, 52, 55, 57, 61: literature of, 83: Sanskrit poetics, 75
"Ayuthaya Wipayok" ("The Perishing of Ayuthaya") (Angkarn), 65–67, 69, 80, 178–80

Bai Mai Thi Hai Pai (The Missing Leaves) (Pitpreecha), 102
Baker, Chris, 16, 17, 18, 125
Bakhtin, Mikhail, 130–31: *Dialogic Imagination, The*, 117–18, 128–29
"Bakhtin on Poetry" (Eskin), 129–30
Bang Bot Jak Suan Kaeo (Passages from the Crystal Garden) (Angkarn), 30, 61
Bangkok, 73 Ginsberg's account of, 146–49; period, 12, 77; as seat of Thai government, 72. *See also under* Angkarn Kallayanapong
Bangkok Kaeo Kamsuan Rue Nirat Nakhon Si Thammarat (Lament for Beloved Bangkok or Nirat Nakhon Si Thammarat) (Angkarn), 6, 30, 35, 60–61, 73, 81, 87, 110, 194–96
Bauer, Christian: on Angkarn's poetry, 4, 22, 26, 30, 31; on Naowarat's poetry, 103

Beat poets, 149, 161. *See also* Allen Ginsberg
belatedness (*Nachträglichkeit*), 50
"Beng Ngan Bat Sop Jop Phop Trai" ("Excreting Work Eternally Vile") (Angkarn), 81
Benjamin, Walter, 134
"Benjasin" ("Five Precepts") (Angkarn), 81–82, 143
Bhawan Ruangsilp, 76
Bing Xin, 140
"Black May"/"Bloody May." *See under* protests
"Bombay poets," 25
boriphat, 80
Buddhadasa Bhikkhu, 51, 162
Buddhism: aesthetics, 4: in literature, 20; *anātman/anattā*, doctrine of, 9, 43; *anātmavāda*, 38; artistic production and, 7, 35; *ātmavāda*, 38; attachment/detachment, 20; Bodhisattvahood, 93; cosmology, 6, 53; counterdoctrinality, in Thailand, 20–21; dimensions of space and time, concern with, 6, 38; in general, 23, 26; impermanence, doctrine of, 7–8, 13, 43, 47: women/femininity and, 64; *khanda*, 44, 49, 101; Mahayana, 6, 93, 144, 145, 163; *paṭiccasamuppāda*, 44, 51; practice, v. textual traditions, 20; *saṃkhāra/saṅkhāra*, 44, 226n7; selfhood/subjectivity and, 9, 38, 43–45, 108; soteriology, doctrine of, 7, 28, 100; *śūnyatā*, 144, 160–63; *śūnyavāda* school, 37–38; temporality in: 3, 5, 7, 11; cyclical time, 52; *kalpa*, 2, 6, 52; substantiality of time, 36, 51; *yuga*, 52; in Thailand, 20, 51, 144; Theravada, 6, 43–44; in the United States, 160; Vajrayana,

Buddhism *(continued)*
144, 151, 163. *See also under* Angkarn Kallayanapong; literary theory; Thai literature
Buddhist-Hindu cultural imaginary, 153
Buddhist studies, 20, 225n41

Cassaniti, Julia: *Living Buddhism: Mind, Self, and Emotion in a Thai Community*, 21; *Remembering the Present: Mindfulness in Buddhist Asia*, 21
Celan, Paul: Angkarn's work and, 25, 122–25, 128; biographical details, 122; "Le Contrescarpe," 135; "Es war Erde in ihnen," 135; in general, 24, 25; loss, in work of, 123–24; Meridian speech, 123; *Die Niemandsrose*, 135; poetic innovations, 123–24, 128; "Psalm," 135; religion, in work of, 134–35; "Die Schleuse," 135; temporality, in work of, 131–34
Central Intelligence Agency: Congress for Cultural Freedom, 143; Thailand and, 144, 148
"CIA Dope Calypso" (Ginsberg), 148
Chakrabarty, Dipesh, 10
Chang Sae Tang (Chang Tang), 70–71
Cheah, Pheng, 10, 11: *What Is a World?*, 163
Chetana Nagavajara, 22, 24, 35, 89: on Buddhism, in work of Angkarn, 95–97, 235n25; on nature, in work of Angkarn, 137; transnationality, in work of Angkarn, 122
China: People's Republic of, and Thailand, 18
Chinese prose poems, 24, 140–41, 169

Chiranan Pitpreecha, 72
Chit Phumisak, 61: *Art for Life, Art for the People*, 71
Cho, Francisca: *Seeing Like the Buddha: Enlightenment through Film*, 21
Chusak Pattarakulvanit, 97–98: "Thruesadi Wannakam Naeo Deconstruction" ("Deconstructionist Literary Theory"), 97
Cindamani, 56, 78, 232n72
Civilized Woman: M. L. Boonlua Debhayasuwan and the Thai Twentieth Century, A (Kepner), 22
Cold War, 3, 13, 15, 143–44, 157. *See also* Southeast Asia Treaty Organization
Collected Poems 1947–1997 (Ginsberg), 156
Collins, Steven, 44–45, 50
communism: in general, 16; in Thailand, 17: Communist Party of Thailand, 72, 102; Marxists, 71
Congress for Cultural Freedom, 143
cosmopolitanism: of Thailand, 4. *See also* Angkarn Kallayanapong
culture: cultural identity in *nirat*, 58–60; recovery/survival of, 5, 11; as site of contestation, 27

Davis, Erik, 21: *Deathpower: Buddhism's Ritual Imagination in Cambodia*, 21
"Death & Fame" (Ginsberg), 161–62
Deathpower: Buddhism's Ritual Imagination in Cambodia (Davis), 21
decolonization, 11
deconstruction, 97

democracy/democratic movements, in Thailand, 13, 15, 31, 231n48: and Thai literature, 119, 157–59
Dhiravat na Pombejra, 76
Dialogic Imagination, The (Bakhtin), 117–18, 128–29
Disturbing Conventions: Decentering Thai Literary Cultures (Harrison), 22

80 Pi Angkarn Kallayanapong (Ruenruethai), 30–31
Eisenhower, Dwight D., 156
emotions: in *nirat*, 59–60. *See also under* Angkarn Kallayanapong
Eshel, Amir, 133, 134
Eskin, Michael: "Bakhtin on Poetry," 129–30
ethics, 2; artistic production and, 7, 9. *See also under* Angkarn Kallayanapong

Feroci, Corrado. *See* Silpa Bhirasri
Fuea Haripitak, 31
Fuhrmann, Arnika: *Ghostly Desires: Queer Sexuality and Vernacular Buddhism in Contemporary Thai Cinema,* 21

gender: gendered landscape, in *nirat*, 57; in work of Angkarn, 27–28
"Genre Occludes the Creation of Genre: Bing Xin, Tagore, and Prose Poetry" (Admussen), 140–41
Ghostly Desires: Queer Sexuality and Vernacular Buddhism in Contemporary Thai Cinema (Fuhrmann), 21
Ginsberg, Allen: Angkarn and: meeting with, 145; translator of, 24–25, 143, 150–55; "Angkor Wat," 146, 155–57; in Bangkok, 145: journal entries on, 146–49; Buddhism, in work of, 144, 145, 151, 156, 160–63; "CIA Dope Calypso," 148; *Collected Poems 1947–1997*, 156; critique, work as: cultural, 143, 149; political, 144, 155–57; "Death & Fame," 161–62; egalitarian ontology of, 150–51; "Howl," 151; leftist politics, 25, 143–44; queerness of, 143, 161; in Saigon, journal entry on, 155; subjectivity, in work of, 161; surrealism, in work of, 148–49; "The Terms in Which I Think of Reality," 151; "Understand That This Is a Dream," 146
globalization: in general, 4, 11; Thailand and, 17, 18, 55
Gombrich, Richard, 20

Hale, Peter, 145
Hall, Stuart, 26–27
Harootunian, Harry, 10, 53
Harrison, Rachel: *Disturbing Conventions: Decentering Thai Literary Cultures*, 22
Hinduism, 6, 111, 235n32
"Howl" (Ginsberg), 151
Hudak, Thomas, 70

India, poetry of, 25
individualism, 10, 116: Buddhism and, 9; in Thailand, 116
International Portland Review, 145, 153
Isan Writers, Thai Literature: Writing and Regionalism in Modern Thailand (Platt), 22

Jao Jan Phom Hom: Nirat Phrathat In Khwaen (Mala), 60

Japan/Japanese, 17–18, 77
"Jaruek Adid" ("Inscription from the Past") (Angkarn), 24, 137–39, 188–89
"Jiaranai Kaeo Mani Haeng Chiwit" ("Cutting the Crystal Gems of Life") (Angkarn), 115–16, 201–2

"Kalajak" ("The Wheel of Time") (Angkarn), 38–39, 183–84
"Kala Khue Arai" ("What Is Time?") (Angkarn), 6, 191–92
"Kamakon Khom Khuen Sak Sop Sau Tang Prathet" ("Workers Rape the Corpse of a Foreign Woman") (Angkarn), 32
Kaphayakantha, 78, 232n72
Kaphayasarawilasini, 78, 232n72
Kawiniphon Khong Angkarn Kallayanapong (The Poetry of Angkarn Kallayanapong) (Angkarn), 6, 7, 30, 35, 38, 40, 61, 75–76, 87, 89, 117, 171–89
"Kawiniphon Khong Angkarn Kallayanapong: Sasana Haeng Sunthari" (Suchitra), 22, 89
"Kawi" ("Poet/ry") (Naowarat), 73, 103–6
Kawi Sri Ayuthaya (Poet of Ayuthaya) (Angkarn), 30, 31–32, 220–21
Kepner, Susan: *Civilized Woman: M. L. Boonlua Debhayasuwan and the Thai Twentieth Century, A*, 22; *Lioness in Bloom: Modern Thai Fiction about Women, The*, 22
"Kha Mi Khru Yu Thua Fa" ("I Have Teachers All over the Heavens") (Angkarn), 95
Kham Yad (Word Drops) (Naowarat), 103
Khled Thai, 31
Khlong Hariphunchai, 57

Khlong Kamsuan Si Prat (Si Prat), 57, 60, 63, 65
Khmer culture, 75, 77
Khomthuan Khanthanu, 70, 72, 230n40: "Nak Khien Nak Sang Sinlapa" ("The Writer: A Creator of Art"), 103, 106–7, 159
"Khwam Fan Khong Thueak Pha Luang" ("Dream of the Rocks") (Angkarn), 38
Klap Ban Koed, 32
"Kroen" ("Foreword") (Angkarn), 110–11, 194–95
Krung Thep Thawarawadi: Jaruek Wai Nai Pi Thi 200 Haeng Krung Rattanakosin (Krung Thep Thawarawadi: Recorded in the 200th Year of the Rattanakosin Era) (Naowarat), 60
"Ku Duang Jai" ("Redeeming the Heart") (Angkarn), 108–9, 186–87

"Laeng Wanakhadi" ("Devoid of Literature") (Angkarn), 7, 98, 109–10, 137, 172–73
"Lak Chai" (Angkarn), 93, 187–88
Lamnam Phu Kradueng (Kradueng Mountain Song) (Angkarn), 5, 6, 30, 35, 60, 87, 95, 190–93, 230n29. *See also under* Suchitra Chongstitvatana
leftism, 25: in Thailand, 13, 17, 61, 71: concept of nationhood, 72. *See also* Art for Life movement; communism; democracy movements
Lim, Bliss Cua, 10–11, 165
linguistic negativism, 123
Lioness in Bloom: Modern Thai Fiction about Women, The (Kepner), 22
literary theory, 14: and Buddhist thought, 89

Living Buddhism: Mind, Self, and Emotion in a Thai Community (Cassaniti), 21
"Lok" ("The World") (Angkarn), 137
loss: language in response to, 29. *See also under* Angkarn Kallayanapong; Paul Celan
Lovelorn Ghost and the Magical Monk, The (McDaniel), 20

Makhawan Rangsan (Makhawan Creation) (Angkarn), 32
Mala Khamjan: *Jao Jan Phom Hom: Nirat Phrathat In Khwaen*, 60
Manas Chitakasem, 57, 227–28n2
manifestos, 87–88. See also *panithan*
Marshall, Cynthia, 108, 116
Mattioli, John, 22
Maurel, Frederic, 10, 18, 22, 109, 113, 116–17
McDaniel, Justin: *Architects of Buddhist Leisure: Socially Disengaged Buddhism in Asia's Museums, Monuments, and Amusement Parks*, 21; *Lovelorn Ghost and the Magical Monk, The*, 20
Melting Men (drawings) (Angkarn), 159
meter, in Thai poetry: *chan*, 79; *chan matraphruet*, 232n72; *chan wanaphruet*, 232n72; *kap*, 70, 79–80, 83, 229n26, 233n85; *kap yani*, 83; *kap yani 11*, 63; *khlong*, 56, 63, 65, 70, 80, 83, 118, 229n26, 233n83; *klon*, 70, 232n75; *klon*, 8, 118; *klon plao* (free verse), 70; *lilit*, 83; in *nirat*, 60; *rai*, 79. *See also* Thai poetry
modernity: European, 39, 53, 124; in general, 3, 52; global, 82; literary, 4, 20; temporality of, 165; in Thailand: 2, 35, 56, 61, 64, 67, 74; cultural, 70, 85
Morgan, Bill, 145
Mortensen, Erik, 160, 161

Naowarat Pongpaiboon, 22, 230n40: "Kawi" ("Poet/ry"), 73, 103–6; *Kham Yad* (Word Drops), 103; *Krung Thep Thawarawadi: Jaruek Wai Nai Pi Thi 200 Haeng Krung Rattanakosin* (Krung Thep Thawarawadi: Recorded in the 200th Year of the Rattanakosin Era), 60; leftism of, 17, 26, 70, 72, 102–4; *panithan* by, 103–5; *Phiang Khwam Khluean Wai* (Mere Movement), 72, 102, 103; "Phiang Khwam Khluean Wai" ("Mere Movement"), 72, 103; *Phleng Khlui Phiu* (Flute Song), 103; subjectivity in work of, 104–5
"Nature of Modern Thai Poetry Considered with Reference to the Works of Angchan Kalayanaphong, Naowarat Phongphaibun and Suchit Wongthet" (Suchitra), 21–22
neoliberalism, 10, 18, 107, 124
Nietzsche, Friedrich, 10, 113, 116–17
"Nimit Nai Sai Rung" ("Nimitta in the Rainbow") (Angkarn), 7, 35, 51, 205–7: ontology of time in, 36–38
nimit/nimitta, 226n1
nirat, 18, 22, 83: *bot chom mueang*, 64; classical, 57; contemporary, 60; definition, 55, 227–28n2; features, 58: love-longing in, 56–57, 60, 64; geocultural landscape of, 55–57; *khlong*

nirat (continued)
nirat, 56, 65; political content of, 59, 69; punning in, 56, 57, 60; subjectivity in, 57, 59–60; as travel narratives, 55, 57: journeys of emotion, 59–60; journeys of identity, 58–59. *See also under* Angkarn Kallayanapong; Mala Khamjan; Naowarat Pongpaiboon; Si Prat; Suchitra Chongstitvatana; Sunthorn Phu; *and* specific works

Nirat Mueang Klaeng (Sunthorn Phu), 58–59

Nirat Nakhon Sawan, 58–59

Nirat Nongkhai, 59

Nirat Phu Khao Thong (Sunthorn Phu), 58

Noakes, Tim, 146

Nopporn Prachakul, 97–98: "Thruesadi Wannakam Naeo Deconstruction" ("Deconstructionist Literary Theory"), 97

"Oh Hok Tula Maha-amahit" ("Oh Brutal Sixth of October") (Angkarn), 159

"Om" (*Kawiniphon*) (Angkarn), 40–41, 186

Ongkan Chaeng Nam Khlong Ha, 83

ontology: of time, 6–7, 36. *See also under* Angkarn Kallayanapong; Buddhism

Ormkaew Kallayanapong, 12, 26, 31, 145: on Angkarn's philosophical outlook, 162; on Angkarn's politics, 32

"Pakka Thip" ("The Divine Pen") (Angkarn), 99–100, 195–96

Panithan Kawi (The Poet's Testament) (Angkarn), 6, 8, 18, 30–31, 35, 40, 61, 80–81, 87, 112, 113, 133, 196–205: globalization and, 125; hybridized vocabulary of, 117–18, 127

"Panithan Kawi" ("The Poet's Testament") (Angkarn), 88, 90–93, 95, 104, 197–99: deconstructive reading of, 97–98; eco-poetics and, 136, 139–40; *klon* 8 meter of, 118; vocabulary of, 119, 126–28

"Panithan Khong Kawi" ("Pledge of the Poet" or "The Poet's Pledge") (Angkarn), 24–25, 87–90, 96–97, 105, 117, 171–72: Ginsberg's version ("The Poet's Testament"), 144, 153; *khlong* meter of, 118; v. "The Poet's Testament," 136

panithan (manifestos): definition, 88, 233–34n5; manifesto-poem, 22; in modern Thai poetry, 14–15, 79, 103–7

Pasuk Pongpaichit, 16, 17, 18, 125

People's Alliance for Democracy, 32

Phali Son Nong, 83

"Phiang Khru Nueng Ko Muai Samoe Fan" ("In One Instant Dead, like in a Dream") (Angkarn), 113, 114, 204–5

Phiang Khwam Khluean Wai (Mere Movement) (Naowarat), 72, 102, 103

"Phiang Khwam Khluean Wai" ("Mere Movement") (Naowarat), 72, 103

"Phi Phung Tai" ("Shooting Star") (Angkarn), 41–42, 182–83

"Phlapphlueng" ("Lily") (Angkarn), 39, 185

Phleng Khlui Phiu (Flute Song) (Naowarat), 103

phranakhon, 82

Phra Narai, 57, 65, 228n3

Phraparamanuchit: *Vutthodaya*, 232n72
"Phutharom" ("Buddhist Spirit") (Angkarn), 8–10, 101, 196–97
Phuthatham Nai Kawiniphon Samai Mai (Suchitra), 22, 162
Platt, Martin B.: *Isan Writers, Thai Literature: Writing and Regionalism in Modern Thailand*, 22
"Pledge of the Poet"/"Poet's Pledge." *See* "Panithan Khong Kawi"
poetology, 12
"Poet's Testament, The." *See* "Panithan Kawi" *and under* Allen Ginsberg
Pollock, Sheldon, 75
postcoloniality: individual and, 3; literature and, 20, 163–64
Prabhu, Gayathri, 149
pranithan, 88
Praphat Charusathien, 72
protests, in Thailand: of 1973, 69, 72–73, 102, 158: massacre in October, 159; of 1976, 69, 72–73, 102, 159; of 1992 ("Black/Bloody May"), 31, 159

Rachasadudi Ming Khwan Prachathipatai (Angkarn), 31
"Raluek Thueng Phra Saphanyu" ("Remembering Phra Saphanyu") (Angkarn), 40
Rama I, 58
Ramathibodi I, 83
Rama III, 232n72
Ramkhamhaeng, 75–76
Rattanakosin period, 58, 228n3
Read Till It Shatters: Nationalism and Identity in Modern Thai Literature (Thak), 22
religion, 29, 135–36, 147, 148, 160. *See also* Buddhism, Suchitra Chongstitvatana *and under*

Angkarn Kallayanapong; Paul Celan
Remembering the Present: Mindfulness in Buddhist Asia (Cassaniti), 21
Reynolds, Craig, 59
rightism, in Thailand: 61, 71
Rotman, Andy: *Thus I Have Seen: Faith in Early Indian Buddhism*, 21
Ruenruthai Sajjaphan: *80 Pi Angkarn Kallayanapong*, 30–31

Saigon, 146, 147, 155
"Sanam Luang" (Angkarn), 73
Sanskrit language: lexicon, in Angkarn's work: 64, 82, 126–28; "Sanskrit cosmopolis," 75
Sarit Thanarat, 15–16: as reactionary modernist, 74: regime, 17, 61, 72, 102; technocratic nationalism of, 77
Sarvāstivādins, 36
Sautrāntikas, 36
Schweisguth, Paul, 228n2
Seeing Like the Buddha: Enlightenment through Film (Cho), 21
Shoah, the, 29, 122–23, 169
"Sia Jao" ("I Lost You") (Angkarn), 24–25, 42–43, 185–86: translation by Ginsberg, 145, 153–55
Siem Reap, 147, 156
Sihanouk, Norodom, 156
Silpa Bhirasri (Corrado Feroci), 141, 235n25
Si Mahosot, 58
"Sinlapa Ayuthaya" ("The Art of Ayuthaya") (Angkarn), 68–69, 80, 175–78
Si Prat, 58: *Khlong Kamsuan Si Prat*, 57, 60, 63, 65
"Si Sachanalai" (Angkarn), 76, 180–82

"Sith Isara Seri Khong Puang Pracharat—Prakat Jetanarom 14 Tula Udomsith Isara" ("The People's Right to Freedom—Statement of Intention 14 October Rights and Freedom") (Angkarn), 32, 158–59, 163, 220–21
social studies textbooks, in Thailand, 76–77
Southeast Asia, 3, 16: Buddhism in, 20; US involvement in, 16, 25, 30, 147, 155
Southeast Asia Treaty Organization (SEATO), 148
subjectivity, 3, 10, 13–14, 20, 51, 108: challenges to, 107, 109, 116; in *nirat*, 57, 59–60; in Thai poetry, 103; contradictions in, 144. See also under Angkarn Kallayanapong; Buddhism
Suchat Sawadsri, 70
Suchitra Chongstitvatana, 35: on Angkarn's work: Buddhism in, 94–96, 162; gender in, 27; on *Lamnam Phu Kradueng*, 64–65, 93; "lexical patterns" of, 131; "Kawiniphon Khong Angkarn Kallayanapong: Sasana Haeng Sunthari," 22, 89; nature in, 137, 139; "Nature of Modern Thai Poetry Considered with Reference to the Works of Angkhan Kalayanaphong, Naowarat Phongphaibun and Suchit Wongthet," 21–22; *nirat* in, 56, 80; ontology of, 94, 137; "Panithan Kawi," 92–93; *panithan* (manifestos), 73; *Phuthatham Nai Kawiniphon Samai Mai*, 22, 162; "religion of aesthetics," 88, 92–98; *thip* in, 94; time in, 39; vocabulary of, 124; on Mahayana Buddhism and Thai literature, 162; on Naowarat's work, 104–5; on *nirat*, 57; on *panithan* (manifestos), 14, 22
Sujit Wongthet, 72
"Sukhothai" (Angkarn), 76
Sukhothai period, 74–75, 77, 83
"Su Krasae Chara" ("Against the Stream of Aging") (Angkarn), 5, 39–40, 192–93
Sulak Sivaraksa, 24–25, 31, 145, 150, 159
Sumalai Poralok (Angkarn), 31
Sunthorn Phu, 58: *Nirat Mueang Klaeng*, 58–59; *Nirat Phu Khao Thong*, 58
surrealism, 148
Swearer, Donald, 20

Tagore, Rabindranath, 140
Tai states, 75
Tamra Chan Wanaphruet lae Matraphruet, 78, 232n72
temporality, 7, 10: developmentalist, 165; heterotemporality, 11, 164–65; "homogeneous empty time," 11, 52–53, 136, 161; in *nirat*, 60; postcoloniality and, 163–64. See also Angkarn Kallayanapong; Buddhism; ontology
"Terms in Which I Think of Reality, The" (Ginsberg), 151
Terwiel, Barend Jan, 78
Thailand: "American era"/US involvement in, 16–17, 25, 72, 148, 231n47, 237n7; Cold War and, 143–44; cosmopolitanism of, 4; developmentalism of, 16–17; "geo-body," 17; globalization and, 17, 18, 55, 102, 119: localist ideologies in response to, 102, 113–14; temporality of, 124; indigenous literary theory, 14;

industrialization of, 18; mass media in, 19; modernity in, 2, 82; monarchy, 17, 74; national identity of, 71, 77; nationalism in, 72; nationhood of, 72; *nirat* and Siamese identity, 58; as noncolonial/semicolonial, 5; *sakdina* culture, 71, 230n43; as technocracy, 77, 125. *See also under* Buddhism; individualism; protests; Thai literature; Thai poetics/poetry

Thai literature: Buddhism and, 21, 103, 106–7; New Wave literature, 70; revolutionary, 72, 102; writers, 71, 144. *See also* Thai poetry *and* specific individuals

Thai poetics/poetry: manuals: *Cindamani*, 56, 73, 232n72; *Kaphayckantha*, 78, 232n72; *Kaphaycsarawilasini*, 78, 232n72; *Tamra Chan Waraphruet lae Matraphruet*, 78, 232n72; modern v. traditional, 78–79; political content, 72, 107, 119; prosody, in general, 78–79; South Asian poetics and, 78–79. *See also* Angkarn Kallayanapong; Art for Life movement; meter; *nirat*; *panithar*

Thak Chaloemtiarana, 61, 74: *Read Till It Shatters: Nationalism and Identity in Modern Thai Literature*, 22

Thanom Kittikachorn, 72

Thawathotsamat, 57–58

Thet Mahachat, 95

"Thruesadi Wannakam Naeo Deconstruction" ("Deconstructionist Literary Theory") (Chusak and Nopporn), 97

Thus I Have Seen: Faith in Early Indian Buddhism (Rotman), 21

Traiphum Phra Ruang, 95

transnationality, in literature: translation and, 140–41. *See also under* Angkarn Kallayanapong

Trigilio, Tony, 156

Trisilpa Boonkhachorn, 14–15, 22, 64: on Thai poetry, 78, 79, 83

trivial, the 26–27

"Tuen Thoet Lok Manut" ("Awake, Humanity!") (Angkarn), 80–81, 101, 199–200: vocabulary of, 126

"Understand That This Is a Dream" (Ginsberg), 146

United States: involvement in Southeast Asia, 147, 155; involvement in Thailand, 16, 25, 72, 144, 148, 231n47

"Unnamed" (p. 39) (Angkarn), 82, 126, 200–201

"Unnamed" (p. 75) (Angkarn), 112, 133, 202

Vietnam War, 16, 72, 148

Vutthodaya (Phraparamanuchit), 232n72

"Waeo Ta Khong Wela" ("The Eye of Time") (Angkarn), 39

"Wak Thale" ("Scoop Up the Sea") (Angkarn), 25: translation by Ginsberg, 144, 150–51, 152–53; translation by Sulak/Woodward, 151–53

Weeks, Marc, 10, 18, 22, 109, 113, 116–17

"Wela Khue Chiwa" ("Time Is Life") (Angkarn), 1–3, 6, 40, 190–91

Weller, Shane, 123, 131–32, 135

Wenk, Klaus, 22, 83, 230n29

Wesling, Donald, 238n10

What Is a World? (Cheah), 163
Wilson, Liz, 64
"Wiman Nam Khang" ("Celestial Mansion of Dew") (Angkarn), 114–15, 203–4
women: in *nirat*, 59; in work of Angkarn, 27, 64, 230n32
Woodward, Hiram, 24
worlding, 11
Wright, Michael, 24

Wyatt, David, 74, 75

Yad Nam Khang Khue Namta Khong Wela (Dew Drops Are the Tears of Time) (Angkarn), 6, 30, 31, 35, 205–20
"Yad Nam Khang Khue Namta Khong Wela" ("Dew Drops Are the Tears of Time") (Angkarn), 45–50, 101, 207–20

www.ingramcontent.com/pod-product-compliance
Lightning Source LLC
Chambersburg PA
CBHW020642230426
43665CB00008B/288